GMS INTENSIVE METHOD
Glossika Mass Sentences

Features: Sound files have A/B/C formats.

A Files	English - Target language 2x
B Files	English - space - Target 1x
C Files	Target language only 1x

 Useful for students with more time to dedicate.

GSR F
Glossi

Features: O
algorithm th
every day, w
for a total of
Requires less than 20 minutes daily.

Useful for people with busy schedules and limited study time.

HOW TO USE
---

1 To familiarise yourself with IPA and spelling, Glossika recommends using the book while listening to A or C sound files and going through all 1000 sentences on your first day. Then you can start your training.

2 Set up your schedule. It's your choice, you can choose 20, 50 or 100 sentences for daily practice. We recommend completing the following four steps.

 Training Step **1**: Try repeating the sentences with the same speed and intonation in the A sound files.

 Training Step **2**: Dictation: use the C sound files (and pausing) to write out each sentence (in script or IPA or your choice). Use the book to check your answers.

 Training Step **3**: Recording: record the sentences as best you can. We recommend recording the same sentences over a 3-day period, and staggering them with new ones.

 Training Step **4**: Use the B sound files to train your interpretation skills. Say your translation in the space provided.

2 Set up your schedule. You can listen to a single GSR file daily or even double up. One book typically takes 3-4 months to complete.

3 You can accompany with the GMS training when you have extra time to practice.

Reminder

Don't forget that if you run into problems, just skip over it! Keep working through the sentences all the way to the end and don't worry about the ones you don't get. You'll probably get it right the second time round. Remember, one practice session separated by *one* sleep session yields the best results!

Glossika Mass Sentences

French

Fluency 3

Complete Fluency Course

Michael Campbell

Maxime Paquin

Glossika

Glossika Mass Sentence Method

French Fluency 3

First published : NOV 2015
via license by Nolsen Bédon, Ltd.
Taipei, Taiwan

Authors: Michael Campbell, Maxime Paquin
Chief Editor: Michael Campbell
Translator: Michael Campbell, Maxime Paquin
Recording: Michael Campbell, Maxime Paquin
Editing Team: Claudia Chen, Sheena Chen
Consultant: Percy Wong
Programming: Edward Greve
Design: Glossika team

glossika.com

Glossika Series

The following languages are available (not all are published in English):

Afroasiatic

AM Amharic
ARE Egyptian Arabic
HA Hausa
IV Hebrew
AR Modern Standard Arabic
ARM Moroccan Arabic

Altaic

AZ Azerbaijani
JA Japanese
KK Kazakh
KR Korean
MN Mongolian
UZ Uzbek

Austroasiatic

KH Khmer
VNN Vietnamese (Northern)
VNS Vietnamese (Southern)

Austronesian

AMP Amis

TYS Atayal
BNN Bunun
ILO Ilokano
SDQ Seediq
TGL Tagalog
THW Thao

Caucasian

Dravidian

KAN Kannada
MAL Malayalam
TAM Tamil
TEL Telugu

IE: Baltic

LAV Latvian
LIT Lithuanian

IE: Celtic

CYM Welsh

IE: Germanic

EN American English
DA Danish
NL Dutch

DE German
IS Icelandic
NO Norwegian
SV Swedish

IE: Indo-Iranian

BEN Bengali
PRS Dari Persian
GUJ Gujarati
HI Hindi
KUR Kurmanji Kurdish
MAR Marathi
NEP Nepali
FA Persian
PAN Punjabi (India)
SIN Sinhala
KUS Sorani Kurdish
TGK Tajik
UR Urdu

IE: Other

SQ Albanian
HY Armenian
EU Basque
EO Esperanto
EL Greek

IE: Romance

PB Brazilian Portuguese
ES Castilian Spanish
CA Catalan
PT European Portuguese
FR French
IT Italian
ESM Mexican Spanish
RO Romanian

IE: Slavic

BEL Belarusian
BOS Bosnian
HR Croatian
CS Czech
MK Macedonian
PL Polish
RU Russian
SRP Serbian
SK Slovak
SL Slovene
UKR Ukrainian

Kartuli

KA Georgian

Niger-Congo

SW Swahili
YO Yoruba

Sino-Tibetan

MY Burmese
YUE Cantonese
ZH Chinese
HAK Hakka
ZS Mandarin Chinese (Beijing)
WUS Shanghainese
MNN Taiwanese
WUW Wenzhounese

Tai-Kadai

LO Lao
TH Thai

Uralic

EST Estonian
FI Finnish
HU Hungarian

Glossika Levels

Many of our languages are offered at different levels (check for availability):

Intro Level	Fluency Level	Expression Level
Pronunciation Courses	Fluency	Business Courses
Intro Course	Daily Life	Intensive Reading
	Travel	
	Business Intro	

Getting Started

For Busy People & Casual Learners

- 20 minutes per day, 3 months per book
- Use the Glossika Spaced Repetition (GSR) MP3 files, 1 per day. The files are numbered for you.
- Keep going and don't worry if you miss something on the first day, you will hear each sentence more than a dozen times over a 5 day period.

For Intensive Study

- 1-2 hours per day, 1 month per book

Log on to our website and download the Self Study Planner at: glossika.com/howto.

Steps:

1. Prepare (GMS-A). Follow the text as you listen to the GMS-A files (in 'GLOSSIKA-XX-GMS-A'). Listen to as many sentences as you can, and keep going even when you miss a sentence or two. Try to focus on the sounds and matching them to the text.
2. Listen (GMS-A). Try to repeat the target sentence with the speaker the second time you hear it.
3. Write (GMS-C). Write down the sentences as quickly as you can, but hit pause when you need to. Check your answers against the text.
4. Record (GMS-C). Listen to each sentence and record it yourself. Record from what you hear, not from reading the text. You can use your mobile phone or computer to do the recording. Play it back, and try to find the differences between the original and your recording.
5. Interpret (GMS-B). Try to recall the target sentence in the gap after you hear it in English. Try to say it out loud, and pause if necessary.

Glossika Mass Sentence Method

French

Fluency 3

This GMS Fluency Series accompanies the GMS recordings and is a supplementary course assisting you on your path to fluency. This course fills in the fluency training that is lacking from other courses. Instead of advancing in the language via grammar, GMS builds up sentences and lets students advance via the full range of expression required to function in the target language.

GMS recordings prepare the student through translation and interpretation to become proficient in speaking and listening.

Glossika Spaced Repetition (GSR) recordings are strongly recommended for those who have trouble remembering the content. Through the hundred days of GSR training, all the text in each of our GMS publications can be mastered with ease.

What is Glossika?

From the creation of various linguists and polyglots headed by Michael Campbell, Glossika is a comprehensive and effective system that delivers speaking and listening training to fluency.

It's wise to use Glossika training materials together with your other study materials. Don't bet everything on Glossika. Always use as many materials as you can get your hands on and do something from all of those materials daily. These are the methods used by some of the world's greatest polyglots and only ensures your success.

If you follow all the guidelines in our method you can also become proficiently literate as well. But remember it's easier to become literate in a language that you can already speak than one that you can't.

Most people will feel that since we only focus on speaking and listening, that the Glossika method is too tough. It's possible to finish one of our modules in one month, in fact this is the speed at which we've been training our students for years: 2 hours weekly for 4 weeks is all you need to complete one module. Our students are expected to do at least a half hour on their own every day through listening, dictation, and recording. If you follow the method, you will have completed 10,000 sentence repetitions by the end of the month. This is sufficient enough to start to feel your fluency come out, but you still have a long way to go.

This training model seems to fit well with students in East Asia learning tough languages like English, because they are driven by the fact that they need a better job or have some pressing issue to use their English. This drive makes them want to succeed.

Non-East Asian users of the Glossika Mass Sentence (GMS) methods are split in two groups: those who reap enormous benefit by completing the course, and others who give up because it's too tough to stick to the schedule. If you feel like our training is too overwhelming or demands too much of your time, then I suggest you get your hands on our Glossika Spaced Repetition (GSR) audio files which are designed for people like you. So if you're ambitious, use GMS. If you're too busy or can't stick to a schedule, use GSR.

Glossika Levels

The first goal we have in mind for you is Fluency. Our definition of fluency is simple and easy to attain: speaking full sentences in one breath. Once you achieve fluency, then we work with you on expanding your expression and vocabulary to all areas of language competency. Our three levels correlate to the European standard:

- Introduction = A Levels
- Fluency = B Levels
- Expression = C Levels

The majority of foreign language learners are satisfied at a B Level and a few continue on. But the level at which you want to speak a foreign language is your choice. There is no requirement to continue to the highest level, and most people never do as a B Level becomes their comfort zone.

Glossika Publications

Each Glossika publication comes in four formats:

- Print-On-Demand paperback text
- E-book text (available for various platforms)
- Glossika Mass Sentence audio files
- Glossika Spaced Repetition audio files

Some of our books include International Phonetic Alphabet (IPA) as well. Just check for the IPA mark on our covers.

We strive to provide as much phonetic detail as we can in our IPA transcriptions, but this is not always possible with every language.

As there are different ways to write IPA, our books will also let you know whether it's an underlying pronunciation (phonemic) with these symbols: / /, or if it's a surface pronunciation (phonetic) with these symbols: [ ].

IPA is the most scientific and precise way to represent the sounds of foreign languages. Including IPA in language training guides is taking a step away from previous decades of language publishing. We embrace the knowledge now available to everybody via online resources like Wikipedia which allow anybody to learn the IPA: something that could not be done before without attending university classes.

To get started, just point your browser to Wikipedia's IPA page to learn more about pronouncing the languages we publish.

4 Secrets of the Mass Sentence Method

When learning a foreign language it's best to use full sentences for a number of reasons:

1. Pronunciation—In languages like English, our words undergo a lot of pronunciation and intonation changes when words get strung together in sentences which has been well analyzed in linguistics. Likewise it is true with languages like Chinese where the pronunciations and tones from individual words change once they appear in a sentence. By following the intonation and prosody of a native speaker saying a whole sentence, it's much easier to learn rather than trying to say string each word together individually.

2. Syntax—the order of words, will be different than your own language. Human thought usually occurs in complete ideas. Every society has developed a way to express those ideas linearly by first saying what happened (the verb), or by first saying who did it (the agent), etc. Paying attention to this will accustom us to the way others speak.

3. Vocabulary—the meanings of words, never have just one meaning, and their usage is always different. You always have to learn words in context and which words they're paired with. These are called collocations. To "commit a crime" and to "commit to a relationship" use two different verbs in most other languages. Never assume that learning "commit" by itself will give you the answer. After a lifetime in lexicography, Patrick Hanks "reached the alarming conclusion that words don't have meaning," but rather that "definitions listed in dictionaries can be regarded as presenting meaning potentials rather than meanings as such." This is why collocations are so important.

4. Grammar—the changes or morphology in words are always in flux. Memorizing rules will not help you achieve fluency. You have to experience them as a native speaker says them, repeat them as a native speaker would, and through mass amount of practice come to an innate understanding of the inner workings of a language's morphology. Most native speakers can't explain their own grammar. It just happens.

How to Use GMS and GSR

The best way to use GMS is to find a certain time of day that works best for you where you can concentrate. It doesn't have to be a lot of time, maybe just 30 minutes at most is fine. If you have more time, even better. Then schedule that time to be your study time every day.

Try to tackle anywhere from 20 to 100 sentences per day in the GMS. Do what you're comfortable with.

Review the first 50 sentences in the book to get an idea of what will be said. Then listen to the A files. If you can, try to write all the sentences down from the files as dictation without looking at the text. This will force you to differentiate all the sounds of the language. If you don't like using the A files, you can switch to the C files which only have the target language.

After dictation, check your work for any mistakes. These mistakes should tell you a lot that you will improve on the next day.

Go through the files once again, repeating all the sentences. Then record yourself saying all the sentences. Ideally, you should record these sentences four to five days in a row in order to become very familiar with them.

All of the activities above may take more than one day or one setting, so go at the pace that feels comfortable for you.

If this schedule is too difficult to adhere to, or you find that dictation and recording is too much, then take a more relaxed approach with the GSR files. The GSR files in most cases are shorter than twenty minutes, some go over due to the length of the sentences. But this is the perfect attention span that most people have anyway. By the end of the GSR files you should feel pretty tired, especially if you're trying to repeat everything.

The GSR files are numbered from Day 1 to Day 100. Just do one every day, as all the five days of review sentences are built in. It's that simple! Good luck.

Sentence Mining

Sentence mining can be a fun activity where you find sentences that you like or feel useful in the language you're learning. We suggest keeping your list of sentences in a spreadsheet that you can re-order how you wish.

It's always a good idea to keep a list of all the sentences you're learning or mastering. They not only encompass a lot of vocabulary and their actual usage, or "collocations", but they give you a framework for speaking the language. It's also fun to keep track of your progress and see the number of sentences increasing.

Based on many tests we've conducted, we've found that students can reach a good level of fluency with only a small number of sentences. For example, with just 3000 sentences, each trained 10 times over a period of 5 days, for a total of 30,000 sentences (repetitions), can make a difference between a completely mute person who is shy and unsure how to speak and a talkative person who wants to talk about everything. More importantly, the reps empower you to become a stronger speaker.

The sentences we have included in our Glossika courses have been carefully selected to give you a wide range of expression. The sentences in our fluency modules target the kinds of conversations that you have discussing day-to-day activities, the bulk of what makes up our real-life conversations with friends and family. For some people these sentences may feel really boring, but these sentences are carefully selected to represent an array of discussing events that occur in the past, the present and the future, and whether those actions are continuous or not, even in languages where such grammar is not explicitly marked—especially in these languages as you need to know how to convey your thoughts. The sentences are transparent enough that they give you the tools to go and create dozens of more sentences based on the models we give you.

As you work your way through our Fluency Series the sentences will cover all aspects of grammar without actually teaching you grammar. You'll find most of the patterns used in all the tenses and aspects, passive and active (or ergative as is the case in some languages we're developing), indirect speech, and finally describing events as if to a policeman. The sentences also present some transformational patterns you can look out for. Sometimes we have more than one way to say something in our own language, but maybe only one in a foreign language. And the opposite is true where we may only have one way to say something whereas a foreign language may have many.

Transformation Drills

A transformation is restating the same sentence with the same meaning, but using different words or phrasing to accomplish this. A transformation is essentially a translation, but inside the same language. A real example from Glossika's business module is:

- Could someone help me with my bags?
- Could I get a hand with these bags?

You may not necessarily say "hand" in a foreign language and that's why direct translation word-for-word can be dangerous. As you can see from these two sentences, they're translations of each other, but they express the same meaning.

To express yourself well in a foreign language, practice the art of restating everything you say in your mother language. Find more ways to say the same thing.

There are in fact two kinds of transformation drills we can do. One is transformation in our mother language and the other is transformation into our target language, known as translation.

By transforming a sentence in your own language, you'll get better at transforming it into another language and eventually being able to formulate your ideas and thoughts in that language. It's a process and it won't happen over night. Cultivate your ability day by day.

Build a bridge to your new language through translation. The better you get, the less you rely on the bridge until one day, you won't need it at all.

Translation should never be word for word or literal. You should always aim to achieve the exact same feeling in the foreign language. The only way to achieve this is by someone who can create the sentences for you who already knows both languages to such fluency that he knows the feeling created is exactly the same.

In fact, you'll encounter many instances in our GMS publications where sentences don't seem to match up. The two languages are expressed completely differently, and it seems it's wrong. Believe us, we've not only gone over and tested each sentence in real life situations, we've even refined the translations several times to the point that this is really how we speak in this given situation.

Supplementary Substitution Drills

Substitution drills are more or less the opposite of transformation drills. Instead of restating the same thing in a different way, you're saying a different thing using the exact same way. So using the example from above we can create this substitution drill:

- Could someone help me with my bags?
- Could someone help me with making dinner?

In this case, we have replaced the noun with a gerund phrase. The sentence has a different meaning but it's using the same structure. This drill also allows the learner to recognize a pattern how to use a verb behind a preposition, especially after being exposed to several instances of this type.

We can also combine transformation and substitution drills:

- Could someone help me with my bags?
- Could someone give me a hand with making dinner?

So it is encouraged that as you get more and more experience working through the Glossika materials, that you not only write out and record more and more of your own conversations, but also do more transformation and substitution drills on top of the sentences we have included in the book.

Memory, The Brain, and Language Acquisition

by Michael Campbell

We encounter a lot of new information every day that may or may not need to be memorized. In fact, we're doing it all the time when we make new friends, remembering faces and other information related to our friends.

After some experience with language learning you'll soon discover that languages are just like a social landscape. Except instead of interconnected friends we have interconnected words. In fact, looking at languages in this way makes it a lot more fun as you get familiar with all the data.

Since languages are natural and all humans are able to use them naturally, it only makes sense to learn languages in a natural way. In fact studies have found, and many students having achieved fluency will attest to, the fact that words are much easier to recognize in their written form if we already know them in the spoken form. Remember that you already own the words you use to speak with. The written form is just a record and it's much easier to transfer what you know into written form than trying to memorize something that is only written.

Trying to learn a language from the writing alone can be a real daunting task. Learning to read a language you already speak is not hard at all. So don't beat yourself up trying to learn how to read a complicated script like Chinese if you have no idea how to speak the language yet. It's not as simple as one word = one character. And the same holds true with English as sometimes many words make up one idea, like "get over it".

What is the relationship between memory and sleep? Our brain acquires experiences throughout the day and records them as memories. If these memories are too common, such as eating lunch, they get lost among all the others and we find it difficult to remember one specific memory from the others. More importantly such memories leave no impact or impression on us. However, a major event like a birth or an accident obviously leaves a bigger impact. We attach importance to those events.

Since our brain is constantly recording our daily life, it collects a lot of useless information. Since this information is both mundane and unimportant to us, our brain has a built-in mechanism to deal with it. In other words, our brains dump the garbage every day. Technically speaking our memories are connections between our nerve cells and these connections lose strength if they are not recalled or used again.

During our sleep cycles our brain is reviewing all the events of the day. If you do not recall those events the following day, the memory weakens. After three sleep cycles, consider a memory gone if you haven't recalled it. Some memories can be retained longer because you may have anchored it better the first time you encountered it. An anchor is connecting your memory with one of your senses or another pre-existing memory. During your language learning process, this won't happen until later in your progress. So what can you do in the beginning?

A lot of memory experts claim that making outrageous stories about certain things they're learning help create that anchor where otherwise none would exist. Some memory experts picture a house in their mind that they're very familiar with and walk around that house in a specific pre-arranged order. Then all the objects they're memorizing are placed in that house in specific locations. In order to recall them, they just walk around the house.

I personally have had no luck making outrageous stories to memorize things. I've found the house method very effective but it's different than the particular way I use it. This method is a form of "memory map", or spatial memory, and for me personally I prefer using real world maps. This probably originates from my better than average ability to remember maps, so if you can, then use it! It's not for everybody though. It really works great for learning multiple languages.

What do languages and maps have in common? Everything can be put on a map, and languages naturally are spoken in locations and spread around and change over time. These changes in pronunciations of words creates a word history, or etymology. And by understanding how pronunciations change over time and where populations migrated, it's quite easy to remember a large number of data with just a memory map. This is how I anchor new languages I'm learning. I have a much bigger challenge when I try a new language family. So I look for even deeper and longer etymologies that are shared between language families, anything to help me establish a link to some core vocabulary. Some words like "I" (think Old English "ic") and "me/mine" are essentially the same roots all over the world from Icelandic (Indo-European) to Finnish (Uralic) to Japanese (Altaic?) to Samoan (Austronesian).

I don't confuse languages because in my mind every language sounds unique and has its own accent and mannerisms. I can also use my memory map to position myself in the location where the language is spoken and imagine myself surrounded by the people of that country. This helps me adapt to their expressions and mannerisms, but more importantly, eliminates interference from other languages. And when I mentally set myself up in this way, the chance of confusing a word from another language simply doesn't happen.

When I've actually used a specific way of speaking and I've done it several days in a row, I know that the connections in my head are now strengthening and taking root. Not using them three days in a row creates a complete loss, however actively using them (not passively listening) three days in a row creates a memory that stays for a lifetime. Then you no longer need the anchors and the memory is just a part of you.

You'll have noticed that the Glossika training method gives a translation for every sentence, and in fact we use translation as one of the major anchors for you. In this way 1) the translation acts as an anchor, 2) you have intelligible input, 3) you easily start to recognize patterns. Pattern recognition is the single most important skill you need for learning a foreign language.

A lot of people think that translation should be avoided at all costs when learning a foreign language. However, based on thousands of tests I've given my students over a ten-year period, I've found that just operating in the foreign language itself creates a false sense of understanding and you have a much higher chance of hurting yourself in the long run by creating false realities.

I set up a specific test. I asked my students to translate back into their mother tongue (Chinese) what they heard me saying. These were students who could already hold conversations in English. I found the results rather shocking. Sentences with certain word combinations or phrases really caused a lot of misunderstanding, like "might as well" or "can't do it until", resulted in a lot of guesswork and rather incorrect answers.

If you assume you can think and operate in a foreign language without being able to translate what's being said, you're fooling yourself into false comprehension. Train yourself to translate everything into your foreign language. This again is an anchor that you can eventually abandon when you become very comfortable with the new language.

Finally, our brain really is a sponge. But you have to create the structure of the sponge. Memorizing vocabulary in a language that you don't know is like adding water to a sponge that has no structure: it all flows out.

In order to create a foreign language structure, or "sponge", you need to create sentences that are natural and innate. You start with sentence structures with basic, common vocabulary that's easy enough to master and start building from there. With less than 100 words, you can build thousands of sentences to fluency, slowly one by one adding more and more vocabulary. Soon, you're speaking with natural fluency and you have a working vocabulary of several thousand words.

If you ever learn new vocabulary in isolation, you have to start using it immediately in meaningful sentences. Hopefully sentences you want to use. If you can't make a sentence with it, then the vocabulary is useless.

Vocabulary shouldn't be memorized haphazardly because vocabulary itself is variable. The words we use in our language are only a tool for conveying a larger message, and every language uses different words to convey the same message. Look for the message, pay attention to the specific words used, then learn those words. Memorizing words from a wordlist will not help you with this task.

Recently a friend showed me his wordlist for learning Chinese, using a kind of spaced repetition flashcard program where he could download a "deck". I thought it was a great idea until I saw the words he was trying to learn. I tried explaining that learning these characters out of context do not have the meanings on his cards and they will mislead him into a false understanding, especially individual characters. This would only work if they were a review from a text he had read, where all the vocabulary appeared in real sentences and a story to tell, but they weren't. From a long-term point of view, I could see that it would hurt him and require twice as much time to re-learn everything. From the short-term point of view, there was definitely a feeling of progress and mastery and he was happy with that and I dropped the issue.

French Background and Pronunciation

- **Classification:** Indo-European Language Family - Romance Branch
- **Writing:** Latin

- **Consonants:**

  /p b f v m t d s z l n ʃ ʒ j ɲ ɥ k g ʁ w/ Unvoiced stops (p, t, k) are not aspirated /pˀ tˀ kˀ/ different from English.

- **Vowels:**

  /i y u e ø ə o ɛ œ ɔ ɛ̃ ɔ̃ ɑ̃ a ɑ/

- **IPA:** Phonetic transcription showing liaison

- **Intonation:** Mostly word-final and even phrase-final
- **Word Order:** Subject - Verb - Object
- **Adjective Order:** Noun - Adjective
- **Possessive Order:** Genitive - Noun
- **Adposition Order:** Preposition - Noun
- **Dependent Clause:** Dependent - Noun, Noun - Relative Clause
- **Verbs:** Tense (present, past, future), Aspect (perfect, imperfect), Mood (indicative, subjunctive)
- **Nouns:** 2 genders, definite/indefinite
- **Pronouns:** 1st/2nd/3rd, masc/feminine/neuter, singular/plural, reflexive, 6 conjugations

Classification

French is closely related to the other Romance languages (languages of the Romans) descended from Latin. Historically all of these languages are generalisations of a dialect continuum from Italy up to France and then down to the Iberian peninsula where Catalan, Spanish and Portuguese are spoken. Today we like to give things labels such as "language" or "dialect", but the difference between them can cause disputes. Historically, there were only dialects. It wasn't until nation states sprung up and communication required a standard that languages were standardized, usually based on the "dialect" of the capital city. In some countries like Italy, when it was unified in the 19th century a national language was created with bits and pieces from various dialects spoken around the new "country". These national, standardized "languages" become a nation's identity to the rest of the world.

So as we can identify a central position among a dialectal region, perhaps a place of commerce or larger city, the speech of areas between these places of commerce become dialectal grey areas where the continuum blends slowly into the next. So from the northern region of Italy where people speak a national Italian language and a local dialect, they can just as easily switch between their local dialect and the neighboring French language, simply because their dialect is at the halfway point between the two national languages. Likewise those in southern France may also be able to communicate with Italians in the border areas. In southern France one finds the language of the "Ocs" because they say "òc" instead of "oui" for the word "yes". This language, Occitan (or Provençal) has its own dialectal regions, but it is gradually blends into the "Catalan" of Spain. Our Glossika course for "Catalan" is based on the speech of Barcelona, but you could still use it to communicate in or acquire "Occitan" in southern France. It should be seen as an intermediary language between French, Spanish and Italian.

One might wonder how dialects came about in the first place. Languages evolve naturally, and like biological evolution, the traits that are adopted by the masses are those that continue to live on from one generation to the next. No one individual can take control over the future course of a language or how it evolves. But then you may wonder, how can a national language be created and how can it be adopted by everyone in the country? The matter is not as simple as you may think. What happens in most cases (or we could say, in most countries) is a dual register. If you are from England, then you will definitely be aware of the regional dialects and how words and sometimes how grammar differs from area to area. The English language also differs between different classes of people, from the poor to the rich, historically one's speech defines a man's social status.

The Académie française, restored in its modern form by Napoleon in 1803, polices the French language as a national standard. So on the one hand we can say that no individual person or "academy" can control a language's evolution, on the other hand it is precisely for this reason that the Académie has been established, so that a standard of speech can be maintained among all the dialects within France. To this day, as in most countries, a dichotomy remains: the local dialects in all their flavours, and the national standard. It is quite possible that as a student of the language you will eventually learn how to recognize and switch between them yourself, depending on the circumstances and your audience.

Due to the dichotomy that exists in most languages (the real world spoken dialect vs. the national standard), most textbooks only teach the national standard and there are peculiarities with the colloquial language that is seldom taught. It is our goal here at Glossika to present you with the real spoken language, not in defiance of the national standard, but to allow you as the student to get as close as humanly possible to communicating comfortably in social settings in your host country. This means that in a language like French which has a lot of tricky pronunciation with liaison, that what you will learn from this course is the relaxed and comfortable liaisons rather than the official ones. This will make it possible to meet people and let them feel comfortable with your style of speech from the very beginning. Oftentimes speaking exactly like a textbook or text-to-speech algorithm will not benefit you socially as much as you would like it to.

Thus the language presented in the Glossika recordings are based on the national standard, but the liaisons are spoken in a relaxed way. We do not need to change the spelling or the text in any way to show this (unlike our Finnish, Armenian and Persian courses which require parallel texts due to the dichotomy), however our phonetic transcription is written in such a way that it matches the surface pronunciation that you will encounter in the sound files.

Grammar

This fluency series of books does not go into grammatical detail. This is why we recommend to use this course as a supplement to other studies, but if you are using it alone, then you can get a lot of the grammatical explanation online from Wikipedia and videos that teachers have shared. Since French is a widely taught language, we will not attempt to replicate any grammatical explanations in this course. The Glossika Fluency series really focus on speaking the language in real life, so all of your effort in this course should be spent on accent and pronunciation improvement, both in speaking and listening.

Since the course is written with syntax structure in mind, it should follow a natural sequence of ever more complex sentences, of which you will find many deliberate iterations therein in order to allow to acquire a true natural and fluent grasp of the language. The goal of this definition of fluency is not a huge vocabulary, but rather complete freedom over your ability to manipulate sentences.

The most important feature of this course is our list of words and all their variable pronunciations that occur throughout the course which we will describe below in more detail.

Due to differences between your language and French, we advise you never to get stuck analyzing just one sentence. Sometimes word orders are different. Oftentimes there is not enough data in one sentence to deduce what is happening. To take this method to heart, start of by going through the whole book listening to all 1000 sentences and take some occasional notes when you notice patterns. By learning how to notice these patterns, you are building the skills you need for natural language acquisition. Don't try to memorize any single sentence or any grammatical rules. Get a feel for how the sentences flow off the tongue.

The native speaker will speak long strings of syllables in such rapid succession that you'll find it impossible to follow or imitate in the beginning. This is due to the aforementioned problem: too small of a data set to extract or deduce what you need to learn. To learn effectively, or whenever you get stuck, just sit back with your book and relax, play through all 1000 sentences in a single setting and let the repetitive parts of the phrases fill your ears and your brain. Soon you'll be on the right track to mimicking these phrases just as a child does. A child will always have a rough approximation of speech before the age of five, but has no problem in saying complete sentences. So always focus first on fluency and continue to work hard on perfecting your pronunciation, intonation, and accent.

As a foreigner, it may take you many years to master the language. We've given you about six to twelve months of training here depending on your personal schedule. Everything included here is just the basic of basics, so you really need to get to the point where all of these sentences become quite easy to manipulate and produce, and then you can spend the next five to ten years conversing in French and learning how to say more and more, learning directly inside the language without the need for translating. We've given you the tools to get to that point.

Structure

French stress evolved out of Latin stress, so the stress patterns are almost identical to those found in Italian, Catalan, Spanish and Portuguese. But since a lot of phonological degradation has occurred in French over the centuries, the penultimate stress you find in Italian and Spanish has become final stress in both French and Catalan (Occitan). French has been moving more and more to a non-stress pattern as words get shorter and shorter getting strung together in rapid succession, and in most cases you'll find that stress on individual words has disappeared and has moved to the end of the phrase. This is usually the case in fluent speech. This has also given rise to innovations in the language, for example "pas" placed after the negated verb, because the negative participle can almost get completely lost in speech due to nasalization and shortening of words. And so in almost every instance of "pas", you'll find it with a strong stress as to make sure the phrase is understood as being negative.

Unlike Italian or Spanish, the diacritics above letters in French do not indicate stress patterns at all. These are used simply to indicate different pronunciations. For example, the letter {e} can very easily disappear or be swallowed by neighboring consonants (in which case we write as a tiny superscript schwa [°] as a possible phonetic realization). If the letter {e} is still to be pronounced, it depends on its position (is it followed by {-s} or {-t} or {-z} at the end of a word?) or it would be written with an acute accent {é}. In this case it should sound like its IPA equivalent /e/. The other two letters {è, ê} are both pronounced like the English short vowel /ɛ/. The letter {ê} in most cases gave rise from a disappearing {-s} as can be observed in "même" (Spanish: mismo) and "forêt" (English: forest) and other evolutions of the language. Likewise the letter {é} can also represent the disappearing {-s} at the beginning of words which can be observed in "étude" (Spanish: estudio, English: study).

Names

The Glossika Fluency series is a global production with over a hundred languages in development, so we include names from all the major languages and cultures around the world. Many of these are foreign to French speakers, and probably including yourself. However, it is of particular interest to us how languages deal with foreign names, both in localizing and dealing with them grammatically. In this edition we have not attempted to write the pronunciation of names, but left the pronunciation up to the native speaker. However, note how word endings are attached to names, because as a foreigner speaking French, you will undoubtedly have to use foreign names. Also use these names to your advantage, as an anchor in each sentence to figure out how all the other parts of speech interact with the name.

The pronunciation guide used in this book (please read the following section for details) does not account for foreign words or borrowings and so we simply do not transcribe the pronunciations in this case.

IPA

Almost all language teaching books over the last century have resorted to awkward explanations of pronunciation. You may have seen lots of strange pronunciation guides over the years in all kinds of publications. The problem with these kinds of publications is many-fold. Many times the pronunciation being taught is very specific to American pronunciation in particular, which means even if you're not American, you'll end up pronouncing the language you're learning like an American. I've seen similar devices used in British publications, but many times when I see a book explain: "pronounce it like the vowel in 'hear'" I have no idea which version of

English they're referring to. The British books often make references to Scottish speakers, which is not really common knowledge for Americans. So I think it is important to consider where your readers are coming from without making assumptions.

The second problem is why would anybody want to pronounce the language they're learning like an American? Isn't the point to learn pronunciation as closely as we can to the way native speakers speak? In any case, it pays off well to work hard at eliminating a trace of one's foreign accent when speaking other languages. It also puts your listeners at ease as they won't have to strain so hard to understand what you're saying. Here we will avoid criticizing all the problems related to the transcription of other pronunciation guides and why they may be misleading, and focus our attention instead to amazing solutions.

Over the last century our knowledge of phonetics has improved greatly. All of this knowledge seems to have been known by the elite few professors and students of Linguistics departments scattered around the globe. But with the internet comes the explosion of information that is now accessible to everybody. Not only that, but language learners, even average language learners, are a lot smarter about the process of going about learning other languages than people were just a mere twenty or thirty years ago. It is now possible for teenagers to achieve fluency in any number of languages they want from the comfort of their own home just by using the resources available on the internet. I personally attempted to do so when I was a teenager without the internet, and trying to make sense of languages with very little data or explanation was quite frustrating.

As well-informed language learners of the twenty-first century, we now have access to all the tools that make languages much easier to learn. If you can read other languages as well, there are literally thousands of blogs, discussion groups, communities and places to go on the internet to learn everything you want to know about language learning. There is still a lot of misinformation getting passed around, but the community is maturing. The days of using such hackneyed pronunciation guides are hopefully over.

All the secrets that linguists have had are now available to the general public. Linguists have been using the International Phonetic Alphabet (IPA) as a standard for recording languages, where every letter is given one and only one sound, what is called a point of articulation. This enables linguists to talk about linguistic phenomena in a scientific and precise way. Since the point of articulation can be slightly different from language to language, a single letter like /t/ does not have a very specific point, but just a general area that we can call "alveolar" the location known as the alveolar ridge behind the teeth. IPA has extra diacritics available to indicate where the /t/ is to be pronounced. In a lot of cases, this information is not necessary for talking about the language in broad terms, especially topics unrelated to pronunciation, so as long as the language has no other kind of /t/ in that same area, there's no need to indicate the precise location: this is known as phonemic.

English is a good example. For example, we don't think about it much that {t} is pronounced differently in "take", "wanted", "letter", "stuff" and "important". If you're North American, the {t} in each of these words is actually pronounced differently: aspirated, as a nasal, as a flap, unaspirated, as a glottal stop. Maybe you never even realized it. But to a foreign learner of English, hearing all these different sounds can get very confusing especially when everybody says "it's a T!" but in reality they're saying different things. It's not that Americans don't hear the different sounds, it's just that they label all of the sounds as {t} which leads them to believe that what they're actually hearing are the same. But it more difficult for the foreigners to learn when a {t} is pronounced as a glottal stop or as a flap, etc. The task for the language learner is often underestimated by teachers and native speakers.

Many letters in English have these variations which are called "allophones" and we can record them as separate letters in IPA or with diacritical marks. In order to indicate that this pronunciation is "precise" I should use square brackets: [tʰ, t̚, ɾ, ʔ]. So we can say that although English has one phonemic /t/, in reality there are many allophones. Actually every language has allophones! So what we learn as spelling, or in a book, usually is just the general phonemic guide, and it differs quite a bit from the way people actually speak with allophones. When I'm learning a foreign language I always ask what the allophones are because it helps me speak that language much clearer and much more like a native.

Why does a language learner need a "precise" pronunciation guide?

Let's take the English learner again. If that person is told to always pronounce {t} exactly the same way, then his speech will actually become very emphatic, unnatural sounding and forced. To native speakers this learner will always have a strong foreign accent, have choppy pronunciation and be difficult to understand. We should always set our goals high enough even if we can't attain them perfectly, but at least we're pushing ourselves to achieve more than we would have otherwise. So if you have an accurate transcription of native speakers which indicates all the variations that they use, you will have access to a wealth of information that no other language learner had access to before. Not only that but you have the tools available for perfecting your pronunciation.

There is no better solution than IPA itself, the secret code of the linguists. Now the IPA is available in Wikipedia with links for each letter to separate pages with recordings and a list of languages that use those sounds.

From the beginning you must take note that French has absolutely no aspirated sounds, so that the English {p, t, k} are completely different from French {p, t, k}. To summarize:

English {p, t, k} = lots of aspiration (puff of air) French {p, t, k} = no aspiration whatsoever. To the untrained English ear, they may actually sound like {b, d, g}, which means you'll need more exposure and practice.

French Pronunciation

The IPA transcription in this book is based on a computer program written by the Glossika staff which produces pronunciation in two steps which is required for all languages: 1) phonemic, 2) phonetic. The computer program is based on the official spelling of the language alone rather than pronunciation guides. Some languages require additional steps of adding stress and tone in order to get the correct phonetic output, as in the case for French "appele" and "appeler", otherwise the unstressed {e} in the second example would get deleted.

Liaison is a big issue that any student of French is acutely aware of. Our transcription works like this:

1. If the ending of a word is not pronounced, the phonemes get deleted.
2. If the ending of a word carries over to the next word, the phoneme moves to the next word and *starts* it.
3. If a word contains the sometimes pronounced schwa, we write it as [°] or which some speakers do not pronounce. This results in consonant "clusters", but consonant clusters occur in two different ways among world languages:

A) Languages with consonant clusters that fuse together: English, Russian, German, etc. B) Languages with consonant clusters where every consonant is spoken individually with an epenthetic [°]: French, Georgian, Atayal, etc.

In other words, consonant clusters in English and French are produced differently. Where you come across [db] in "debout" does not sound like the [db] in English "bad boy", but rather spoken slightly separately as [d°b]. An English speaker would consider "bad° boy" with an epenthetic [°] an incorrect pronunciation, whereas this is not the case in French.

Last two pieces of advice: Please consult the IPA transcription whenever in doubt.

Don't forget that if you ever get frustrated, just go back through all 1000 sentences and relax while you listen. No need to force yourself to remember or repeat during this. This is just to help clear your mind of a few problematic sentences. Chances are, if you keep moving through all the sentences, those troublesome sentences will no longer be troublesome when you loop back around again.

Vocabulary Index

1. The vocabulary index does not include foreign names and places, or words without an IPA transcription.
2. The index lists every variation of every French word found in this book. However, for common words, we do not list every single sentence in which they occur in order to save space. The first few sentences that we do list should be enough of a resource for you to check that special occurrence or pronunciation pattern.
3. Words that are combined in transcription in the text are separated in the index for individual lookup.
4. All words that have a change in liaison can be looked up in the index by observing the IPA transcription. Do you want to know when "tous" is pronounced [tu] or [tus]? Do you want to know when "allé" is pronounced [ale] or [zale] or [tale] because of the preceding liaison? Do you want to know how many different conjugations appear in our text? All of these are listed as separate entries in the index for your convenience.

We sincerely hope that our unique way of presenting the language will be useful for both students and teachers alike and will remain as a useful reference and tool for years to come.

Vocabulary: French

Prepositions

about	sur
above	au-dessus
according to	selon
across	à travers
after	après
against	contre
among	entre
around	autour de
as	comme
as far as	autant que
as well as	aussi bien que
at	à
because of	en raison de
before	avant
behind	derrière
below	en dessous
beneath	sous
beside	à côté de
between	entre
beyond	au-delà
but	mais
by	par
close to	près de
despite	malgré

down	vers le bas
due to	à cause de
during	au cours de
except	sauf
except for	à l'exception de
far from	loin d'être
for	pour
from	à partir de
in	dans
in addition to	en plus de
in front of	en face de
in spite of	en dépit de
inside	à l'intérieur
inside of	l'intérieur de
instead of	au lieu de
into	dans
near	près de
near to	près de
next	prochain
next to	à côté de
of	de
on	sur
on behalf of	au nom de
on top of	au sommet de
opposite	opposé
out	à
outside	à l'extérieur
outside of	en dehors des
over	sur

per	par
plus	plus
prior to	avant
round	tour
since	depuis
than	que
through	par
till	jusqu'à
to	à
toward	vers
under	sous
unlike	contrairement à
until	jusqu'à ce que
up	jusqu'à
via	via
with	avec
within	dans
without	sans

Adjectives

a few	quelques
bad	mauvais
big	grand
bitter	amer
clean	propre
correct	correct
dark	sombre
deep	profond

difficult	difficile
dirty	sale
dry	sec
easy	facile
empty	vide
expensive	cher
fast	rapide
few	peu
foreign	étranger
fresh	frais
full	plein
good	bon
hard	dur
heavy	lourd
inexpensive	peu coûteux
light	léger
little	peu
local	local
long	long
many	beaucoup
much	beaucoup
narrow	étroit
new	nouveau
noisy	bruyant
old	vieux
part	partie
powerful	puissant
quiet	calme
short person	salé

small	court
salty	lent
slow	petit
soft	doux
some	certains
sour	aigre
spicy	épicé
sweet	doux
tall	haut
thick	épais
thin	mince
very	très
weak	faible
wet	humide
whole	ensemble
wide	large
wrong	faux
young	jeune

Adverbs

absolutely	absolument
ago	il y a
almost	presque
alone	seul
already	déjà
always	toujours
anywhere	n'importe où
away	loin

barely	à peine
carefully	soigneusement
everywhere	partout
fast	rapide
frequently	fréquemment
hard	dur
hardly	à peine
here	ici
home	maison
immediately	immédiatement
last night	dernière nuit
lately	récemment
later	plus tard
mostly	surtout
never	jamais
next week	semaine prochaine
now	maintenant
nowhere	nulle part
occasionally	de temps en temps
out	dehors
over there	là-bas
pretty	joli
quickly	rapidement
quite	tout à fait, assez
rarely	rarement
really	vraiment
recently	récemment
right now	pour le moment, en ce moment
seldom	rarement

slowly	lentement
sometimes	parfois
soon	bientôt
still	encore
then	puis
there	là
this morning	ce matin
today	aujourd'hui
together	ensemble
tomorrow	demain
tonight	ce soir
usually	habituellement
very	très
well	bien
yesterday	hier, la vielle
yet	encore

Glossika Mass Sentences

GMS #2001 - 2100

2001

EN Can you remind me to call Sandra tomorrow?

FR Peux-tu me rappeler d'appeler Sandra demain?
IPA [pø ty mø ʁapᵊle d‿apᵊle (...) dᵊmɛ̆ ‖]

2002

EN Who taught you to drive?

FR Qui t'a appris à conduire?
IPA [ki t‿a apʁi a kɔ̃dɥiʁ ‖]

2003

EN I didn't move the piano by myself. I got somebody to help me.

FR Je n'ai pas déplacé le piano par moi-même. J'ai demandé à quelqu'un de m'aider.
IPA [ʒø n‿ɛ pa deplase lø pjano paʁ mwamɛm ‖ ʒ‿ɛ dᵊmɑ̃de a kɛlkœ̃ dø m‿ede ‖]

2004

EN Diego said the switch was dangerous, and warned me not to touch it.

FR Diego a dit que l'interrupteur était dangereux et m'a prévenu de ne pas y toucher.

IPA [(...) a di kø l‿ɛ̃tɛʁyptœʁ etɛ dɑ̃ʒ°ʁø e m‿a pʁɛv°ny dø nø pa z‿i tuʃe ‖]

2005

EN I was warned not to touch the switch.

FR J'ai été prévenu de ne pas toucher à l'interrupteur.

IPA [ʒ‿ɛ ete pʁɛv°ny dø nø pa tuʃe a l‿ɛ̃tɛʁyptœʁ ‖]

2006

EN Stan suggested I ask you for advice.

FR Stan a suggéré que je te demandes ton avis.

IPA [stan a sygʒeʁe kø ʒø tø d°mɑ̃d tɔ̃ n‿avi ‖]

2007

EN I wouldn't advise staying in that hotel. > I wouldn't advise anybody to stay in that hotel.

FR Je ne te recommanderais pas de séjourner dans cet hôtel. > Je ne recommanderais pas à personne de séjourner dans cet hôtel.

IPA [ʒø nø tø ʁ°komɑ̃d°ʁɛ pa dø seʒuʁne dɑ̃ sɛ t‿otɛl ‖ > ʒø nø ʁ°komɑ̃d°ʁɛ pa a pɛʁsɔn dø seʒuʁne dɑ̃ sɛ t‿otɛl ‖]

2008

EN They don't allow parking in front of the building. > They don't allow people to park in front of the building.

FR Ils interdisent qu'on se gare devant l'édifice. > Ils interdisent aux gens de se garer devant l'édifice.

IPA [i l‿ɛ̃tɛʁdiz k‿ɔ̃ sø gaʁ d‿ə vɑ̃ l‿edifis ‖ > i l‿ɛ̃tɛʁdiz o ʒɑ̃ dø sø gaʁe d‿ə vɑ̃ l‿edifis ‖]

2009

EN Parking isn't allowed in front of the building. > You aren't allowed to park in front of the building.

FR Il est interdit de se garer devant l'édifice. > Tu ne peux pas te garer devant l'édifice.

IPA [i l‿e t‿ɛ̃tɛʁdi dø sø gaʁe d‿ə vɑ̃ l‿edifis ‖ > ty nø pø pa tø gaʁe d‿ə vɑ̃ l‿edifis ‖]

2010

EN I made him promise that he wouldn't tell anybody what happened.

FR Je l'ai fait promettre de ne raconter à personne ce qui s'était passé.

IPA [ʒø l‿e fɛ pʁomɛtʁ dø nø ʁakɔ̃te a pɛʁsɔn sø ki s‿ete pase ‖]

2011

EN Hot weather makes me feel tired.

FR La chaleur me fatigue.
IPA [la ʃalœʁ mø fatig ||]

2012

EN Her parents wouldn't let her go out alone.

FR Ses parents ne la laissaient pas sortir seule.
IPA [se paʁɑ̃ nø la lɛsɛ pa sɔʁtiʁ sœl ||]

2013

EN Let me carry your bag for you.

FR Laisse-moi porter ton sac.
IPA [lɛs mwa pɔʁte tɔ̃ sak ||]

2014

EN We were made to wait for two (2) hours.

FR On nous a fait attendre deux heures.
IPA [ɔ̃ nu z‿a fɛ atɑ̃dʁ dø z‿œʁ ||]

2015

EN My lawyer said I shouldn't say anything to the police. > My lawyer advised me not to say anything to the police.

FR Mon avocat a dit que je ne devrais rien dire à la police. > Mon avocat m'a recommandé de ne rien dire à la police.

IPA [mɔ̃ n̪avoka a di kø ʒø nø dᵊvʁɛ ʁjɛ̃ diʁ a la polis ||
> mɔ̃ n̪avoka m̪a ʁᵊkomɑ̃de dø nø ʁjɛ̃ diʁ a la polis
||]

2016

EN I was told that I shouldn't believe everything he says. > I was warned not to believe anything he says.

FR On m'a dit de ne pas croire tout ce qu'il dit. > J'ai été prévenu (♀prévenue) de ne pas croire tout ce qu'il dit.

IPA [ɔ̃ m̪a di dø nø pa kʁwaʁ tu sø k̪il di || > ʒ̪ɛ ete
pʁɛvᵊny (♀pʁɛvᵊny) dø nø pa kʁwaʁ tu sø k̪il di ||]

2017

EN If you have a car, you're able to get around more easily. > Having a car enables you to get around more easily.

FR Si tu as une voiture, tu peux te déplacer plus facilement. > Avoir une voiture te permet de te déplacer plus facilement.

IPA [si ty a z̪yn vwatyʁ | ty pø tø deplase plys fasilᵊmɑ̃
|| > avwa ʁ̪yn vwatyʁ tø pɛʁmɛ dø tø deplase plys
fasilᵊmɑ̃ ||]

2018

EN I know I locked the door. I clearly remember locking it. > I remembered to lock the door, but I forgot to shut the windows.

FR Je sais que j'ai verrouillé la porte. Je me souviens clairement l'avoir verrouillée. > J'ai pensé à verrouiller la porte, mais j'ai oublié de fermer les fenêtres.

IPA [ʒø sɛ kø ʒ‿ɛ veʁuje la pɔʁt ‖ ʒø mø suvjɛ̃ klɛʁ°mɑ̃ l‿avwaʁ veʁuje ‖ > ʒ‿ɛ pɑ̃se a veʁuje la pɔʁt | mɛ ʒ‿ɛ ublije dø fɛʁme le f°nɛtʁ ‖]

2019

EN He could remember driving along the road just before the accident, but he couldn't remember the accident itself.

FR Il se souvenait avoir conduit le long de la route juste avant l'accident, mais il n'arrivait pas à se souvenir de l'accident lui-même.

IPA [il sø suv°nɛ avwaʁ kɔ̃dɥi lø lɔ̃ dø la ʁut ʒyst avɑ̃ l‿aksidɑ̃ | mɛ il n‿aʁive pa a sø suv°niʁ dø l‿aksidɑ̃ lɥimɛm ‖]

2020

EN Please remember to mail the letter on your way to work.

FR N'oublie pas de poster la lettre en te rendant au travail s'il te plaît.

IPA [n‿ubli pa dø pɔste la lɛtʁ ɑ̃ tø ʁɑ̃dɑ̃ o tʁavaj s‿il tø plɛ ‖]

2021

EN I now regret saying what I said. I shouldn't have said it.

FR Je regrette maintenant d'avoir dit ce que j'ai dit. Je n'aurais pas dû le dire.

IPA [ʒø ʁ°gʁɛt mɛ̃t°nɑ̃ d̯avwaʁ di sø kø ʒ̯ɛ di ‖ ʒø n̯ɔʁɛ pa dy lø diʁ ‖‖]

2022

EN It began to get cold, and he regretted not wearing his coat.

FR Il a commencé à faire froid et il a regretté de ne pas porter son manteau.

IPA [i l̯a komɑ̃se a fɛʁ fʁwa e i l̯a ʁ°gʁete dø nø pa poʁte sɔ̃ mɑ̃to ‖‖]

2023

EN We regret to inform you that we cannot offer you the job.

FR Nous avons le regret de vous informer que nous ne pouvons pas vous offrir l'emploi.

IPA [nu z̯avɔ̃ lø ʁ°gʁɛ dø vu z̯ɛ̃fɔʁme kø nu nø puvɔ̃ pa vu z̯ofʁiʁ l̯ɑ̃plwa ‖‖]

2024

EN The president went on talking for hours.

FR Le président a continué à parler pendant des heures.

IPA [lø pʁezidɑ̃ a kɔ̃tinɥe a paʁle pɑ̃dɑ̃ de z̯œʁ ‖‖]

2025

EN After discussing the economy, the president then went on to talk about foreign policy.

FR Après avoir discuté d'économie, le président a ensuite parlé de politique étrangère.

IPA [apʁɛ z‿avwaʁ diskyte d‿ekonomi | lø pʁezidɑ̃ a ɑ̃sɥit paʁle dø politik etʁɑ̃ʒɛʁ ||]

2026

EN We need to change. We can't go on living like this.

FR Nous devons changer. Nous ne pouvons pas continuer à vivre comme ça. > On doit changer. On ne peut pas continuer à vivre comme ça.

IPA [nu dᵊvɔ̃ ʃɑ̃ʒe || nu nø puvɔ̃ pa kɔ̃tinɥe a vivʁ kɔm sa || > ɔ̃ dwa ʃɑ̃ʒe || ɔ̃ nø pø pa kɔ̃tinɥe a vivʁ kɔm sa ||]

2027

EN Don't bother locking the door. I'll be right back.

FR Ne t'embête pas à verrouiller la porte. Je reviens tout de suite.

IPA [nø t‿ɑ̃bɛt pa a veʁuje la pɔʁt || ʒø ʁᵊvjɛ̃ tu dø sɥit ||]

2028

EN I lent you some money a few months ago. — Are you sure? I don't remember you lending me money.

FR Je t'ai prêté de l'argent il y a quelques mois. — En es-tu sûr (♀ sûre)? Je ne me souviens pas que tu m'aies prêté de l'argent.

IPA [ʒø t̪ɛ pʁete dø l̪aʁʒɑ̃ i l̪i a kɛlk mwa || — ɑ̃ ɛ ty syʁ (♀ syʁ) || ʒø nø mø suvjɛ̃ pa kø ty m̪ɛ pʁete dø l̪aʁʒɑ̃ ||]

2029

EN Did you remember to call your mother? — Oh no, I completely forgot. I'll call her tomorrow.

FR T'es-tu souvenu d'appeler ta mère? — Oh non, j'ai complètement oublié. Je l'appellerai demain.

IPA [t̪ɛ ty suvᵊny d̪apᵊle ta mɛʁ || — o nɔ̃ | ʒ̪ɛ kɔ̃plɛtᵊmɑ̃ t̪ublije || ʒø l̪apɛlᵊʁɛ d̪ᵊmɛ̃ ||]

2030

EN Chandra joined the company nine (9) years ago and became assistant manager after two (2) years.

FR Chandra s'est joint à l'entreprise il y a neuf ans et est devenu manager adjoint après deux ans.

IPA [(...) s̪e ʒwɛ̃ a l̪ɑ̃tʁᵊpʁiz i l̪i a nœ v̪ɑ̃ e e d̪ᵊvᵊny manadʒe adʒwɛ̃ apʁɛ dø z̪ɑ̃ ||]

2031

EN A few years later, he went on to become the manager of the company.

FR Quelques années plus tard, il est devenu le manager de l'entreprise.

IPA [kɛl k‿ane plys taʁ | i l‿e dᵊvᵊny lø manadʒe dø l‿ãtʁᵊpʁiz ‖]

2032

EN I tried to keep my eyes open, but I couldn't.

FR J'ai essayé de garder mes yeux ouverts, mais je n'ai pas pu.

IPA [ʒ‿ɛ esɛje dø gaʁde me z‿jø uvɛʁ | mɛ ʒø n‿ɛ pa py ‖]

2033

EN Please try to be quiet when you come home. Everyone will be asleep.

FR Essaie d'être silencieux (♀ silencieuse) lorsque tu rentreras à la maison s'il te plaît. Tout le monde dormira.

IPA [esɛ d‿ɛtʁ silãsjø (♀ silãsjøz) lɔʁskᵊ ty ʁãtʁᵊʁa a la mɛzõ s‿il tø plɛ ‖ tu lø mõd dɔʁmiʁa ‖]

2034

EN We couldn't find anywhere to stay. We tried every hotel in town, but they were all full.

FR On n'a pas pu trouver nulle part où dormir. Nous avons essayé tous les hôtels du village, mais ils affichaient tous complet.

IPA [ɔ̃ n‿a pa py tʁuve nyl paʁ‿u dɔʁmiʁ ‖ nu z‿avɔ̃ eseje tu le otɛl dy vilaʒ | mɛ i l‿afiʃe tu kɔ̃plɛ ‖]

2035

EN The photocopier doesn't seem to be working. — Try pressing the green button.

FR Le photocopieur ne semble pas fonctionner. — Essaie d'appuyer sur le bouton vert.

IPA [lø fotokopjœʁ nø sãbl pa fɔ̃ksjone ‖ — ɛsɛ d‿apɥije syʁ lø butɔ̃ vɛʁ ‖]

2036

EN I need to get more exercise. > I need to start working out more.

FR J'ai besoin de faire plus d'exercice. > J'ai besoin de m'entraîner plus.

IPA [ʒ‿ɛ bøzwɛ̃ dø fɛʁ plys d‿ɛgzeʁsis ‖ > ʒ‿ɛ bøzwɛ̃ dø m‿ãtʁene plys ‖]

2037

EN He needs to work harder if he wants to make progress.

FR Il doit travailler plus fort s'il veut faire des progrès.

IPA [il dwa tʁavaje plys fɔʁ s‿il vø fɛʁ de pʁogʁɛ |||]

2038

EN My cellphone needs to be charged. > My cellphone needs charging.

FR Mon portable a besoin d'être rechargé.

IPA [mɔ̃ pɔʁtabl a bøzwɛ̃ d‿etʁ ʁ°ʃaʁʒe |||]

2039

EN Do you think my pants need to be washed? > Do you think my pants need washing?

FR Penses-tu que mon pantalon a besoin d'être lavé?

IPA [pɑ̃s ty kø mɔ̃ pɑ̃talɔ̃ a bøzwɛ̃ d‿etʁ lave |||]

2040

EN They needed help to clean up after the party, so everybody helped clean up.

FR Ils (♀elles) avaient besoin d'aide pour nettoyer après la fête, alors tout le monde a aidé à nettoyer.

IPA [il (♀ɛl) avɛ bøzwɛ̃ d‿ed puʁ netwaje apʁɛ la fɛt | alɔʁ tu lø mɔ̃d a ɛde a netwaje |||]

2041

EN I need your help to move this table. > Do you think you could help me move this table?

FR J'ai besoin de ton aide pour déplacer cette table. > Penses-tu que tu pourrais m'aider à déplacer cette table?

IPA [ʒ‿ɛ bøzwɛ̃ dø tɔ̃ n‿ɛd puʁ deplase sɛt tabl ‖ > pɑ̃s ty kø ty puʁɛ m‿ede a deplase sɛt tabl ‖]

2042

EN I don't like him, but he has a lot of problems. I can't help feeling sorry for him.

FR Je ne l'aime pas, il a beaucoup de problèmes. Je ne peux pas m'empêcher d'avoir pitié de lui.

IPA [ʒø nø l‿em pa | i l‿a boku dø pʁoblɛm ‖ ʒø nø pø pa m‿ɑ̃peʃe d‿avwaʁ pitje dø lɥi ‖]

2043

EN She tried to be serious, but she couldn't help laughing.

FR Elle a essayé d'être sérieuse, mais elle ne pouvait pas s'empêcher de rire.

IPA [ɛ l‿a eseje d‿etʁ seʁjøz | mɛ ɛl nø puvɛ pa s‿ɑ̃peʃe dø ʁiʁ ‖]

2044

EN I'm sorry I'm so nervous. I can't help it.

FR Je suis désolé (♀désolée) d'être aussi nerveux
(♀nerveuse). Je ne peux rien y faire.

IPA [ʒø sɥi dezole (dezole) d‿etʁ osi nɛʁvø (nɛʁvøz) ‖ ʒø
nø pø ʁjɛ̃ i fɛʁ ‖]

2045

EN Do you like getting up early? > Do you like to get
up early?

FR Aimes-tu te lever tôt?

IPA [ɛm ty tø lᵊve to ‖]

2046

EN Vadim hates flying. > Vadim hates to fly.

FR Vadim déteste prendre l'avion.

IPA [(...) detɛst pʁɑ̃dʁ l‿avjɔ̃ ‖]

2047

EN I love meeting people. > I love to meet people.

FR J'adore rencontrer des gens.

IPA [ʒ‿adoʁ ʁɑ̃kɔ̃tʁe de ʒɑ̃ ‖]

2048

EN I don't like being kept waiting. > I don't like to be kept waiting.

FR Je n'aime pas qu'on me fasse attendre.
IPA [ʒø n‿ɛm pa k‿ɔ̃ mø fas atɑ̃dʁ ‖]

2049

EN I don't like friends calling me at work. > I don't like friends to call me at work.

FR Je n'aime pas que mes amis (♀amies) m'appellent au travail.
IPA [ʒø n‿ɛm pa kø me z‿ami (♀ami) m‿apɛl o tʁavaj ‖]

2050

EN Silvia likes living in London.

FR Silvia aime vivre à Londres.
IPA [(...) ɛm vivʁ a lɔ̃dʁ° ‖]

2051

EN The office I worked at was horrible. I hated working there.

FR Le bureau où j'ai travaillé était horrible. J'ai détesté travailler là-bas.
IPA [lø byʁo u ʒ‿ɛ tʁavaje etɛ oʁibl ‖ ʒ‿ɛ detɛste tʁavaje laba ‖]

2052

EN It's not my favorite job, but I like cleaning the kitchen as often as possible.

FR Ce n'est pas ma tâche préférée, mais j'aime nettoyer la cuisine aussi souvent que possible.

IPA [sø n̩e pa ma taʃ pʁefeʁe | mɛ ʒ̊em netwaje la kɥizin osi suvɑ̃ kø posibl ||]

2053

EN I enjoy cleaning the kitchen. > I don't mind cleaning the kitchen.

FR J'aime nettoyer la cuisine. > Ça ne me dérange pas de nettoyer la cuisine.

IPA [ʒ̊em netwaje la kɥizin || > sa nø mø deʁɑ̃ʒ pa dø netwaje la kɥizin ||]

2054

EN I'd love to meet your family.

FR J'adorerais rencontrer ta famille.

IPA [ʒ̊adɔʁ°ʁɛ ʁɑ̃kɔ̃tʁe ta famij ||]

2055

EN Would you prefer to have dinner now or later? — I'd prefer later.

FR Préférerais-tu dîner maintenant ou plus tard? — Je préférerais plus tard.

IPA [pʁefeʁ°ʁɛ ty dine mɛ̃t°nɑ̃ t̪u plys taʁ || — ʒø pʁefeʁ°ʁɛ plys taʁ ||]

2056

EN Would you mind closing the door, please? — Not at all.

FR Aurais-tu l'obligeance de fermer la porte, s'il te plaît? — Oui, bien sûr.

IPA [oʁɛ ty l‿obliʒɑ̃s dø fɛʁme la pɔʁt | s‿il tø plɛ || — wi | bjɛ̃ syʁ ||]

2057

EN It's too bad we didn't see Hideki when we were in Tokyo. I would have liked to have seen him again.

FR C'est dommage que nous n'ayons pas vu Hideki lorsque nous étions à Tokyo. J'aurais aimé le revoir.

IPA [sɛ domaʒ kø nu n‿ɛjɔ̃ pa vy (...) lɔʁskᵊ nu z‿etjɔ̃ a (...) || ʒ‿oʁɛ eme lø ʁᵊvwaʁ ||]

2058

EN We'd like to have gone on vacation, but we didn't have enough money.

FR Nous aurions aimé aller en vacances, mais nous n'avions pas assez d'argent.

IPA [nu z‿oʁjɔ̃ eme ale ʁ‿ɑ̃ vakɑ̃s | mɛ nu n‿avjɔ̃ pa z‿ase d‿aʁʒɑ̃ ||]

2059

EN Poor Hanako! I would hate to have been in her position.

FR Pauvre Hanako! Je n'aurais pas aimé être dans sa situation.

IPA [povʁ (...) || ʒø n‿oʁɛ pa z‿eme ɛtʁ dɑ̃ sa sitɥasjɔ̃ ||]

2060

EN I'd love to have gone to the party, but it was impossible.

FR J'aurais aimé aller à la fête, mais c'était impossible.

IPA [ʒ‿oʁɛ eme ale a la fɛt | mɛ se ete ɛ̃posibl ||]

2061

EN I prefer driving over traveling by train. > I prefer to drive rather than travel by train.

FR Je préfère conduire à voyager en train. > Je préfère conduire plutôt que de voyager en train.

IPA [ʒø pʁefɛʁ kɔ̃dɥiʁ a vwajaʒe ʁ‿ɑ̃ tʁɛ̃ || > ʒø pʁefɛʁ kɔ̃dɥiʁ plyto kø dø vwajaʒe ʁ‿ɑ̃ tʁɛ̃ ||]

2062

EN Tamara prefers to live in the country rather than in the city.

FR Tamara préfère vivre à la campagne plutôt qu'en ville.

IPA [(...) pʁefɛʁ vivʁ a la kɑ̃paɲ plyto k‿ɑ̃ vil ||]

2063

EN I'd prefer to stay at home tonight rather than go to the movies. > I'd rather stay at home tonight than go to the movies.

FR Je préférerais rester à la maison ce soir plutôt que d'aller au cinéma. > Je préfère rester à la maison ce soir plutôt que d'aller au cinéma.

IPA [ʒø pʁefeʁ°ʁɛ ʁɛste a la mɛzɔ̃ sø swaʁ plyto kø d‿alc o sinema || > ʒø pʁefeʁ ʁɛste a la mɛzɔ̃ sø swaʁ plyto kø d‿ale o sinema ||]

2064

EN I'm tired. I'd rather not go out tonight, if you don't mind.

FR Je suis fatigué (♀ fatiguée). Je préfère ne pas sortir ce soir, si ça ne te dérange pas.

IPA [ʒø sɥi fatige (♀ fatige) || ʒø pʁefeʁ nø pa sɔʁtiʁ sø swaʁ | si sa nø tø deʁɑ̃ʒ pa ||]

2065

EN I'll fix your car tomorrow. — I'd rather you did it today.

FR Je vais réparer ta voiture demain. — Je préférerais que tu le fasses aujourd'hui.

IPA [ʒø vɛ ʁepaʁe ta vwatyʁ d°mɛ̃ || — ʒø pʁefeʁ°ʁɛ kø ty lø fas oʒuʁdɥi ||]

2066

EN Should I tell them, or would you rather they didn't know? — No, I'll tell them.

FR Devrais-je leur dire, ou préférerais-tu qu'ils (♀elles) ne le sachent pas? — Non, je vais leur dire.

IPA [dᵊvʁɛ ʒø lœʁ diʁ | u pʁefeʁᵊʁɛ ty k‿il (♀ɛl) nø lø saʃ pa || — nɔ̃ | ʒø ve lœʁ diʁ |||]

2067

EN I'd rather you didn't tell anyone what I said.

FR Je préférerais que tu ne dises pas à personne ce que j'ai dit.

IPA [ʒø pʁefeʁᵊʁɛ kø ty nø diz pa a pɛʁsɔn sø kø ʒ‿ɛ di |||]

2068

EN I'd prefer to take a taxi rather than walk home.

FR Je préférerais prendre un taxi plutôt que de rentrer à pied.

IPA [ʒø pʁefeʁᵊʁɛ pʁɑ̃dʁ œ̃ taksi plyto kø dø ʁɑ̃tʁe a pje |||]

2069

EN I'd prefer to go swimming rather than playing basketball.

FR Je préférerais aller nager plutôt que de jouer au basketball.

IPA [ʒø pʁefeʁᵊʁɛ ale naʒe plyto kø dø ʒwe o (...) |||]

2070

EN Are you going to tell Vladimir what happened or would you rather I told him? — No, I'll tell him.

FR Vas-tu dire à Vladimir ce qui s'est passé ou préfères-tu que je lui dise? — Non, je vais lui dire.

IPA [va ty diʁ a (...) sø ki s‿e pase u pʁefeʁ ty kø ʒø lɥi diz || — nɔ̃ | ʒø vɛ lɥi diʁ ||]

2071

EN Before going out, I called Jianwen.

FR Avant de sortir, j'ai appelé Jianwen.

IPA [avɑ̃ dø sɔʁtiʁ | ʒ‿ɛ apˀle (...) ||]

2072

EN What did you do after finishing school?

FR Qu'as-tu fait après avoir fini l'école?

IPA [k‿a ty fɛ apʁɛ z‿avwaʁ fini l‿ekɔl ||]

2073

EN The burglars got into the house by breaking a window and climbing in.

FR Les cambrioleurs se sont introduits dans la maison en fracassant une fenêtre et en y grimpant.

IPA [le kɑ̃bʁijolœʁ sø sɔ̃ ɛ̃tʁodɥi dɑ̃ la mɛzɔ̃ ɑ̃ fʁakasɑ̃ t‿yn fˀnɛtʁ e ɑ̃ n‿i gʁɛ̃pɑ̃ ||]

2074

EN You can improve your language skills by reading more.

FR Tu peux améliorer tes compétences linguistiques en lisant plus.

IPA [ty pø ameljoʁe te kõpetãs lẽgɥistik ã lizã plys ||]

2075

EN She made herself sick by not eating properly.

FR Elle s'est rendue malade en ne mangeant pas bien.

IPA [ɛl s̺e ʁãdy malad ã nø mãʒã pa bjẽ ||]

2076

EN Many accidents are caused by people driving too fast.

FR Plusieurs accidents sont causés par des gens qui conduisent trop vite.

IPA [plyzjœ ʁ̺aksidã sõ koze paʁ de ʒã ki kõdɥiz tʁo vit ||]

2077

EN We ran ten (10) kilometers without stopping.

FR Nous avons couru dix kilomètres sans arrêt.

IPA [nu z̺avõ kuʁy dis kilomɛtʁ sã z̺aʁɛ ||]

2078

EN It was a stupid thing to say. I said it without thinking.

FR C'était une chose idiote à dire. Je l'ai dite sans réfléchir.

IPA [se etɛ yn ʃoz idjɔt a diʁ ‖ ʒø l̩ɛ dit sɑ̃ ʁefleʃiʁ ‖]

2079

EN She needs to work without people disturbing her.

FR Elle a besoin de travailler sans gens qui la dérangent.

IPA [ɛ l̩a bøzwɛ̃ dø tʁavaje sɑ̃ ʒɑ̃ ki la deʁɑ̃ʒ ‖]

2080

EN I have enough problems of my own without having to worry about yours.

FR J'ai assez de mes propres problèmes sans avoir à me soucier des tiens.

IPA [ʒ̩ɛ ase dø me pʁɔpʁ pʁɔblɛm sɑ̃ z̩avwaʁ a mø susje de tjɛ̃ ‖]

2081

EN Would you like to meet for lunch tomorrow? — Sure, let's do lunch.

FR Aimerais-tu qu'on se rencontre pour déjeuner demain midi? — D'accord, déjeunons.

IPA [ɛmᵊʁɛ ty k̩ɔ̃ sø ʁɑ̃kɔ̃tʁ puʁ deʒœne dᵊmɛ̃ midi ‖ — d̩akɔʁ | deʒœnɔ̃ ‖]

2074

EN You can improve your language skills by reading more.

FR Tu peux améliorer tes compétences linguistiques en lisant plus.

IPA [ty pø ameljoʁe te kɔ̃petɑ̃s lɛ̃gɥistik ɑ̃ lizɑ̃ plys ||]

2075

EN She made herself sick by not eating properly.

FR Elle s'est rendue malade en ne mangeant pas bien.

IPA [ɛl s‿e ʁɑ̃dy malad ɑ̃ nø mɑ̃ʒɑ̃ pa bjɛ̃ ||]

2076

EN Many accidents are caused by people driving too fast.

FR Plusieurs accidents sont causés par des gens qui conduisent trop vite.

IPA [plyzjœʁ ʁ‿aksidɑ̃ sɔ̃ koze paʁ de ʒɑ̃ ki kɔ̃dɥiz tʁo vit ||]

2077

EN We ran ten (10) kilometers without stopping.

FR Nous avons couru dix kilomètres sans arrêt.

IPA [nu z‿avɔ̃ kuʁy dis kilomɛtʁ sɑ̃ z‿aʁɛ ||]

2078

EN It was a stupid thing to say. I said it without thinking.

FR C'était une chose idiote à dire. Je l'ai dite sans réfléchir.

IPA [se etɛ yn ʃoz idjɔt a diʁ ‖ ʒø l̪ɛ dit sã ʁefleʃiʁ ‖]

2079

EN She needs to work without people disturbing her.

FR Elle a besoin de travailler sans gens qui la dérangent.

IPA [ɛ l̪a bøzwɛ̃ dø tʁavaje sã ʒã ki la deʁɑ̃ʒ ‖]

2080

EN I have enough problems of my own without having to worry about yours.

FR J'ai assez de mes propres problèmes sans avoir à me soucier des tiens.

IPA [ʒ̪ɛ ase dø me pʁɔpʁ pʁoblɛm sã z̪avwaʁ a mø susje de tjɛ̃ ‖]

2081

EN Would you like to meet for lunch tomorrow? — Sure, let's do lunch.

FR Aimerais-tu qu'on se rencontre pour déjeuner demain midi? — D'accord, déjeunons.

IPA [ɛmᵊʁɛ ty k̪ɔ̃ sø ʁãkɔ̃tʁ puʁ deʒœne dᵊmɛ̃ midi ‖ — d̪akɔʁ | deʒœnɔ̃ ‖]

2082

EN Are you looking forward to the weekend? — Yes, I
am.

FR As-tu hâte au week-end? — Oui, j'ai hâte.

IPA [a ty at o wikɛnd || — wi | ʒ‿ɛ at ||]

2083

EN Why don't you go out instead of sitting at home all
the time?

FR Pourquoi ne sors-tu pas au lieu de toujours rester à la
maison?

IPA [puʁkwa nə sɔʁ ty pa o ljø də tuʒuʁ ʁeste a la mɛzɔ̃
||]

2084

EN We got into the exhibition without having to wait in
line.

FR Nous sommes entrés dans l'exposition sans avoir à
attendre en ligne.

IPA [nu sɔm ɑ̃tʁe dɑ̃ l‿ekspozisjɔ̃ sɑ̃ z‿avwaʁ a atɑ̃dʁ ɑ̃ liɲ
||]

2085

EN Victor got himself into financial trouble by borrowing too much money.

FR Victor s'est mis dans le pétrin financier en empruntant trop d'argent.

IPA [(...) s‿e mi dɑ̃ lø petʁɛ̃ finɑ̃sje ɑ̃ n‿ɑ̃pʁœ̃tɑ̃ tʁo d‿aʁʒɑ̃ ||]

2086

EN Ramona lives alone. She's lived alone for fifteen (15) years. It's not strange for her.

FR Ramona vit seule. Elle a vécu seule pendant quinze ans. Ce n'est pas bizarre pour elle.

IPA [(...) vi sœl || ɛ l‿a veky sœl pɑ̃dɑ̃ kɛ̃z ɑ̃ || sø n‿e pa bizaʁ pu ʁ‿el ||]

2087

EN She's used to it. She's used to living alone.

FR Elle y est habituée. Elle est habituée à vivre seule.

IPA [ɛ l‿i e t‿abitɥe || ɛ l‿e t‿abitɥe a vivʁ sœl ||]

2082

EN Are you looking forward to the weekend? — Yes, I am.

FR As-tu hâte au week-end? — Oui, j'ai hâte.
IPA [a ty at o wikɛnd || — wi | ʒ‿ɛ at ||]

2083

EN Why don't you go out instead of sitting at home all the time?

FR Pourquoi ne sors-tu pas au lieu de toujours rester à la maison?
IPA [puʁkwa nø sɔʁ ty pa o ljø dø tuʒuʁ ʁɛste a la mɛzɔ̃ ||]

2084

EN We got into the exhibition without having to wait in line.

FR Nous sommes entrés dans l'exposition sans avoir à attendre en ligne.
IPA [nu sɔm ɑ̃tʁe dɑ̃ l‿ɛkspozisjɔ̃ sɑ̃ z‿avwaʁ a atɑ̃dʁ ɑ̃ liɲ ||]

2085

EN Victor got himself into financial trouble by borrowing too much money.

FR Victor s'est mis dans le pétrin financier en empruntant trop d'argent.

IPA [(...) s‿e mi dã lø petʁɛ̃ finãsje ã n‿ãpʁɶ̃tã tʁo d‿aʁʒã ||]

2086

EN Ramona lives alone. She's lived alone for fifteen (15) years. It's not strange for her.

FR Ramona vit seule. Elle a vécu seule pendant quinze ans. Ce n'est pas bizarre pour elle.

IPA [(...) vi sœl || ɛ l‿a veky sœl pãdã kɛ̃z ã || sø n‿e pa bizaʁ pu ʁ‿ɛl ||]

2087

EN She's used to it. She's used to living alone.

FR Elle y est habituée. Elle est habituée à vivre seule.

IPA [ɛ l‿i e t‿abitɥe || ɛ l‿e t‿abitɥe a vivʁ sœl ||]

2088

EN I bought some new shoes. They felt strange at first because I wasn't used to them.

FR J'ai acheté de nouvelles chaussures. Elles étaient étranges au début, car je n'étais pas habitué (♀habituée) à elles.

IPA [ʒ‿ɛ aʃᵊte dø nuvɛl ʃosyʁ || ɛ l‿etɛ etʁɑ̃ʒ o deby | kaʁ ʒø n‿etɛ pa z‿abitɥe (♀abitɥe) a ɛl ||]

2089

EN Our new apartment is on a very busy street. I expect we'll get used to the noise, but for now it's very annoying.

FR Notre nouvel appartement est sur une rue très passante. Je m'attends à ce qu'on s'habitue au bruit, mais pour le moment, c'est très ennuyeux.

IPA [nɔtʁ nuvɛ l‿apaʁtᵊmɑ̃ e sy ʁ‿yn ʁy tʁɛ pasɑ̃t || ʒø m‿atɑ̃ a sø k‿ɔ̃ s abity o bʁɥi | mɛ puʁ lø momɑ̃ | sɛ tʁɛ z‿ɑ̃nɥijø ||]

2090

EN Jamaal has a new job. He has to get up much earlier now than before. He finds it difficult because he isn't used to getting up so early.

FR Jamaal a un nouvel emploi. Il doit maintenant se lever beaucoup plus tôt qu'avant. Il trouve ça difficile, parce qu'il n'est pas habitué de se lever si tôt.

IPA [(...) a œ̃ nuvɛ l‿ɑ̃plwa || il dwa mɛ̃tᵊnɑ̃ sø lᵊve boku plys to k avɑ̃ || il tʁuv sa difisil | paʁs k‿il n‿e pa z‿abitɥe dø sø lᵊve si to ||]

2091

EN Malika's husband is often away. She doesn't mind. She's used to him being away.

FR Le mari de Malika est souvent parti. Ça ne la dérange pas. Elle est habituée à ce qu'il soit parti.

IPA [lø maʁi dø (...) e suvɑ̃ paʁti || sa nø la deʁɑ̃ʒ pa || ɛ l̩e t̩abitɥe a sø k̩il swa paʁti ||]

2092

EN Keiko had to get used to driving on the left when she moved back to Japan.

FR Keiko a dû s'habituer à conduire à gauche lorsqu'elle est redéménagée au Japon.

IPA [(...) a dy s abitɥe a kɔ̃dɥiʁ a goʃ lɔʁsk ɛl e ʁ°demenaʒe o ʒapɔ̃ ||]

2093

EN I'm used to driving on the left because I grew up in England.

FR Je suis habitué (♀habituée) à conduire à gauche, parce que j'ai grandi en Angleterre.

IPA [ʒø sɥi abitɥe (♀abitɥe) a kɔ̃dɥiʁ a goʃ | paʁs kø ʒ̩ɛ gʁɑ̃di ɑ̃ n̩ɑ̃gløteʁ ||]

2094

EN I used to drive to work every day, but these days I usually ride my bike.

FR Je suis habitué (♀habituée) à me rendre au travail en voiture chaque jour, mais ces jours-ci, j'utilise mon vélo.

IPA [ʒø sɥi abitɥe (♀abitɥe) a mø ʁɑ̃dʁ o tʁavaj ɑ̃ vwatyʁ ʃak ʒuʁ | mɛ se ʒuʁ si | ʒ‿ytiliz mɔ̃ velo ‖]

2095

EN We used to live in a small town, but now we live in Los Angeles.

FR Nous habitions dans une petite maison, mais maintenant nous vivons à Los Angeles.

IPA [nu z‿abitjɔ̃ dɑ̃ z‿yn pᵊtit mɛzɔ̃ | mɛ mɛ̃tᵊnɑ̃ nu vivɔ̃ a (...) ‖]

2096

EN We talked about the problem.

FR Nous avons parlé du problème.

IPA [nu z‿avɔ̃ paʁle dy pʁoblɛm ‖]

2097

EN You should apologize for what you said.

FR Tu devrais t'excuser pour ce que tu as dit.

IPA [ty dᵊvʁɛ t‿ɛkskyze puʁ sø kø ty a di ‖]

2098

EN You should apologize for not telling the truth.

FR Tu devrais t'excuser de ne pas avoir dit la vérité.
IPA [ty dᵊvʁɛ tˌɛkskyze dø nø pa zˌavwaʁ di la veʁite ‖]

2099

EN Have you succeeded in finding a job yet?

FR As-tu réussi à te trouver un emploi?
IPA [a ty ʁeysi a tø tʁuve ʁˌœ̃ nˌɑ̃plwa ‖]

2100

EN They insisted on paying for dinner.

FR Ils (♀elles) ont insisté pour payer le dîner.
IPA [il (♀ɛl) ɔ̃ ɛ̃siste puʁ peje lø dine ‖]

GMS #2101 - 2200

2101

EN I'm thinking of buying a house.

FR Je songe à m'acheter une maison.
IPA [ʒø sɔ̃ʒ a m‿aʃ°te yn mɛzɔ̃ ‖]

2102

EN I wouldn't dream of asking them for money.

FR Je n'oserais pas leur demander de l'argent.
IPA [ʒø n‿oz°ʁɛ pa lœʁ d°mɑ̃de dø l‿aʁʒɑ̃ ‖]

2103

EN He doesn't approve of swearing.

FR Il n'aime pas les jurons.
IPA [il n‿ɛm pa le ʒyʁɔ̃ ‖]

2104

EN We've decided against moving to Australia.

FR Nous avons décidé de ne pas déménager en Australie.
IPA [nu z‿avɔ̃ deside dø nø pa demenaʒe ʁ‿ɑ̃ ostʁali ‖]

2105

EN Do you feel like going out tonight?

FR As-tu envie de sortir ce soir?

IPA [a ty ɑ̃vi də sɔʁtiʁ sə swaʁ ‖]

2106

EN I'm looking foward to meeting her.

FR J'ai hâte de la rencontrer.

IPA [ʒ‿ɛ at də la ʁɑ̃kɔ̃tʁe ‖]

2107

EN I congratulated Mira on getting a new job.

FR J'ai félicité Mira pour l'obtention de son nouvel emploi.

IPA [ʒ‿ɛ felisite (...) puʁ l‿ɔptɑ̃sjɔ̃ də sɔ̃ nuvɛ l‿ɑ̃plwa ‖]

2108

EN They accused us of telling lies.

FR Ils nous ont accusés (♀accusées) de mentir.

IPA [il nu z‿ɔ̃ akyze (♀akyze) də mɑ̃tiʁ ‖]

2109

EN Nobody suspected the employee of being a spy.

FR Personne ne soupçonnait l'employé (♀l'employée) d'être un espion (♀une espionne).

IPA [pɛʁsɔn nø supsɔnɛ l‿ɑ̃plwaje (♀l‿ɑ̃plwaje) d‿ɛtʁ œ̃ n‿ɛspjɔ̃ (♀yn ɛspjɔn) ||]

2110

EN What prevented you from coming to see us?

FR Qu'est-ce qui t'a empêché de venir nous voir?

IPA [kɛsᵊ ki t‿a ɑ̃peʃe dø vᵊniʁ nu vwaʁ ||]

2111

EN The noise keeps me from falling asleep.

FR Le bruit m'empêche de m'endormir.

IPA [lø bʁɥi m‿ɑ̃peʃ dø m‿ɑ̃dɔʁmiʁ ||]

2112

EN The rain didn't stop us from enjoying our vacation.

FR La pluie ne nous a pas empêchés (♀empêchées) de profiter de nos vacances.

IPA [la plɥi nø nu z‿a pa z‿ɑ̃peʃe (♀ɑ̃peʃe) dø pʁofite dø no vakɑ̃s ||]

2113

EN I forgot to thank them for helping me.

FR J'ai oublié de les remercier de m'avoir aidé.
IPA [ʒ‿ɛ ublije dø le ʁ°mɛʁsje dø m‿avwaʁ ɛde ‖]

2114

EN Please excuse me for not returning your call.

FR Veuillez m'excuser de ne pas vous avoir rappelé.
IPA [vœje m‿ɛkskyze dø nø pa vu z‿avwaʁ ʁap°le ‖]

2115

EN There's no point in having a car if you never use it.

FR Il est inutile d'avoir une voiture si tu ne l'utilises jamais.
IPA [i l‿e t‿inytil d‿avwaʁ yn vwatyʁ si ty nø l‿ytiliz ʒamɛ ‖]

2116

EN There was no point in waiting any longer, so we left.

FR Il était inutile d'attendre plus longtemps, alors nous sommes partis.
IPA [i l‿etɛ inytil d‿atãdʁ plys lõtã | alɔʁ nu sɔm paʁti ‖]

2117

EN There's nothing you can do about the situation, so there's no use worrying about it.

FR Il n'y a rien que tu puisses faire à propos de la situation, alors il est inutile de t'en faire.

IPA [il n‿i a ʁjɛ̃ kø ty pɥis fɛʁ a pʁopo dø la sitɥasjɔ̃ | alɔ ʁ‿i l‿e t‿inytil dø t‿ɑ̃ fɛʁ ‖]

2118

EN I live only a short walk from here, so it's not worth taking a taxi.

FR J'habite à seulement quelques pas d'ici, alors il est inutile de prendre un taxi.

IPA [ʒ‿abit a sœl°mɑ̃ kɛlk pa d‿isi | alɔ ʁ‿i l‿e t‿inytil dø pʁɑ̃dʁ œ̃ taksi ‖]

2119

EN Our flight was very early in the morning, so it wasn't worth going to bed.

FR Notre vol était très tôt en matinée, alors il était inutile d'aller au lit.

IPA [nɔtʁ vɔl ete tʁɛ to t‿ɑ̃ matine | alɔ ʁ‿i l‿ete inytil d‿ale o li ‖]

2120

EN What was the movie like? Was it worth seeing?

FR Comment était le film? Valait-il d'être vu?

IPA [kɔmɑ̃ t‿ete lø film ‖ valɛ t‿il d‿etʁ vy ‖]

2121

EN Thieves broke into the house, but there was nothing worth stealing.

FR Des cambrioleurs se sont introduits dans la maison, mais il n'y avait rien qui méritait d'être volé.

IPA [de kɑ̃bʁijolœʁ sø sɔ̃ ɛ̃tʁodɥi dɑ̃ la mɛzɔ̃ | mɛ il n‿i avɛ ʁjɛ̃ ki meʁitɛ d‿etʁ vole ||]

2122

EN I had no trouble finding a place to live.

FR Je n'ai pas eu de mal à trouver un endroit où vivre.

IPA [ʒø n‿ɛ pa z‿y dø mal a tʁuve ʁ‿œ̃ n‿ɑ̃dʁwa u vivʁ ||]

2123

EN Did you have any trouble getting a visa?

FR As-tu eu de la difficulté à obtenir un visa?

IPA [a ty y dø la difikylte a ɔptᵊni ʁ‿œ̃ viza ||]

2124

EN People often have a lot of trouble reading my handwriting.

FR Les gens ont souvent de la difficulté à lire mon écriture.

IPA [le ʒɑ̃ ɔ̃ suvɑ̃ dø la difikylte a liʁ mɔ̃ n‿ekʁityʁ ||]

2125

EN I had trouble finding a place to live. > I had difficulty finding a place to live.

FR J'ai eu du mal à trouver un endroit où vivre. > J'ai eu de la difficulté à trouver un endroit où vivre.

IPA [ʒ‿ɛ y dy mal a tʁuve ʁ‿œ̃ n‿ɑ̃dʁwa u vivʁ ‖ > ʒ‿ɛ y dø la difikylte a tʁuve ʁ‿œ̃ n‿ɑ̃dʁwa u vivʁ ‖]

2126

EN He spent hours trying to repair the clock.

FR Il a passé des heures à essayer de réparer l'horloge.

IPA [i l‿a pase de z‿œʁ a eseje dø ʁepaʁe l‿ɔʁlɔʒ ‖]

2127

EN I waste a lot of time daydreaming.

FR Je perds beaucoup de temps à rêvasser.

IPA [ʒø pɛʁ boku dø tɑ̃ a ʁevase ‖]

2128

EN How often do you go swimming?

FR À quelle fréquence vas-tu nager?

IPA [a kɛl fʁekɑ̃s va ty naʒe ‖]

2129

EN When was the last time you went shopping?

FR Quand es-tu allé faire du shopping pour la dernière fois?

IPA [kɑ̃ ɛ ty ale fɛʁ dy ʃɔpiŋ puʁ la dɛʁnjɛʁ fwa ||]

2130

EN I have a problem remembering people's names.

FR J'ai du mal à me souvenir des noms des gens.

IPA [ʒ‿ɛ dy mal a mø suv°niʁ de nɔ̃ de ʒɑ̃ ||]

2131

EN She had no difficulty getting a job.

FR Elle n'a pas eu de difficulté à se trouver un emploi.

IPA [ɛl n‿a pa z‿y dø difikylte a sø tʁuve ʁ‿œ̃ n‿ɑ̃plwa ||]

2132

EN You won't have any trouble getting a ticket for the game.

FR Tu n'auras pas de mal à obtenir un billet pour la partie.

IPA [ty n‿oʁa pa dø mal a ɔpt°ni ʁ‿œ̃ bijɛ puʁ la paʁti ||]

2133

EN I think you waste too much time watching television.

FR Je pense que tu perds trop de temps à regarder la télé.

IPA [ʒø pɑ̃s kø ty pɛʁ tʁo dø tɑ̃ a ʁ°gaʁde la tele ‖]

2134

EN It's hard to find a place to park downtown.

FR C'est dur de trouver un endroit où se garer au centre-ville.

IPA [sɛ dyʁ dø tʁuve ʁ‿œ̃ n‿ɑ̃dʁwa u sø gaʁe o sɑ̃tʁ°vil ‖]

2135

EN I get lonely if there's nobody to talk to.

FR Je me sens seul (♀ seule) s'il n'y a personne à qui parler.

IPA [ʒø mø sɑ̃s sœl (♀ sœl) s‿il n‿i a pɛʁsɔn a ki paʁle ‖]

2136

EN I need something to open this bottle with.

FR J'ai besoin de quelque chose pour ouvrir cette bouteille.

IPA [ʒ‿ɛ bøzwɛ̃ dø kɛlk ʃoz pu ʁ‿uvʁiʁ sɛt butɛj ‖]

2137

EN They gave us some money to buy some food.

FR Ils (♀elles) nous ont donné de l'argent pour acheter de la nourriture.

IPA [il (♀ɛl) nu z̪ɔ̃ done dø l̪aʁʒɑ̃ pu ʁ̪aʃ°te dø la nuʁityʁ ‖]

2138

EN Do you have much opportunity to practice your foreign language?

FR As-tu beaucoup d'occasions pour pratiquer ta langue étrangère?

IPA [a ty boku d̪okazjɔ̃ puʁ pʁatike ta lɑ̃g etʁɑ̃ʒɛʁ ‖]

2139

EN I need a few days to think about your proposal.

FR J'ai besoin de quelques jours pour penser à ta proposition.

IPA [ʒ̪ɛ bøzwɛ̃ dø kɛlk ʒuʁ puʁ pɑ̃se a ta pʁopozisjɔ̃ ‖]

2140

EN Since there weren't any chairs for us to sit on, we had to sit on the floor.

FR Puisqu'il n'y avait pas de chaises où nous asseoir, nous avons dû nous asseoir par terre.

IPA [pɥisk il n̪i avɛ pa dø ʃɛz u nu z̪aswaʁ | nu z̪avɔ̃ dy nu z̪aswaʁ paʁ tɛʁ ‖]

2141

EN I hurried so that I wouldn't be late.

FR Je me suis dépêché (♀ dépêchée) pour ne pas être en retard.

IPA [ʒø mø sɥi depeʃe (♀ depeʃe) puʁ nø pa z‿ɛtʁ ɑ̃ ʁ°taʁ ‖]

2142

EN Leave early so that you won't miss the bus.

FR Pars tôt pour ne pas manquer le bus.

IPA [paʁ to puʁ nø pa mɑ̃ke lø bys ‖]

2143

EN She's learning English so that she can study in Australia.

FR Elle apprend l'anglais pour pouvoir étudier en Australie.

IPA [ɛ l‿apʁɑ̃ l‿ɑ̃glɛ puʁ puvwaʁ etydje ʁ‿ɑ̃ ostʁali ‖]

2144

EN We moved to the city so that we could see our children more often.

FR Nous sommes déménagés pour pouvoir voir nos enfants plus souvent.

IPA [nu sɔm demenaʒe puʁ puvwaʁ vwaʁ no z‿ɑ̃fɑ̃ plys suvɑ̃ ‖]

2145

EN I put on warmer clothes so I wouldn't feel cold.

FR J'ai enfilé des vêtements plus chauds pour ne pas avoir froid.

IPA [ʒ‿ɛ ãfile de vɛt°mã plys ʃo puʁ nø pa z‿avwaʁ fʁwa ||]

2146

EN I left Kenji my phone number so he'd be able to contact me.

FR J'ai laissé mon numéro de téléphone à Kenji pour qu'il puisse communiquer avec moi.

IPA [ʒ‿ɛ lese mɔ̃ nymeʁo dø telefɔn a (...) puʁ k‿il pɥis komynike avɛk mwa ||]

2147

EN We whispered so that nobody could hear our conversation.

FR Nous avons murmuré pour que personne ne puisse entendre notre conversation.

IPA [nu z‿avɔ̃ myʁmyʁe puʁ kø pɛʁsɔn nø pɥis ãtãdʁ nɔtʁ kɔ̃vɛʁsasjɔ̃ ||]

2154

EN This is a difficult question for me to answer.

FR C'est une question à laquelle il m'est difficile de répondre.

IPA [sɛ t‿yn kɛstjɔ̃ a lakɛ l‿il m‿e difisil dø ʁepɔ̃dʁ ‖]

2155

EN It was nice of you to take me to the airport.

FR C'était gentil de ta part de m'emmener à l'aéroport.

IPA [se etɛ ʒɑ̃ti dø ta paʁ dø m‿ɑ̃mᵊne a l‿aeʁopɔʁ ‖]

2156

EN It's foolish of Liting to quit her job when she needs the money.

FR Il est insensé de la part de Liting de quitter son emploi alors qu'elle a besoin de cet argent.

IPA [i l‿e t‿ɛ̃sɑ̃se dø la paʁ dø (...) dø kite sɔ̃ n‿ɑ̃plwa alɔʁ k‿ɛl a bøzwɛ̃ dø sɛ t‿aʁʒɑ̃ ‖]

2157

EN I think it was very unfair of him to criticize me.

FR Je pense qu'il était vraiment injuste de sa part de me critiquer.

IPA [ʒø pɑ̃s k‿il etɛ vʁɛmɑ̃ t‿ɛ̃ʒyst dø sa paʁ dø mø kʁitike ‖]

2158

EN I was sorry to hear that your father is ill.

FR J'ai été désolé d'apprendre que ton père est malade.
IPA [ʒ‿ɛ ete dezole d‿apʁɑ̃dʁ kø tɔ̃ pɛʁ e malad ‖]

2159

EN Was Adrian surprised to see you?

FR Adrian était-il surpris de te voir?
IPA [(...) etɛ t‿il syʁpʁi dø tø vwaʁ ‖]

2160

EN It was a long and tiring trip. We were glad to get home.

FR Ce fut un voyage long et fatigant. Nous étions contents de rentrer à la maison.
IPA [sø fy t‿œ̃ vwajaʒ lɔ̃ g‿e fatigɑ̃ ‖ nu z‿etjɔ̃ kɔ̃tɑ̃ dø ʁɑ̃tʁe a la mɛzɔ̃ ‖]

2161

EN If I have any more news, you'll be the first person to know.

FR Si j'ai plus de nouvelles, tu seras la première personne à le savoir.
IPA [si ʒ‿ɛ plys dø nuvɛl | ty sᵊʁa la pʁømjɛʁ pɛʁsɔn a lø savwaʁ ‖]

2162

EN The next plane to arrive at Gate Four (4) will be
Flight five-one-two (512) from Beijing.

FR Le prochain avion à arriver à la porte numéro quatre
sera le vol cinq un deux (512) de Pékin.

IPA [lø pʁoʃɛ̃ n‿avjɔ̃ a aʁive a la pɔʁt nymeʁo katʁ sᵊʁa
lø vɔl sɛ̃k œ̃ dø (512) dø pekɛ̃ ‖]

2163

EN Everybody was late except me. I was the only one to
arrive on time.

FR Tout le monde était en retard, sauf moi. J'étais le seul
à être arrivé à l'heure.

IPA [tu lø mɔ̃d etɛ t‿ɑ̃ ʁᵊtaʁ | sof mwa ‖ ʒ‿ete lø sœl a etʁ
aʁive a l‿œʁ ‖]

2164

EN Anastasia's a very good student. She's bound to pass
the exam.

FR Anastasia est une très bonne élève. Elle est destinée à
passer l'examen.

IPA [(...) e t‿yn tʁɛ bɔn elev ‖ ɛ l‿e destine a pase
l‿egzamɛ̃ ‖]

2165

EN I'm likely to get home late tonight.

FR Je risque de rentrer tard ce soir.

IPA [ʒø ʁisk dø ʁɑ̃tʁe taʁ sø swaʁ ‖]

2166

EN I was the second customer to complain to the restaurant manager.

FR J'étais le deuxième client à me plaindre au gérant du restaurant.

IPA [ʒ‿ete lø døzjɛm klijɑ̃ a mø plɛ̃dʁ o ʒeʁɑ̃ dy ʁɛstoʁɑ̃ ||]

2167

EN That chair is not safe to stand on.

FR Cette chaise n'est pas assez sécuritaire pour monter dessus.

IPA [sɛt ʃɛz n‿e pa z‿ase sekyʁitɛʁ puʁ mɔ̃te dᵊsy ||]

2168

EN After such a long trip, you're bound to be tired.

FR Après un si long voyage, tu es destiné (♀ destinée) à être fatigué (♀ fatiguée).

IPA [apʁɛ z‿œ̃ si lɔ̃ vwajaʒ | ty ɛ destine (♀ destine) a etʁ fatige (♀ fatige) ||]

2169

EN Since the holiday begins this Friday, there's likely going to be a lot of traffic on the roads.

FR Comme la fête commence ce vendredi, il y aura probablement beaucoup de circulation sur les routes.

IPA [kɔm la fɛt komɑ̃s sø vɑ̃dʁᵊdi | i l‿i oʁa pʁobablᵊmɑ̃ boku dø siʁkylasjɔ̃ syʁ le ʁut ||]

2170

EN This part of town is dangerous. People are afraid to walk here at night.

FR Cette partie de la ville est dangereuse. Les gens ont peur de marcher ici la nuit.

IPA [sɛt paʁti də la vil e dɑ̃ʒ°ʁøz || le ʒɑ̃ ɔ̃ pøʁ də maʁʃe isi la nɥi ||]

2171

EN Aleksey was afraid to tell his parents what happened.

FR Aleksey avait peur de raconter à ses parents ce qui s'était passé.

IPA [(...) avɛ pøʁ də ʁakɔ̃te a se paʁɑ̃ sø ki s‿ete pase ||]

2172

EN The sidewalk was icy, so we walked very carefully. We were afraid of falling.

FR Le trottoir était glacé, alors nous avons marché très attentivement. Nous avions peur de tomber.

IPA [lø tʁotwaʁ ete glase | alɔʁ nu z‿avɔ̃ maʁʃe tʁɛ z‿atɑ̃tiv°mɑ̃ || nu z‿avjɔ̃ pøʁ də tɔ̃be ||]

2173

EN I don't like dogs. I'm always afraid of getting bitten.

FR Je n'aime pas les chiens. J'ai toujours peur de me faire mordre.

IPA [ʒø n‿em pa le ʃjɛ̃ || ʒ‿ɛ tuʒuʁ pøʁ də mø feʁ mɔʁdʁ ||]

2174

EN I was afraid to go near the dog because I was afraid of getting bitten.

FR J'avais peur d'aller près du chien, parce que j'avais peur de me faire mordre.

IPA [ʒ‿avɛ pøʁ d‿ale pʁɛ dy ʃjɛ̃ | paʁs kø ʒ‿avɛ pøʁ dø mø fɛʁ mɔʁdʁ ‖]

2175

EN Let me know if you're interested in joining the club.

FR Fais-moi savoir si tu souhaites joindre le club.

IPA [fɛ mwa savwaʁ si ty swɛt ʒwɛ̃dʁ lø klœb ‖]

2176

EN I tried to sell my car, but nobody was interested in buying it.

FR J'ai essayé de vendre ma voiture, mais personne ne souhaitait l'acheter.

IPA [ʒ‿ɛ eseje dø vɑ̃dʁ ma vwatyʁ | mɛ pɛʁsɔn nø swɛtɛ l‿aʃ°te ‖]

2177

EN I was interested to hear that Arturo quit his job. — I, on the other hand, was surprised to hear it.

FR J'ai trouvé intéressant d'entendre qu'Arturo a quitté son emploi. — Moi, en contrepartie, j'ai été surpris (♀ surprise) de l'entendre.

IPA [ʒ‿ɛ tʁuve ɛ̃teʁesɑ̃ d‿ɑ̃tɑ̃dʁ k (...) a kite sɔ̃ n‿ɑ̃plwa ‖ — mwa | ɑ̃ kɔ̃tʁ°paʁti | ʒ‿ɛ ete syʁpʁi (♀ syʁpʁiz) dø l‿ɑ̃tɑ̃dʁ ‖]

2178

EN Ask Anna for her opinion. I'd be interested to know what she thinks.

FR Demande à Anna quelle est son opinion. Je serais intéressé (♀ intéressée) de savoir ce qu'elle pense.

IPA [d°mɑ̃d a anna kɛ l‿e sɔ̃ n‿opinjɔ̃ ‖ ʒø s°ʁɛ ɛ̃teʁese (♀ ɛ̃teʁese) dø savwaʁ sø k‿ɛl pɑ̃s ‖]

2179

EN I was sorry to hear that Boris lost his job.

FR J'ai été désolé (♀ désolée) d'apprendre que Boris a perdu son emploi.

IPA [ʒ‿ɛ ete dezole (♀ dezole) d‿apʁɑ̃dʁ kø (...) a peʁdy sɔ̃ n‿ɑ̃plwa ‖]

2180

EN I've enjoyed my stay here. I'll be sorry to leave.

FR J'ai apprécié mon séjour ici. Je serai triste de partir.

IPA [ʒ‿ɛ apʁesje mɔ̃ seʒuʁ isi ‖ ʒø s°ʁɛ tʁist dø paʁtiʁ ‖]

2181

EN I'm sorry to call you so late, but I need to ask you something.

FR Je suis désolé de vous appeler si tard, mais je dois vous demander quelque chose.

IPA [ʒø sɥi dezole dø vu z‿ap°le si taʁ | mɛ ʒø dwa vu d°mɑ̃de kɛlk ʃoz ‖]

2182

EN I'm sorry for shouting at you yesterday. > I'm sorry I shouted at you yesterday.

FR Je suis désolé d'avoir crié contre toi hier.

IPA [ʒø sɥi dezole d‿avwaʁ kʁije kɔ̃tʁ twa jɛʁ ‖]

2183

EN We weren't allowed to leave the building. > We were prevented from leaving the building.

FR Nous n'étions pas autorisés (♀ autorisées) à quitter le bâtiment. > On nous a empêché de quitter le bâtiment.

IPA [nu n‿etjɔ̃ pa z‿otoʁize (♀ otoʁize) a kite lø batimɑ̃ ‖ > ɔ̃ nu z‿a ɑ̃peʃe dø kite lø batimɑ̃ ‖]

2184

EN Daisuke failed to solve the problem, whereas Aiko succeeded in solving the problem.

FR Daisuke n'a pas réussi à résoudre le problème, tandis qu'Aiko a réussi à résoudre le problème.

IPA [(...) n‿a pa ʁeysi a ʁezudʁ lø pʁɔblɛm | tandis k (...) a ʁeysi a ʁezudʁ lø pʁɔblɛm ‖]

2185

EN Fabio promised to buy me lunch. > Fabio insisted on buying me lunch.

FR Fabio a promis de m'inviter à déjeuner. > Fabio a insisté pour payer mon déjeuner.

IPA [(...) a pʁomi dø m‿ɛ̃vite a deʒœne ‖ > (...) a ɛ̃siste puʁ peje mɔ̃ deʒœne ‖]

2186

EN I saw Donna get into her car and drive away.

FR J'ai vu Donna entrer dans sa voiture et s'en aller.

IPA [ʒ‿ɛ vy dona ɑ̃tʁe dɑ̃ sa vwatyʁ e s‿ɑ̃ ale ‖]

2187

EN I saw Fyodor waiting for a bus.

FR J'ai vu Fyodor attendant un bus.

IPA [ʒ‿ɛ vy (...) atɑ̃dɑ̃ t‿œ̃ bys ‖]

2188

EN I saw him fall off his bike.

FR Je l'ai vu tomber de son vélo.
IPA [ʒø l̯ɛ vy tɔ̃be dø sɔ̃ velo ‖]

2189

EN Did you see the accident happen?

FR Avez-vous vu l'accident se produire?
IPA [ave vu vy l̯aksidɑ̃ sø pʁodɥiʁ ‖]

2190

EN I saw him walking along the street.

FR Je l'ai vu marcher le long de la rue.
IPA [ʒø l̯ɛ vy maʁʃe lø lɔ̃ dø la ʁy ‖]

2191

EN I didn't hear you come in.

FR Je ne t'ai pas entendu (♀entendue) entrer.
IPA [ʒø nø t̯ɛ pa z̯ɑ̃tɑ̃dy (♀ɑ̃tɑ̃dy) ɑ̃tʁe ‖]

2192

EN Xenia suddenly felt somebody touch her on the shoulder.

FR Xenia a soudainement senti quelqu'un lui toucher l'épaule.
IPA [(...) a sudɛnᵊmɑ̃ sɑ̃ti kɛlkœ̃ lɥi tuʃe l̯epol ‖]

2193

EN Did you notice anyone go out?

FR Avez-vous aperçu quelqu'un sortir?
IPA [ave vu apɛʁsy kɛlkœ̃ sɔʁtiʁ ‖]

2194

EN I could hear it raining.

FR Je pouvais entendre la pluie.
IPA [ʒø puvɛ ãtãdʁ la plɥi ‖]

2195

EN The missing children were last seen playing near the river.

FR Les enfants disparus ont été vus pour la dernière fois en train de jouer près de la rivière.
IPA [le z‿ãfã dispaʁy ɔ̃ ete vy puʁ la dɛʁnjɛʁ fwa ã tʁɛ̃ dø ʒwe pʁɛ dø la ʁivjɛʁ ‖]

2196

EN Can you smell something burning?

FR Sens-tu quelque chose en train de brûler?
IPA [sãs ty kɛlk ʃoz ã tʁɛ̃ dø bʁyle ‖]

2197

EN I found Franz in my room reading my email.

FR J'ai trouvé Franz dans ma chambre en train de lire mes courriels.

IPA [ʒ‿ɛ tʁuve (...) dã ma ʃãbʁ ã tʁɛ̃ dø liʁ me kuʁjɛl ‖]

2198

EN Everyone heard the bomb explode.

FR Tout le monde a entendu la bombe exploser.

IPA [tu lø mɔ̃d a ãtãdy la bɔ̃b ɛksploze ‖]

2199

EN I heard someone slamming the door in the middle of the night.

FR J'ai entendu quelqu'un claquer la porte au milieu de la nuit.

IPA [ʒ‿ɛ ãtãdy kɛlkœ̃ klake la pɔʁt o miljø dø la nɥi ‖]

2200

EN Heidi hurt her knee playing volleyball.

FR Heidi s'est blessée au genou en jouant au volleyball.

IPA [(...) s‿e blese o ʒ°nu ã ʒwã o (...) ‖]

GMS #2201 - 2300

2201

EN Takahiro's in the kitchen making coffee.

FR Takahiro est dans la cuisine en train de faire du café.
IPA [(...) e dã la kɥizin ã tʁɛ̃ dø fɛʁ dy kafe ||]

2202

EN A man ran out of the house shouting.

FR Un homme est sorti de la maison en criant.
IPA [œ̃ n‿ɔm e sɔʁti dø la mɛzɔ̃ ã kʁijã ||]

2203

EN Do something! Don't just stand there doing nothing.

FR Fais quelque chose! Ne reste pas là à ne rien faire.
IPA [fɛ kɛlk ʃoz || nø ʁɛst pa la a nø ʁjɛ̃ fɛʁ ||]

2204

EN Did you cut yourself shaving?

FR T'es-tu coupé en te rasant?
IPA [t‿ɛ ty kupe ã tø ʁazã ||]

2205

EN Be careful when crossing the street.

FR Fais attention en traversant la rue.

IPA [fɛ atɑ̃sjɔ̃ ɑ̃ tʁavɛʁsɑ̃ la ʁy ||]

2206

EN Having finally found a hotel, we looked for some place to have dinner.

FR Ayant enfin trouvé un hôtel, nous avons cherché un endroit pour dîner.

IPA [ɛjɑ̃ ɑ̃fɛ̃ tʁuve œ̃ n‿otɛl | nu z‿avɔ̃ ʃɛʁʃe œ̃ n‿ɑ̃dʁwa puʁ dine ||]

2207

EN After getting off work, she went straight home.

FR Après avoir fini de travailler, elle est allée directement à la maison.

IPA [apʁɛ z‿avwaʁ fini dø tʁavaje | ɛ l‿e t‿ale diʁɛktᵊmɑ̃ a la mɛzɔ̃ ||]

2208

EN Taking a key out of his pocket, he unlocked the door.

FR Sortant une clé de sa poche, il déverrouilla la porte.

IPA [sɔʁtɑ̃ t‿yn kle dø sa pɔʃ | il devᵊʁuija la pɔʁt ||]

2209

EN Feeling tired, I went to bed early.

FR Me sentant fatigué (♀fatiguée), je suis allé (♀allée) au lit tôt.

IPA [mø sãtã fatige (♀fatige) | ʒø sɥi ale (♀ale) o li to ‖]

2210

EN Being unemployed means he doesn't have much money.

FR Qu'il soit au chômage signifie qu'il n'a pas beaucoup d'argent.

IPA [k‿il swa o ʃomaʒ siɲifi k‿il n‿a pa boku d‿aʁʒã ‖]

2211

EN Not having a car can make getting around difficult in some places.

FR Ne pas avoir de voiture peut rendre le fait de se déplacer difficile dans certains endroits.

IPA [nø pa z‿avwaʁ dø vwatyʁ pø ʁãdʁ lø fɛ dø sø deplase difisil dã sɛʁtẽ z‿ãdʁwa ‖]

2212

EN Having already seen the movie twice, I didn't want to go again with my friends.

FR Ayant déjà vu le film deux fois, je ne voulais pas y retourner avec mes amis.

IPA [ɛjɑ̃ deʒa vy lø film dø fwa | ʒø nø vulɛ pa z‿i ʁ°tuʁne avɛk me z‿ami ||]

2213

EN Not being able to speak the local language meant that I had trouble communicating.

FR Ne pas être en mesure de parler la langue locale signifie que j'ai eu du mal à communiquer.

IPA [nø pa z‿ɛtʁ ɑ̃ m°zyʁ dø paʁle la lɑ̃g lokal siɲifi kø ʒ‿ɛ y dy mal a komynike ||]

2214

EN Being a vegetarian, Mitsuko doesn't eat any kind of meat.

FR Étant végétarien, Mitsuko ne mange aucun type de viande.

IPA [etɑ̃ veʒetaʁjɛ̃ | (...) nø mɑ̃ʒ okœ̃ tip dø vjɑ̃d ||]

2215

EN The police want to talk to anybody who saw the accident.

FR La police veut parler à quiconque a vu l'accident.

IPA [la polis vø paʁle a kikɔ̃k a vy l‿aksidɑ̃ ||]

2216

EN The new city hall isn't a very beautiful building. Most people don't like it.

FR Le nouvel hôtel de ville n'est pas un très beau bâtiment. La plupart des gens ne l'aiment pas.

IPA [lø nuvɛ l̩ otɛl dø vil n̩ e pa z ̃œ tʁɛ bo batimɑ̃ || la plypaʁ de ʒɑ̃ nø l̩ em pa ||]

2217

EN The people were injured in the accident.

FR Les personnes ont été blessées dans l'accident.

IPA [le pɛʁsɔn ɔ̃ ete blese dɑ̃ l̩ aksidɑ̃ ||]

2218

EN Do the police know the cause of the explosion?

FR Les policiers connaissent-ils la cause de l'explosion?

IPA [le polisje konɛ s̩ il la koz dø l̩ ɛksplozjɔ̃ ||]

2219

EN The police are looking for the stolen car.

FR Les policiers sont à la recherche de la voiture volée.

IPA [le polisje sɔ̃ a la ʁᵊʃɛʁʃ dø la vwatyʁ vole ||]

2220

EN I need my glasses, but I can't find them.

FR J'ai besoin de mes lunettes, mais je ne peux pas les trouver.

IPA [ʒ‿ɛ bøzwɛ̃ dø me lynɛt | mɛ ʒø nø pø pa le tʁuve ‖]

2221

EN I'm going to buy some new jeans today.

FR Je vais acheter de nouveaux jeans aujourd'hui.

IPA [ʒø vɛ aʃᵊte dø nuvo dʒins oʒuʁdɥi ‖]

2222

EN Did you hear a noise just now?

FR Avez-vous entendu un bruit tout à l'heure?

IPA [ave vu ɑ̃tɑ̃dy œ̃ bʁɥi tu a l‿œʁ ‖]

2223

EN I can't work here. There's too much noise.

FR Je ne peux pas travailler ici. Il y a trop de bruit.

IPA [ʒø nø pø pa tʁavaje isi ‖ i l‿i a tʁo dø bʁɥi ‖]

2224

EN There's a hair in my soup.

FR Il y a un cheveu dans ma soupe.

IPA [i l‿i a œ̃ ʃᵊvø dɑ̃ ma sup ‖]

2225

EN You've got very long hair.

FR Tu as les cheveux très longs.
IPA [ty a le ʃᵊvø tʁɛ lɔ̃ ‖]

2226

EN You can stay with us. We have a spare room.

FR Tu peux séjourner chez nous. Nous avons une chambre d'amis.
IPA [ty pø seʒuʁne ʃe nu ‖ nu z‿avɔ̃ z‿yn ʃɑ̃bʁ d‿ami ‖]

2227

EN You can't sit here. There isn't any room.

FR Tu ne peux pas t'asseoir ici. Il n'y a pas de place.
IPA [ty nø pø pa t‿aswaʁ isi ‖ il n‿i a pa dø plas ‖]

2228

EN I had some interesting experiences while I was traveling.

FR J'ai eu quelques expériences intéressantes pendant que je voyageais.
IPA [ʒ‿ɛ y kɛl k‿ekspeʁjɑ̃s ɛ̃teʁesɑ̃t pɑ̃dɑ̃ kø ʒø vwajaʒɛ ‖]

2229

EN They offered me the job because I had a lot of experience.

FR Ils m'ont offert le poste parce que j'avais beaucoup d'expérience.
IPA [il m‿ɔ̃ ofɛʁ lø pɔst paʁs kø ʒ‿ave boku d‿ɛkspeʁjɑ̃s ‖]

2230

EN I'm going to go buy a loaf of bread.

FR Je vais aller acheter une miche de pain.
IPA [ʒø vɛ ale aʃ°te ʁ‿yn miʃ dø pɛ̃ ‖]

2231

EN Enjoy your vacation. I hope you have good weather.

FR Profite de tes vacances. J'espère que tu auras du beau temps.
IPA [pʁofit dø te vakɑ̃s ‖ ʒ‿espeʁ kø ty oʁa dy bo tɑ̃ ‖]

2232

EN Where are you going to put all your furniture?

FR Où vas-tu mettre tous tes meubles?
IPA [u va ty mɛtʁ tu te mœbl ‖]

2233

EN Let me know if you need more information.

FR Fais-moi savoir si tu as besoin de plus amples informations.

IPA [fɛ mwa savwaʁ si ty a bøzwɛ̃ dø ply s‿ãp l‿ɛ̃fɔʁmasjɔ̃ ‖]

2234

EN The news was very depressing.

FR Les nouvelles étaient très déprimantes.

IPA [le nuvɛl ete tʁɛ depʁimãt ‖]

2235

EN They spend a lot of money on travel.

FR Ils dépensent beaucoup d'argent sur leurs voyages.

IPA [il depãs boku d‿aʁʒã syʁ lœʁ vwajaʒ ‖]

2236

EN We had a very good trip.

FR Nous avons passé un très beau voyage.

IPA [nu z‿avɔ̃ pase œ̃ tʁɛ bo vwajaʒ ‖]

2237

EN It's a nice day today. > It's nice weather today.

FR C'est une belle journée aujourd'hui. > Il fait beau aujourd'hui.

IPA [sε t‿yn bεl ʒuʀne oʒuʀdɥi || > il fε bo oʒuʀdɥi ||]

2238

EN We had a lot of bags and suitcases. > We had a lot of baggage.

FR Nous avions beaucoup de sacs et de valises. > Nous avions beaucoup de bagages.

IPA [nu z‿avjɔ̃ boku dø sak e dø valiz || > nu z‿avjɔ̃ boku dø bagaʒ ||]

2239

EN These chairs are mine. > This furniture is mine.

FR Ces chaises sont à moi. > Ce mobilier est à moi.

IPA [se ʃεz sɔ̃ a mwa || > sø mobilje ʀ‿e a mwa ||]

2240

EN That's a good suggestion. > That's good advice.

FR C'est une bonne suggestion. > C'est un bon conseil.

IPA [sε t‿yn bɔn sygʒεstjɔ̃ || > sε t‿œ̃ bɔ̃ kɔ̃sεj ||]

2241

EN My neighbor drives an SUV.

FR Mon voisin conduit un VUS.
IPA [mɔ̃ vwazɛ̃ kɔ̃dɥi t‿œ̃ vy ‖]

2242

EN My neighbor is an FBI agent.

FR Mon voisin est un agent du FBI.
IPA [mɔ̃ vwazɛ̃ n‿e t‿œ̃ n‿aʒɑ̃ dy (...) ‖]

2243

EN He got a university degree.

FR Il a obtenu un diplôme universitaire.
IPA [i l‿a ɔptᵊny œ̃ diplom yniveʁsitɛʁ ‖]

2244

EN He was an NYU student.

FR Il était un étudiant de NYU.
IPA [i l‿etɛ t‿œ̃ n‿etydjɑ̃ dø (...) ‖]

2245

EN If you want to leave early, you have to ask for permission.

FR Si tu souhaites partir plus tôt, tu dois demander la permission.

IPA [si ty swɛt paʁtiʁ plys to | ty dwa dᵊmɑ̃de la pɛʁmisjɔ̃ ||]

2246

EN I don't think Marco will get the job, because he doesn't have enough experience.

FR Je ne pense pas que Marco va obtenir l'emploi, parce qu'il n'a pas assez d'expérience.

IPA [ʒø nø pɑ̃s pa kø (...) va ɔptᵊniʁ l̥ɑ̃plwa | paʁs k̩il n̩a pa z̩ase d̩ɛkspeʁjɑ̃s ||]

2247

EN Can I talk to you? I need some advice.

FR Puis-je te parler? J'ai besoin de quelques conseils.

IPA [pɥi ʒø tø paʁle || ʒ̩ɛ bøzwɛ̃ dø kɛlk kɔ̃sɛj ||]

2248

EN I'd like some information about hotels in Paris.

FR J'aimerais avoir de l'information sur les hôtels à Paris.

IPA [ʒ̩ɛmᵊʁɛ avwaʁ dø l̩ɛ̃fɔʁmasjɔ̃ syʁ le otɛl a (...) ||]

2249

EN English has one (1) alphabet with twenty-six (26) letters.

FR L'anglais a un alphabet de vingt-six (26) lettres.
IPA [l‿ɑ̃glɛ a œ̃ n‿alfabɛ də vɛ̃tsis (26) lɛtʁ ‖]

2250

EN English has a lot of vocabulary.

FR L'anglais a beaucoup de vocabulaire.
IPA [l‿ɑ̃glɛ a boku də vokabylɛʁ ‖]

2251

EN Today I learned twenty (20) new vocabulary words.

FR Aujourd'hui, j'ai appris vingt nouveaux mots de vocabulaire.
IPA [oʒuʁdɥi | ʒ‿ɛ apʁi vɛ̃ nuvo mo də vokabylɛʁ ‖]

2252

EN I've got a new job, and it's hard work.

FR J'ai un nouvel emploi, et c'est un travail difficile.
IPA [ʒ‿ɛ œ̃ nuvɛ l‿ɑ̃plwa | e sɛ t‿œ̃ tʁavaj difisil ‖]

2253

EN I need some money to buy some food.

FR J'ai besoin d'argent pour acheter de la nourriture.
IPA [ʒ‿ɛ bøzwɛ̃ d‿aʁʒɑ̃ pu ʁ‿aʃᵊte də la nuʁityʁ ‖]

2254

EN We met a lot of interesting people at the party.

FR Nous avons rencontré beaucoup de gens intéressants à la fête.

IPA [nu z‿avɔ̃ ʁãkɔ̃tʁe boku də ʒã ɛ̃teʁesã a la fɛt ‖]

2255

EN I'm going to open a window to get some fresh air.

FR Je vais ouvrir une fenêtre pour faire entrer un peu d'air frais.

IPA [ʒø vɛ uvʁi ʁ‿yn fᵊnɛtʁ puʁ fɛʁ ãtʁe ʁ‿œ̃ pø d‿ɛʁ fʁɛ ‖]

2256

EN I'd like to give you some advice before you go off to college.

FR Je voudrais te donner quelques conseils avant que tu partes pour l'université.

IPA [ʒø vudʁe tø done kɛlk kɔ̃sɛj avã kø ty paʁt puʁ l‿ynivɛʁsite ‖]

2257

EN The tour guide gave us some information about the city.

FR Le guide nous a donné de l'information sur la ville.

IPA [lø gid nu z‿a done də l‿ɛ̃fɔʁmasjɔ̃ syʁ la vil ‖]

2258

EN We've had wonderful weather this last month.

FR Nous avons eu du très beau temps ce mois dernier.
IPA [nu z‿avɔ̃ y dy tʁɛ bo tɑ̃ sø mwa dɛʁnje ‖]

2259

EN Some children learn very quickly.

FR Certains enfants apprennent très vite.
IPA [sɛʁtɛ̃ z‿ɑ̃fɑ̃ apʁɛn tʁɛ vit ‖]

2260

EN Tomorrow there'll be rain in some places, but most of the country will be dry.

FR Demain, il y aura de la pluie dans certains endroits, mais la plus grande partie du pays sera au sec.
IPA [d°mɛ̃ | i l‿i oʁa dø la plɥi dɑ̃ sɛʁtɛ̃ z‿ɑ̃dʁwa | mɛ la plys gʁɑ̃d paʁti dy pei s°ʁa o sɛk ‖]

2261

EN I have to go to the bank today. — Is there a bank near here?

FR Je dois aller à la banque aujourd'hui. — Y a-t-il une banque près d'ici?
IPA [ʒø dwa ale a la bɑ̃k oʒuʁdɥi ‖ — i a t‿il yn bɑ̃k pʁɛ d‿isi ‖]

2262

EN I don't like going to the dentist. — My sister's a dentist.

FR Je n'aime pas aller chez le dentiste. — Ma sœur est dentiste.

IPA [ʒø n‿em pa z‿ale ʃe lø dɑ̃tist || — ma sœʁ e dɑ̃tist ||]

2263

EN I have to go to the bank, and then I'm going to the post office.

FR Je dois aller à la banque et puis je vais au bureau de poste.

IPA [ʒø dwa ale a la bɑ̃k e pɥi ʒø vɛ o byʁo dø pɔst ||]

2264

EN Two people were taken to the hospital after the accident.

FR Deux personnes ont été emmenées à l'hôpital après l'accident.

IPA [dø pɛʁsɔn ɔ̃ ete ɑ̃mᵊne a l‿opital apʁɛ l‿aksidɑ̃ ||]

2265

EN Flora works eight (8) hours a day, six (6) days a week.

FR Flora travaille huit heures par jour, six jours par semaine.

IPA [(...) tʁavaj ɥi t‿œʁ paʁ ʒuʁ | sis ʒuʁ paʁ sᵊmɛn ||]

2266

EN What's the longest river in the world?

FR Quel est le fleuve le plus long au monde?
IPA [kɛ l̩e lø flœv lø plys lɔ̃ o mɔ̃d ‖]

2267

EN The earth goes around the sun, and the moon goes around the earth.

FR La Terre tourne autour du Soleil, et la Lune tourne autour de la Terre.
IPA [la tɛʁ tuʁn otuʁ dy solɛj | e la lyn tuʁn otuʁ dø la tɛʁ ‖]

2268

EN Have you ever crossed the equator?

FR As-tu déjà traversé l'équateur?
IPA [a ty deʒa tʁavɛʁse l̩ekwatœʁ ‖]

2269

EN We looked up at all the stars in the sky.

FR Nous avons recherché toutes les étoiles du ciel.
IPA [nu z̩avɔ̃ ʁ°ʃɛʁʃe tut le z̩etwal dy sjɛl ‖]

2270

EN We must do more to protect the environment.

FR Nous devons faire davantage pour protéger l'environnement.

IPA [nu dᵊvɔ̃ fɛʁ davɑ̃taʒ puʁ pʁoteʒe lᷓãviʁɔnᵊmã ‖]

2271

EN There are millions of stars in space.

FR Il y a des millions d'étoiles dans l'espace.

IPA [i l̯i a de miljɔ̃ dᷓetwal dã lᷓɛspas ‖]

2272

EN Milena's brother's in prison for robbery. > He's in jail.

FR Le frère de Milena est en prison pour vol. > Il est en prison.

IPA [lø fʁɛʁ dø (...) e tᷓã pʁizɔ̃ puʁ vɔl ‖ > i lᷓe tᷓã pʁizɔ̃ ‖]

2273

EN Milena went to the prison to visit her brother.

FR Milena est allé à la prison pour rendre visite à son frère.

IPA [(...) e ale a la pʁizɔ̃ puʁ ʁãdʁ vizit a sɔ̃ fʁɛʁ ‖]

2274

EN When I finish high school, I want to go to college.

FR Quand je finirai l'école secondaire, je veux aller à l'université.

IPA [kɑ̃ ʒø finiʁɛ l̩ekɔl sᵊgɔ̃dɛʁ | ʒø vø ale a l̩ynivɛʁsite ‖]

2275

EN Konstantin is a student at the college where I used to work.

FR Konstantin est un étudiant à l'université où j'ai déjà travaillé.

IPA [(...) e t‿œ̃ n̩etydjɑ̃ a l̩ynivɛʁsite u ʒ‿ɛ deʒa tʁavaje ‖]

2276

EN I was in class for five (5) hours today.

FR J'étais en classe durant cinq heures aujourd'hui.

IPA [ʒ‿ete ɑ̃ klas dyʁɑ̃ sɛ̃ k‿œʁ oʒuʁdɥi ‖]

2277

EN Who's the youngest student in the class?

FR Qui est le plus jeune élève de la classe?

IPA [ki e lø plys ʒœn elɛv dø la klas ‖]

2278

EN Do you ever have breakfast in bed?

FR As-tu déjà pris le petit déjeuner au lit?
IPA [a ty deʒa pʁi lø pᵊti deʒœne o li ‖]

2279

EN What time do you usually finish work?

FR À quelle heure finis-tu généralement de travailler?
IPA [a kɛ l̩ œʁ fini ty ʒeneʁalᵊmã dø tʁavaje ‖]

2280

EN Will you be home tomorrow afternoon?

FR Seras-tu à la maison demain après-midi?
IPA [sᵊʁa ty a la mɛzõ dᵊmɛ̃ apʁɛ midi ‖]

2281

EN The economy was bad, so a lot of people were out of work.

FR L'économie allait mal, alors beaucoup de gens étaient sans emploi.
IPA [l̩ekonomi alɛ mal | alɔʁ boku dø ʒã etɛ sã z̩ãplwa ‖]

2282

EN Do you like strong black coffee?

FR Aimes-tu le café noir corsé?
IPA [ɛm ty lø kafe nwaʁ kɔʁse ‖]

2283

EN Did you like the coffee we had after dinner last night?

FR As-tu aimé le café que nous avons bu après dîner hier soir?
IPA [a ty eme lø kafe kø nu z‿avɔ̃ by apʁɛ dine jɛʁ swaʁ ‖]

2284

EN Some people are afraid of spiders.

FR Certaines personnes ont peur des araignées.
IPA [sɛʁten pɛʁsɔn ɔ̃ pøʁ de z‿aʁɛɲe ‖]

2285

EN A vegetarian is someone who doesn't eat meat.

FR Un végétarien est quelqu'un qui ne mange pas de viande.
IPA [œ̃ veʒetaʁjɛ̃ n‿e kɛlkœ̃ ki nø mɑ̃ʒ pa dø vjɑ̃d ‖]

2286

EN Do you know the people who live next door?

FR Connais-tu les gens qui vivent à côté?

IPA [konɛ ty le ʒɑ̃ ki viv a kote ‖]

2287

EN History is the study of the past.

FR L'histoire est l'étude du passé.

IPA [l̬istwaʁ e l̬etyd dy pase ‖]

2288

EN The water in the pool didn't look clean, so we didn't go swimming.

FR L'eau de la piscine n'avait pas l'air propre, alors nous ne sommes pas allés (♀allées) nager.

IPA [l̬o dø la pisin n̬avɛ pa l̬ɛʁ pʁɔpʁ | alɔʁ nu nø sɔm pa z̬ale (♀ale) naʒe ‖]

2289

EN You need patience to teach young children.

FR Tu as besoin d'être patient pour enseigner à de jeunes enfants.

IPA [ty a bøzwɛ̃ d̬etʁ pasjɑ̃ pu ʁ̬ɑ̃seɲe a dø ʒœ n̬ɑ̃fɑ̃ ‖]

2290

EN Paolo and Giuliana got married, but the marriage didn't last very long.

FR Paolo et Giuliana se sont mariés, mais leur mariage n'a pas duré très longtemps.

IPA [(...) e (...) sø sɔ̃ maʁje | mɛ lœʁ maʁjaʒ n‿a pa dyʁe tʁɛ lɔ̃tã ||]

2291

EN A pacifist is a person who is against war.

FR Un pacifiste est une personne qui est contre la guerre.

IPA [œ̃ pasifist e t‿yn pɛʁsɔn ki e kɔ̃tʁ la gɛʁ ||]

2292

EN Do you think the rich should pay higher taxes?

FR Penses-tu que les riches devraient payer plus d'impôts?

IPA [pãs ty kø le ʁiʃ dᵊvʁe peje plys d‿ɛ̃po ||]

2293

EN The government has promised to provide more money to help the homeless.

FR Le gouvernement a promis de fournir plus d'argent pour aider les sans-abri.

IPA [lø guvɛʁnᵊmã a pʁomi dø fuʁniʁ plys d‿aʁʒã pu ʁ‿ede le sã z‿abʁi ||]

2294

EN The French are famous for their food.

FR Les Français sont reconnus pour leur cuisine.
IPA [le fʁɑ̃sɛ sɔ̃ ʁ°kony puʁ lœʁ kɥizin ‖]

2295

EN The Chinese invented printing.

FR Les Chinois ont inventé l'imprimerie.
IPA [le ʃinwa ɔ̃ ɛ̃vɑ̃te l‿ɛ̃pʁim°ʁi ‖]

2296

EN The dollar is the currency of many countries.

FR Le dollar est la monnaie de nombreux pays.
IPA [lø dolaʁ e la monɛ dø nɔ̃bʁø pei ‖]

2297

EN Life is all right if you have a job, but things are not so easy for the unemployed.

FR La vie n'est pas si mal si tu as un emploi, mais les choses ne sont pas si faciles pour les chômeurs.
IPA [la vi n‿e pa si mal si ty a z‿œ̃ n‿ɑ̃plwa | mɛ le ʃoz nø sɔ̃ pa si fasil puʁ le ʃomœʁ ‖]

2298

EN It is said that Robin Hood took money from the rich and gave it to the poor.

FR Il est dit que Robin des Bois a pris l'argent des riches et l'a donné aux pauvres.

IPA [i l̩e di kø ʁobẽ de bwa a pʁi l̩aʁʒã de ʁiʃ e l̩a done o povʁ ‖]

2299

EN Cairo's the capital of Egypt.

FR Le Caire est la capitale de l'Égypte.

IPA [lø kaiʁ e la kapital dø l̩eʒypt ‖]

2300

EN The Atlantic Ocean is between Africa and America.

FR L'océan Atlantique est entre l'Afrique et l'Amérique.

IPA [l̩oseã atlãtik e ãtʁ l afrique e l̩ameʁik ‖]

GMS #2301 - 2400

2301

EN Sweden is a country in northern Europe.

FR La Suède est un pays en Europe du Nord.
IPA [la sɥɛd e t‿œ̃ pei ã øʁop dy nɔʁ ||]

2302

EN The Amazon is a river in South America.

FR L'Amazone est un fleuve en Amérique du Sud.
IPA [l‿amazon e t‿œ̃ flœv ã n‿ameʁik dy syd ||]

2303

EN Asia is the largest continent in the world.

FR L'Asie est le plus grand continent du monde.
IPA [l asie e lø plys gʁã kõtinã dy mõd ||]

2304

EN The Pacific is the largest ocean.

FR Le Pacifique est le plus grand océan.
IPA [lø pasifik e lø plys gʁã d‿oseã ||]

2305

EN The Rhine is a river in Europe.

FR Le Rhin est un fleuve d'Europe.
IPA [lø ʁin e t‿œ̃ flœv d‿øʁɔp ‖]

2306

EN Kenya is a country in East Africa.

FR Le Kenya est un pays d'Afrique de l'Est.
IPA [lø (...) e t‿œ̃ pei afrique dø l‿e ‖]

2307

EN The United States is between Canada and Mexico.

FR Les États-Unis sont entre le Canada et le Mexique.
IPA [le z‿etazuni sɔ̃ ɑ̃tʁ lø kanada e lø meksik ‖]

2308

EN The Andes are mountains in South America.

FR Les Andes sont des montagnes en Amérique du Sud.
IPA [lø (...) sɔ̃ de mɔ̃taɲ ɑ̃ n‿ameʁik dy syd ‖]

2309

EN Bangkok is the capital of Thailand.

FR Bangkok est la capitale de la Thaïlande.
IPA [(...) e la kapital dø la tailand ‖]

2310

EN The Alps are mountains in central Europe.

FR Les Alpes sont des montagnes d'Europe centrale.
IPA [le z‿alp sɔ̃ de mɔ̃taɲ d‿øʁop sɑ̃tʁal ‖]

2311

EN The Sahara is a desert in northern Africa.

FR Le Sahara est un désert en Afrique du Nord.
IPA [lø (...) e t‿œ̃ dezɛʁ ɑ̃ afʁik dy nɔʁ ‖]

2312

EN The Philippines is a group of islands near Taiwan.

FR Les Philippines sont un groupe d'îles proches de Taïwan.
IPA [le filipin sɔ̃ t‿œ̃ gʁup d‿il pʁɔʃ dø taiwan ‖]

2313

EN Have you ever been to the south of France?

FR Es-tu déjà allé (♀ allée) dans le sud de la France?
IPA [ɛ ty deʒa ale (♀ ale) dɑ̃ lø syd dø la fʁɑ̃s ‖]

2314

EN I hope to go to the United Kingdom next year.

FR J'espère aller au Royaume-Uni l'année prochaine.
IPA [ʒ‿ɛspeʁ ale o ʁwajom yni l‿ane pʁoʃɛn ‖]

2315

EN Scotland, Britain (England), and Wales are all in the United Kingdom.

FR L'Écosse, la Grande-Bretagne (Angleterre) et le Pays de Galles sont tous au Royaume-Uni.

IPA [l̩ekɔs | la gʁɑ̃d bʁ°taɲ (ɑ̃gløtɛʁ) e lø pei dø gal sɔ̃ tu o ʁwajom yni ||]

2316

EN The Great Wall of China is in China.

FR La Grande Muraille de Chine est en Chine.

IPA [la gʁɑ̃d myʁaj dø ʃin e t̪ɑ̃ ʃin ||]

2317

EN UCLA is in L.A.

FR UCLA est à Los Angeles.

IPA [(...) e a (...) ||]

2318

EN The Guggenheim Museum is in New York.

FR Le musée Guggenheim est à New York.

IPA [lø myze (...) e a nuw jɔʁk ||]

2319

EN   The Acropolis is in Athens.

FR   L'Acropole est à Athènes.
IPA [l̩akʁopɔl e a atɛn ‖]

2320

EN   The Kremlin is in Moscow.

FR   Le Kremlin est à Moscou.
IPA [lø kʁɛmlɛ̃ e a mɔsku ‖]

2321

EN   The Pentagon is in Washington, D.C.

FR   Le Pentagone est à Washington, dans le district
     fédéral de Columbia.
IPA [lø pɛ̃tagon e a (...) | dɑ̃ lø distʁikt fedeʁal dø (...) ‖]

2322

EN   The bicycle and the car are means of transportation.

FR   La bicyclette et la voiture sont des moyens de
     transport.
IPA [la bisiklɛt e la vwatyʁ sɔ̃ de mwajɛ̃ dø tʁɑ̃spɔʁ ‖]

2323

EN The police want to interview two (2) men about the robbery last week.

FR La police veut interroger deux hommes à propos du cambriolage de la semaine dernière.

IPA [la polis vø ɛ̃tɛʁɔʒe dø ɔm a pʁopo dy kɑ̃bʁijolaʒ dø la sᵊmɛn dɛʁnjɛʁ ‖]

2324

EN Fortunately, the news wasn't as bad as we expected.

FR Heureusement, les nouvelles n'étaient pas aussi mauvaises que ce à quoi nous nous attendions.

IPA [øʁøzᵊmɑ̃ | le nuvɛl n̩ete pa z̩osi movɛz kø sø a kwa nu nu z̩atɑ̃djɔ̃ ‖]

2325

EN Do the police know how the accident happened?

FR Les policiers savent-ils comment l'accident s'est produit?

IPA [le polisje sa v̩il kɔmɑ̃ l̩aksidɑ̃ s̩e pʁodɥi ‖]

2326

EN I don't like hot weather. Ninety degrees is too hot for me. > I don't like hot weather. Thirty-two (32) degrees is too hot for me.

FR Je n'aime pas la chaleur. Trente-deux degrés, c'est trop chaud pour moi.

IPA [ʒø n‿ɛm pa la ʃalœʁ ‖ tʁɑ̃tdø dᵊgʁe | sɛ tʁo ʃo puʁ mwa ‖]

2327

EN I need more than ten (10) dollars. Ten dollars isn't enough. > I need more than six (6) euros. Six euros isn't enough.

FR J'ai besoin de plus de six euros. Six euros ne suffisent pas.

IPA [ʒ‿ɛ bøzwɛ̃ dø plys dø si z‿øʁo ‖ si z‿øʁo nø syfiz pa ‖]

2328

EN Do you think two (2) days is enough time to visit New York?

FR Penses-tu que deux jours suffisent pour visiter New York?

IPA [pɑ̃s ty kø dø ʒuʁ syfiz puʁ vizite nuw jɔʁk ‖]

2329

EN Problems concerning health are health problems.

FR Les problèmes concernant la santé sont des problèmes de santé.

IPA [le pʁoblɛm kɔ̃sɛʁnɑ̃ la sɑ̃te sɔ̃ de pʁoblɛm də sɑ̃te ‖]

2330

EN Chocolate made from milk is milk chocolate.

FR Du chocolat fait à partir de lait, c'est du chocolat au lait.

IPA [dy ʃokola fɛ a paʁtiʁ də lɛ | sɛ dy ʃokola o lɛ ‖]

2331

EN Someone whose job is to inspect factories is a factory inspector.

FR Quelqu'un dont le travail consiste à inspecter les usines est un inspecteur d'usines.

IPA [kɛlkœ̃ dɔ̃ lø tʁavaj kɔ̃sist a ɛ̃spɛkte le z‿yzin e t‿œ̃ n‿ɛ̃spɛktœʁ d‿yzin ‖]

2332

EN The results of your exams are your exam results.

FR Les résultats de tes examens sont tes résultats d'examen.

IPA [le ʁezylta də te z‿ɛgzamɛ̃ sɔ̃ te ʁezylta d‿ɛgzamɛ̃ ‖]

2333

EN A scandal involving an oil company is an oil company scandal.

FR Un scandale impliquant une compagnie pétrolière est un scandale de compagnie pétrolière.

IPA [œ̃ skãdal ɛ̃plikã t‿yn kɔ̃paɲi petʁoljɛʁ e t‿œ̃ skãdal dø kɔ̃paɲi petʁoljɛʁ ‖]

2334

EN A building with five (5) stories is a five-story building.

FR Un bâtiment comprenant cinq étages est un bâtiment de cinq étages.

IPA [œ̃ batimã kɔ̃pʁ°nã sɛ̃ k‿etaʒ e t‿œ̃ batimã dø sɛ̃ k‿etaʒ ‖]

2335

EN A man who is thirty (30) years old is a thirty-year-old man.

FR Un homme qui a trente ans est un homme de trente ans.

IPA [œ̃ n‿ɔm ki a tʁãt ã e t‿œ̃ n‿ɔm dø tʁãt ã ‖]

2336

EN A course that lasts twelve (12) weeks is a twelve-week course.

FR Un cours qui dure douze semaines est un cours de douze semaines.

IPA [œ̃ kuʁ ki dyʁ duz sᵊmɛn e t‿œ̃ kuʁ dø duz sᵊmɛn ‖]

2337

EN A drive that takes two (2) hours is a two-hour drive.

FR Un trajet qui dure deux heures est un trajet de deux heures.

IPA [œ̃ tʁaʒɛ ki dyʁ dø z‿œʁ e t‿œ̃ tʁaʒɛ dø dø z‿œʁ ‖]

2338

EN A question that has two (2) parts is a two-part question.

FR Une question qui a deux parties est une question à deux parties.

IPA [yn kɛstjɔ̃ ki a dø paʁti e t‿yn kɛstjɔ̃ a dø paʁti ‖]

2339

EN The meeting tomorrow has been canceled. > Tomorrow's meeting has been canceled.

FR La réunion de demain a été annulée.

IPA [la ʁeynjɔ̃ dø dᵊmɛ̃ n‿a ete anyle ‖]

2340

EN The storm last week caused a lot of damage. > Last week's storm caused a lot of damage.

FR La tempête de la semaine dernière a causé beaucoup de dommages.

IPA [la tɑ̃pɛt dø la sᵊmɛn dɛʀnjɛʀ a koze boku dø domaʒ ‖]

2341

EN Tourism is the main industry in the region. > The region's main industry is tourism.

FR Le tourisme est la principale industrie de la région. > La principale industrie de la région est le tourisme.

IPA [lø tuʀizm e la pʀɛ̃sipal ɛ̃dystʀi dø la ʀeʒjɔ̃ ‖ > la pʀɛ̃sipal ɛ̃dystʀi dø la ʀeʒjɔ̃ e lø tuʀizm ‖]

2342

EN I bought enough groceries at the supermarket last night for a week. > I bought a week's worth of groceries last night.

FR J'ai acheté suffisamment de choses au supermarché hier soir pour durer une semaine. > J'ai acheté l'équivalent d'une semaine de courses la nuit dernière.

IPA [ʒ‿ɛ aʃᵊte syfizamɑ̃ dø ʃoz o sypɛʀmaʀʃe jɛʀ swaʀ puʀ dyʀe ʀ‿yn sᵊmɛn ‖ > ʒ‿ɛ aʃᵊte l‿ekivalɑ̃ d‿yn sᵊmɛn dø kuʀs la nɥi dɛʀnjɛʀ ‖]

2343

EN I haven't been able to rest for even a minute all day.
> I haven't had a minute's rest all day.

FR Je n'ai même pas été en mesure de me reposer pour une minute de toute la journée. > Je n'ai pas eu une minute de repos de toute la journée.

IPA [ʒø n‿ɛ mɛm pa z‿ete ɑ̃ mᵊzyʁ dø mø ʁᵊpoze pu ʁ‿yn minyt dø tut la ʒuʁne || > ʒø n‿ɛ pa z‿y yn minyt dø ʁᵊpo dø tut la ʒuʁne ||]

2344

EN I don't want you to pay for me. I'll pay for myself.

FR Je ne veux pas que tu paies pour moi. Je vais payer moi-même.

IPA [ʒø nø vø pa kø ty pɛ puʁ mwa || ʒø vɛ peje mwamɛm ||]

2345

EN Do you talk to yourself sometimes?

FR Te parles-tu parfois à toi-même?
IPA [tø paʁl ty paʁfwa a twamɛm ||]

2346

EN If you want more to eat, help yourselves.

FR Si tu veux manger plus, sers-toi.
IPA [si ty vø mɑ̃ʒe plys | se twa ||]

2347

EN It's not our fault. You can't blame us.

FR Ce n'est pas notre faute. Tu ne peux pas nous blâmer.

IPA [sø n‿e pa nɔtʁ fot || ty nø pø pa nu blame ||]

2348

EN It's our own fault. We should blame ourselves.

FR C'est notre faute. Nous devrions nous blâmer nous-mêmes.

IPA [sɛ nɔtʁ fot || nu dᵊvʁijɔ̃ nu blame numɛm ||]

2349

EN I feel nervous. I can't relax.

FR Je me sens nerveux. Je ne peux pas me détendre.

IPA [ʒø mø sɑ̃s nɛʁvø || ʒø nø pø pa mø detɑ̃dʁ ||]

2350

EN You have to try and concentrate.

FR Tu devrais essayer de te concentrer.

IPA [ty dᵊvʁɛ eseje dø tø kɔ̃sɑ̃tʁe ||]

2351

EN What time should we meet?

FR À quelle heure devrions-nous nous rencontrer?

IPA [a kɛ l‿œʁ dᵊvʁijɔ̃ nu nu ʁɑ̃kɔ̃tʁe ||]

2352

EN He got up, washed, shaved, and got dressed.

FR Il s'est levé, s'est lavé, s'est rasé et s'est habillé.
IPA [il s‿e l°ve | s‿e lave | s‿e ʁaze e s‿e abije ||]

2353

EN How long have you and Kenichi known each other?
> How long have you known one another?

FR Depuis combien de temps Kenichi et toi vous connaissez-vous? > Depuis combien de temps vous connaissez-vous l'un l'autre?
IPA [d°pɥi kɔ̃bjɛ̃ dø tɑ̃ (...) e twa vu konɛse vu || > d°pɥi kɔ̃bjɛ̃ dø tɑ̃ vu konɛse vu lœ̃ l‿otʁ ||]

2354

EN Kasumi and Linda don't like each other. > They don't like one another.

FR Kasumi et Linda ne s'aiment pas. > Elles ne s'aiment pas l'une l'autre.
IPA [(...) e (...) nø s‿em pa || > ɛl nø s‿em pa lyn l‿otʁ ||]

2355

EN Do you and Henrik live near each other? > Do you two (2) live near one another?

FR Est-ce qu'Henrik et toi habitez près l'un de l'autre? > Est-ce que vous deux habitez près l'un de l'autre?
IPA [ɛs° k (...) e twa abite pʁɛ lœ̃ dø l‿otʁ || > ɛs° kø vu dø abite pʁɛ lœ̃ dø l‿otʁ ||]

2356

EN I'm not going to do your work for you. You can do it yourself.

FR Je ne vais pas faire ton travail pour toi. Tu peux le faire toi-même.

IPA [ʒø nø ve pa fɛʀ tɔ̃ tʀavaj puʀ twa ‖ ty pø lø fɛʀ twamɛm ‖]

2357

EN The movie itself wasn't very good, but I loved the music.

FR Le film n'était pas très bon, mais j'ai aimé la musique.

IPA [lø film n‿etɛ pa tʀɛ bɔ̃ | mɛ ʒ‿ɛ eme la myzik ‖]

2358

EN Even Magda herself doesn't think she'll get the new job.

FR Même Magda ne pense pas qu'elle obtiendra le nouvel emploi. > Magda elle-même ne pense pas qu'elle obtiendra le nouvel emploi.

IPA [mɛm (...) nø pãs pa k‿ɛl ɔptjɛ̃dʀa lø nuvɛ l‿ãplwa ‖ > (...) ɛlmɛm nø pãs pa k‿ɛl ɔptjɛ̃dʀa lø nuvɛ l‿ãplwa ‖]

2359

EN She climbed out of the swimming pool and dried herself off with a towel.

FR Elle sortit de la piscine et se sécha avec une serviette.

IPA [ɛl sɔʁti dø la pisin e sø seʃa avɛk yn sɛʁvjɛt ‖]

2360

EN I tried to study, but I couldn't concentrate.

FR J'ai essayé d'étudier, mais je ne pouvais pas me concentrer.

IPA [ʒ‿ɛ eseje d‿etydje | mɛ ʒø nø puvɛ pa mø kɔ̃sãtʁe ‖]

2361

EN If somebody attacks you, you need to be able to defend yourself.

FR Si quelqu'un t'attaque, tu dois être capable de te défendre.

IPA [si kɛlkœ̃ t‿atak | ty dwa ɛtʁ kapabl dø tø defãdʁ ‖]

2362

EN You're always rushing around. Why don't you sit down and relax?

FR Tu es toujours pressé. Pourquoi ne pas t'asseoir et te détendre?

IPA [ty ɛ tuʒuʁ pʁese ‖ puʁkwa nø pa t‿aswaʁ e tø detãdʁ ‖]

2363

EN Some people are very selfish. They think only of themselves.

FR Certaines personnes sont très égoïstes. Elles ne pensent qu'à elles-mêmes.

IPA [sɛʁten pɛʁsɔn sõ tʁɛ z‿egoist ‖ ɛl nø pãs k a ɛlmɛm ‖]

2364

EN We couldn't get back into the house because we had locked ourselves out.

FR Nous ne pouvions pas revenir dans la maison parce que nous nous étions enfermés (♀enfermées) à l'extérieur.

IPA [nu nø puvjõ pa ʁ°v°niʁ dã la mɛzõ paʁs kø nu nu z‿etjõ ãfɛʁme (♀ãfɛʁme) a l‿ɛksteʁjœʁ ‖]

2365

EN They're not speaking to each other anymore.

FR Ils ne se parlent plus.

IPA [il nø sø paʁl plys ‖]

2366

EN We'd never met before, so we introduced ourselves to one another.

FR Nous ne nous étions jamais rencontrés (♀rencontrées) auparavant, alors nous nous sommes présentés l'un à l'autre (♀présentées l'une à l'autre).

IPA [nu nø nu z‿etjɔ̃ ʒamɛ ʁɑ̃kɔ̃tʁe (♀ʁɑ̃kɔ̃tʁe) opaʁavɑ̃ | alɔʁ nu nu sɔm pʁezɑ̃te lœ̃ a l‿otʁ (♀pʁezɑ̃te lyn a l‿otʁ) ||]

2367

EN A friend of mine is getting married this Saturday.

FR Un de mes amis se marie ce samedi.

IPA [œ̃ dø me z‿ami sø maʁi sø samˈdi ||]

2368

EN We took a trip with some friends of ours.

FR Nous avons fait un voyage avec quelques-uns (♀unes) de nos amis (♀amies).

IPA [nu z‿avɔ̃ fɛ t‿œ̃ vwajaʒ avɛk kɛlkˈzœ̃ (♀yn) dø no z‿ami (♀ami) ||]

2369

EN Pietro had an argument with a neighbor of his.

FR Pietro a eu une altercation avec un (♀une) de ses voisins (♀voisines).

IPA [(...) a y yn altɛʁkasjɔ̃ avɛk œ̃ (♀yn) dø se vwazɛ̃ (♀vwazin) ||]

2370

EN That woman over there is a friend of my sister's.

FR Cette femme là-bas est une amie de ma sœur.

IPA [sɛt fam laba z‿e t‿yn ami dø ma sœʁ ‖]

2371

EN My sister graduated from college, and is living on her own. > She's living by herself.

FR Ma sœur a terminé l'université et vit par ses propres moyens. > Elle vit par ses propres moyens.

IPA [ma sœʁ a tɛʁmine l‿ynivɛʁsite e vi paʁ se pʁɔpʁ mwajɛ̃ ‖ > ɛl vi paʁ se pʁɔpʁ mwajɛ̃ ‖]

2372

EN I don't want to share a room with anybody. I want my own room.

FR Je ne veux pas partager ma chambre avec quelqu'un. Je veux ma propre chambre.

IPA [ʒø nø vø pa paʁtaʒe ma ʃɑ̃bʁ avɛk kɛlkœ̃ ‖ ʒø vø ma pʁɔpʁ ʃɑ̃bʁ ‖]

2373

EN It's a shame that the apartment doesn't have its own parking space.

FR C'est une honte que l'appartement ne dispose pas de son propre espace de stationnement.

IPA [sɛ t‿yn ɔ̃t kø l‿apaʁtᵊmɑ̃ nø dispoz pa dø sɔ̃ pʁɔpʁ ɛspas dø stasjɔnᵊmɑ̃ ‖]

2374

EN Why do you want to borrow my car? Why don't you use your own?

FR Pourquoi veux-tu emprunter ma voiture? Pourquoi n'utilises-tu pas la tienne?

IPA [puʁkwa vø ty ɑ̃pʁœte ma vwatyʁ || puʁkwa n‿ytiliz ty pa la tjɛn ||]

2375

EN I'd like to have a garden so that I could grow my own vegetables.

FR J'aimerais avoir un jardin pour pouvoir faire pousser mes propres légumes.

IPA [ʒ‿ɛmᵊʁɛ avwa ʁ‿œ̃ ʒaʁdɛ̃ puʁ puvwaʁ fɛʁ puse me pʁopʁ legym ||]

2376

EN I traveled around Japan on my own.

FR J'ai voyagé à travers le Japon par mes propres moyens.

IPA [ʒ‿ɛ vwajaʒe a tʁavɛʁ lø ʒapɔ̃ paʁ me pʁopʁ mwajɛ̃ ||]

2377

EN She raises her children as a single mother on her own.

FR Elle élève ses enfants comme une mère célibataire par ses propres moyens.

IPA [ɛ l̪elev se z̪ɑ̃fɑ̃ kɔm yn mɛʁ selibateʁ paʁ se pʁɔpʁ mwajɛ̃ ||]

2378

EN Student drivers are not allowed to drive by themselves.

FR Les apprentis conducteurs (♀apprenties conductrices) ne sont pas autorisés (♀autorisées) à conduire par eux-mêmes (♀elles-mêmes).

IPA [le z̪apʁɑ̃ti kɔ̃dyktœʁ (♀apʁɑ̃ti kɔ̃dyktʁis) nø sɔ̃ pa z̪otoʁize (♀otoʁize) a kɔ̃dɥiʁ pa ʁ̪ømɛm (♀ɛl mɛm) ||]

2379

EN Sorry I'm late. There was a lot of traffic.

FR Désolé, je suis en retard. Il y avait beaucoup de circulation.

IPA [dezole | ʒø sɥi z̪ɑ̃ ʁ°taʁ || i l̪i avɛ boku dø siʁkylasjɔ̃ ||]

ENFR

2380

EN Things are more expensive now. There's been a big increase in the cost of living.

FR Les choses sont plus chères maintenant. Il y a eu une forte augmentation du coût de la vie.

IPA [le ʃoz sɔ̃ plys ʃɛʁ mɛ̃tᵊnɑ̃ ‖ i l ̬i a y yn fɔʁt ogmɑ̃tasjɔ̃ dy ku dø la vi ‖]

2381

EN I wasn't expecting them to come. It was a complete surprise.

FR Je ne m'attendais pas à ce qu'ils (♀ elles) viennent. Ce fut une complète surprise.

IPA [ʒø nø m ̬atɑ̃dɛ pa a sø k ̬il (♀ ɛl) vjɛn ‖ sø fy t ̬yn kɔ̃plɛt syʁpʁiz ‖]

2382

EN The new restaurant is very good. I went there last night.

FR Le nouveau restaurant est très bon. J'y suis allé (♀ allée) hier soir.

IPA [lø nuvo ʁɛstoʁɑ̃ e tʁɛ bɔ̃ ‖ ʒ ̬i sɥi ale (♀ ale) jɛʁ swaʁ ‖]

2383

EN Is there a flight to Madrid tonight? — There might be, let me check.

FR Y a-t-il un vol pour Madrid ce soir? — Ça se pourrait, laissez-moi vérifier.

IPA [i a t‿il œ̃ vɔl puʁ (...) sø swaʁ ‖ — sa sø puʁɛ | lɛse mwa veʁifje ‖]

2384

EN If people drove more carefully, there wouldn't be so many accidents.

FR Si les gens conduisaient plus attentivement, il n'y aurait pas tant d'accidents.

IPA [si le ʒɑ̃ kɔ̃dɥizɛ ply s‿atɑ̃tiv°mɑ̃ | il n‿i oʁɛ pa tɑ̃ d‿aksidɑ̃ ‖]

2385

EN I heard music, so there must have been somebody at home.

FR J'ai entendu de la musique, alors il devait y avoir quelqu'un à la maison.

IPA [ʒ‿ɛ ɑ̃tɑ̃dy dø la myzik | alɔ ʁ‿il d°vɛ t‿i avwaʁ kɛlkœ̃ a la mɛzɔ̃ ‖]

2386

EN They live on a big street, so there must be a lot of noise from the traffic.

FR Ils vivent sur une grande rue, alors il doit y avoir beaucoup de bruit provenant de la circulation.

IPA [il viv sy ʁ‿yn gʁɑ̃d ʁy | alɔ ʁ‿il dwa t‿i avwaʁ boku dø bʁɥi pʁovᵊnɑ̃ dø la siʁkylasjɔ̃ ‖]

2387

EN That building is now a supermarket. It used to be a movie theater.

FR Ce bâtiment est maintenant un supermarché. C'était une salle de cinéma.

IPA [sø batimɑ̃ e mɛ̃tᵊnɑ̃ t‿œ̃ sypɛʁmaʁʃe ‖ se etɛ yn sal dø sinema ‖]

2388

EN There's bound to be a flight to Madrid tonight.

FR Il y a forcément un vol pour Madrid ce soir.

IPA [i l‿i a fɔʁsemɑ̃ t‿œ̃ vɔl puʁ (...) sø swaʁ ‖]

2389

EN After the lecture, there will be an opportunity to ask questions.

FR Après la conférence, il y aura la possibilité de poser des questions.

IPA [apʁɛ la kɔ̃feʁɑ̃s | i l‿i oʁa la posibilite dø poze de kɛstjɔ̃ ‖]

2390

EN I like the place where I live, but it'd be nicer to live by the ocean.

FR J'aime l'endroit où je vis, mais ce serait plus agréable de vivre au bord de l'océan.

IPA [ʒ‿em l‿ɑ̃dʁwa u ʒø vis | mɛ sø s°ʁɛ ply s‿agʁeabl dø vivʁ o bɔʁ dø l‿oseɑ̃ ||]

2391

EN I was told that there'd be someone to meet me at the airport, but there wasn't.

FR On m'a dit qu'il y aurait quelqu'un qui m'accueillerait à l'aéroport, mais il n'y avait personne.

IPA [ɔ̃ m‿a di k‿il i oʁɛ kɛlkœ̃ ki m‿akœj°ʁɛ a l‿aeʁopɔʁ | mɛ il n‿i avɛ pɛʁsɔn ||]

2392

EN She went out without any money.

FR Elle est sortie sans argent.

IPA [ɛ l‿e sɔʁti sɑ̃ z‿aʁʒɑ̃ ||]

2393

EN He refused to eat anything.

FR Il a refusé de manger quoi que ce soit.

IPA [i l‿a ʁ°fyze dø mɑ̃ʒe kwa kø sø swa ||]

2394

EN Hardly anybody passed the examination.

FR Presque personne n'a réussi l'examen.
IPA [pʁɛsk pɛʁsɔn n‿a ʁeysi l‿ɛgzamɛ̃ ‖]

2395

EN If anyone has any questions, I'll be glad to answer them.

FR Si quelqu'un a des questions, je serai heureux d'y répondre.
IPA [si kɛlkœ̃ n‿a de kɛstjɔ̃ ǀ ʒø s°ʁɛ øʁø d‿i ʁepɔ̃dʁ ‖]

2396

EN Let me know if you need anything.

FR Fais-moi savoir si tu as besoin de quoi que ce soit.
IPA [fɛ mwa savwaʁ si ty a bøzwɛ̃ dø kwa kø sø swa ‖]

2397

EN I'm sorry for any trouble I've caused.

FR Je suis désolé pour tout problème que j'aie pu causer.
IPA [ʒø sɥi dezole puʁ tu pʁɔblɛm kø ʒ‿ɛ py koze ‖]

2398

EN Anyone who wants to take the exam should tell me by Friday.

FR Quiconque souhaite passer l'examen doit me le dire d'ici vendredi.

IPA [kikɔk swɛt pase l̪ɛgzamɛ̃ dwa mø lø diʁ d̪isi vãdʁ°di ‖]

2399

EN Someone has forgotten their umbrella.

FR Quelqu'un a oublié son parapluie.

IPA [kɛlkœ̃ n̪a ublije sɔ̃ paʁaplɥi ‖]

2400

EN We had to walk home because there was no bus.

FR Nous avons dû marcher jusqu'à la maison parce qu'il n'y avait pas de bus.

IPA [nu z̪avɔ̃ dy maʁʃe ʒyska la mɛzɔ̃ paʁs k̪il n̪i avɛ pa dø bys ‖]

GMS #2401 - 2500

2401

EN She'll have no difficulty finding a job.

FR Elle n'aura aucune difficulté à se trouver un emploi.
IPA [ɛl n‿oʁa okyn difikylte a sø tʁuve ʁ‿œ̃ n‿ɑ̃plwa ‖]

2402

EN There were no stores open.

FR Il n'y avait pas de magasins ouverts.
IPA [il n‿i avɛ pa dø magazɛ̃ uvɛʁ ‖]

2403

EN All the tickets have been sold. There are none left.

FR Tous les billets ont été vendus. Il n'en reste plus.
IPA [tu le bijɛ ɔ̃ ete vɑ̃dy ‖ il n‿ɑ̃ ʁɛst plys ‖]

2404

EN This money is all yours. None of it is mine.

FR Cet argent est à toi. Rien de tout cela n'est à moi.
IPA [sɛ t‿aʁʒɑ̃ t‿e a twa ‖ ʁjɛ̃ dø tu sᵊla n'est a mwa ‖]

2405

EN None of the stores were open.

FR Aucun des magasins n'était ouvert.
IPA [okœ̃ de magazɛ̃ n‿etɛ uvɛʁ ‖]

2406

EN The house is empty. There's no one living there.

FR La maison est vide. Il n'y a personne qui y vit.
IPA [la mɛzɔ̃ e vid ‖ il n‿i a pɛʁsɔn ki i vi ‖]

2407

EN We had nothing to eat.

FR Nous n'avions rien à manger.
IPA [nu n‿avjɔ̃ ʁjɛ̃ a mɑ̃ʒe ‖]

2408

EN Herman didn't tell anyone about his plans.

FR Herman n'a parlé de ses plans à personne.
IPA [(...) n‿a paʁle dø se plɑ̃ a pɛʁsɔn ‖]

2409

EN No one did what I asked them to do, did they?

FR Personne n'a fait ce que je leur ai demandé de faire,
n'est-ce pas?
IPA [pɛʁsɔn n‿a fɛ sø kø ʒø lœ ʁ‿ɛ dᵊmɑ̃de dø fɛʁ | n‿e sø
pa ‖]

2410

EN The accident looked serious, but fortunately nobody was injured.

FR L'accident avait l'air grave, mais heureusement personne n'a été blessé.

IPA [l‿aksidɑ̃ avɛ l‿ɛʁ gʁav | mɛ øʁøz°mɑ̃ pɛʁsɔn n‿a ete blese ‖]

2411

EN I don't know anything about economics.

FR Je ne connais rien à l'économie.

IPA [ʒø nø konɛ ʁjɛ̃ a l‿ekonomi ‖]

2412

EN We didn't spend much money.

FR Nous n'avons pas dépensé beaucoup d'argent.

IPA [nu n‿avɔ̃ pa depɑ̃se boku d‿aʁʒɑ̃ ‖]

2413

EN There's no need to hurry. We've got plenty of time.

FR Nul besoin de se dépêcher. Nous avons amplement de temps.

IPA [nyl bøzwɛ̃ dø sø depeʃe ‖ nu z‿avɔ̃ ɑ̃pl°mɑ̃ dø tɑ̃ ‖]

2414

EN There aren't many tourists here. > There aren't a lot of tourists here.

FR Il n'y a pas beaucoup de touristes ici.
IPA [il n‿i a pa boku dø tuʁist isi ‖]

2415

EN Do you know many people? > Do you know a lot of people?

FR Connais-tu beaucoup de gens?
IPA [konɛ ty boku dø ʒã ‖]

2416

EN Monika's very busy with her job. She has little time for other things.

FR Monika est très occupée par son emploi. Elle a peu de temps pour autre chose.
IPA [(...) e tʁɛ z‿okype paʁ sɔ̃ n‿ãplwa ‖ ɛ l‿a pø dø tã pu ʁ‿otʁ ʃoz ‖]

2417

EN Kimiko has very few friends in London.

FR Kimiko a très peu d'amis à Londres.
IPA [(...) a tʁɛ pø d‿ami a lɔ̃dʁ° ‖]

2418

EN Let's get something to drink. We still have a little
time before the train comes.

FR Achetons quelque chose à boire. Nous avons encore
un peu de temps avant que le train n'arrive.

IPA [aʃᵊtɔ̃ kɛlk ʃoz a bwaʁ ‖ nu z̺avɔ̃ ɑ̃kɔʁ œ̃ pø də tɑ̃
avɑ̃ kø lø tʁɛ̃ n̺aʁiv ‖]]

2419

EN He spoke little English, so it was difficult to
communicate with him.

FR Il parlait peu anglais, alors il était difficile de
communiquer avec lui.

IPA [il paʁlɛ pø ɑ̃glɛ | alɔ ʁ̺i l̺ete difisil də komynike
avɛk lɥi ‖]]

2420

EN We have only a little time left.

FR Il nous reste seulement un peu de temps.

IPA [il nu ʁɛst sœlᵊmɑ̃ t̺œ̃ pø də tɑ̃ ‖]]

2421

EN Everybody was surprised that he won. Few people
expected him to win.

FR Tout le monde a été surpris qu'il gagne. Peu de gens
s'attendaient à le voir gagner.

IPA [tu lø mɔ̃d a ete syʁpʁi k̺il gaɲ ‖ pø də ʒɑ̃ s̺atɑ̃dɛ a
lø vwaʁ gaɲe ‖]]

2422

EN I can't give you a decision yet. I need more time to think about it.

FR Je ne peux pas encore te donner de décision. J'ai besoin de plus de temps pour y penser.

IPA [ʒø nø pø pa z‿ãkɔʁ tø done dø desizjɔ̃ || ʒ‿ɛ bøzwɛ̃ dø plys dø tã pu ʁ‿i pãse ||]

2423

EN It was a very boring place to live. There was little to do.

FR C'était un endroit très ennuyeux où vivre. Il y avait peu à faire.

IPA [se etɛ œ̃ n‿ãdʁwa tʁɛ z‿ãnɥijø u vivʁ || i l‿i avɛ pø a fɛʁ ||]

2424

EN I don't go out very often. I stay home most days.

FR Je ne sors pas très souvent. Je reste à la maison la plupart du temps.

IPA [ʒø nø sɔʁ pa tʁɛ suvã || ʒø ʁɛst a la mɛzɔ̃ la plypaʁ dy tã ||]

2425

EN Some people learn languages more easily than others.

FR Certaines personnes apprennent des langues plus facilement que d'autres.

IPA [sɛʁten pɛʁsɔn apʁɛn de lãg plys fasilᵊmã kø dotʁ ||]

2426

EN Some of the people I work with are not very friendly.

FR Certaines des personnes avec qui je travaille ne sont pas très sympathiques.

IPA [sɛʁtɛn de pɛʁsɔn avɛk ki ʒø tʁavaj nø sɔ̃ pa tʁɛ sɛ̃patik ||]

2427

EN Have you read any of these books?

FR As-tu lu l'un de ces livres?

IPA [a ty ly lœ̃ dø se livʁ ||]

2428

EN I was sick yesterday, so I spent most of the day in bed.

FR J'étais malade hier, j'ai passé la grande majorité de la journée au lit.

IPA [ʒ‿ete malad jɛʁ | ʒ‿e pase la gʁɑ̃d maʒɔʁite dø la ʒuʁne o li ||]

2429

EN All the flowers in this garden are beautiful.

FR Toutes les fleurs de ce jardin sont magnifiques.

IPA [tut le flœʁ dø sø ʒaʁdɛ̃ sɔ̃ maɲifik ||]

2430

EN We're able to solve most of the problems we have.

FR Nous sommes en mesure de résoudre la plupart des problèmes que nous avons.

IPA [nu sɔm ɑ̃ məzyʁ də ʁezudʁ la plypaʁ de pʁoblɛm kø nu z‿avɔ̃ ‖]

2431

EN Do any of you want to go to a party tonight?

FR Est-ce que l'un d'entre vous veut aller à une fête ce soir?

IPA [ɛsᵒ kø ty lœ̃ d‿ɑ̃tʁ vu vø ale a yn fɛt sø swaʁ ‖]

2432

EN Half this money is mine, and half of it is yours.

FR La moitié de cet argent est à moi, et l'autre moitié est à toi.

IPA [la mwatje də sɛ t‿aʁʒɑ̃ t‿e a mwa | e l‿otʁ mwatje e a twa ‖]

2433

EN When she got married, she kept it a secret. She didn't tell any of her friends.

FR Quand elle s'est mariée, elle en a gardé le secret. Elle ne l'a pas dit à aucun (♀aucune) de ses amis (♀amies).

IPA [kɑ̃ d‿ɛl s‿e maʁje | ɛ l‿ɑ̃ a gaʁde lø sᵒkʁɛ ‖ ɛl nø l‿a pa di a okœ̃ (♀okyn) də se z‿ami (♀ami) ‖]

2426

EN Some of the people I work with are not very friendly.

FR Certaines des personnes avec qui je travaille ne sont pas très sympathiques.

IPA [sɛʁten de pɛʁsɔn avɛk ki ʒø tʁavaj nø sɔ̃ pa tʁɛ sẽpatik ||]

2427

EN Have you read any of these books?

FR As-tu lu l'un de ces livres?

IPA [a ty ly lœ̃ dø se livʁ ||]

2428

EN I was sick yesterday, so I spent most of the day in bed.

FR J'étais malade hier, j'ai passé la grande majorité de la journée au lit.

IPA [ʒ‿ete malad jɛʁ | ʒ‿ɛ pase la gʁɑ̃d maʒɔʁite dø la ʒuʁne o li ||]

2429

EN All the flowers in this garden are beautiful.

FR Toutes les fleurs de ce jardin sont magnifiques.

IPA [tut le flœʁ dø sø ʒaʁdɛ̃ sɔ̃ maɲifik ||]

2430

EN   We're able to solve most of the problems we have.

FR   Nous sommes en mesure de résoudre la plupart des problèmes que nous avons.

IPA   [nu sɔm ɑ̃ mᵊzyʁ dø ʁezudʁ la plypaʁ de pʁɔblɛm kø nu z̬avɔ̃ ‖]

2431

EN   Do any of you want to go to a party tonight?

FR   Est-ce que l'un d'entre vous veut aller à une fête ce soir?

IPA   [ɛsᵊ kø ty lœ̃ d̬ɑ̃tʁ vu vø ale a yn fɛt sø swaʁ ‖]

2432

EN   Half this money is mine, and half of it is yours.

FR   La moitié de cet argent est à moi, et l'autre moitié est à toi.

IPA   [la mwatje dø sɛ t̬aʁʒɑ̃ t̬e a mwa | e l̬otʁ mwatje e a twa ‖]

2433

EN   When she got married, she kept it a secret. She didn't tell any of her friends.

FR   Quand elle s'est mariée, elle en a gardé le secret. Elle ne l'a pas dit à aucun (♀ aucune) de ses amis (♀ amies).

IPA   [kɑ̃ d̬ɛl s̬e maʁje | ɛ l̬ɑ̃ a gaʁde lø sᵊkʁɛ ‖ ɛl nø l̬a pa di a okœ̃ (♀ okyn) dø se z̬ami (♀ ami) ‖]

2434

EN Deepak and I have very different ideas. I don't agree with many of his opinions.

FR Deepak et moi avons des idées très différentes. Je ne suis pas d'accord avec plusieurs de ses opinions.

IPA [(...) e mwa avɔ̃ de z‿ide tʁɛ difeʁɑ̃t ‖ ʒø nø sɥi pa d‿akɔʁ avɛk plyzjœʁ dø se z‿opinjɔ̃ ‖]

2435

EN Not all the tourists in the group were Spanish. Some of them were French.

FR Pas tous les touristes du groupe étaient espagnols. Certains d'entre eux étaient français.

IPA [pa tu le tuʁist dy gʁup ete ɛspaɲɔl ‖ sɛʁtɛ̃ d‿ɑ̃tʁ ø z‿ete fʁɑ̃sɛ ‖]

2436

EN I watched most of the movie, but not all of it.

FR J'ai regardé la plus grande partie du film, mais pas la totalité.

IPA [ʒ‿ɛ ʁ°gaʁde la plys gʁɑ̃d paʁti dy film | mɛ pa la totalite ‖]

2437

EN I asked some people for directions, but none of them were able to help me.

FR J'ai demandé des indications à des gens, mais aucun d'entre eux n'était en mesure de m'aider.

IPA [ʒ‿ɛ dᵊmɑ̃de de z‿ɛ̃dikasjɔ̃ a de ʒɑ̃ | mɛ okɶ̃ d‿ɑ̃tʁ ø n‿etɛ ɑ̃ mᵊzyʁ də m‿ede ||]

2438

EN Both restaurants are very good. > Both of these restaurants are very good.

FR Les deux restaurants sont très bons. > Ces deux restaurants sont très bons.

IPA [le dø ʁestoʁɑ̃ sɔ̃ tʁɛ bɔ̃ || > se dø ʁestoʁɑ̃ sɔ̃ tʁɛ bɔ̃ ||]

2439

EN Neither restaurant is expensive. > Neither of the restaurants we went to was expensive.

FR Aucun de ces restaurants n'est cher. > Aucun des restaurants où nous sommes allés (♀ allées) n'était cher.

IPA [okɶ̃ dø se ʁestoʁɑ̃ n‿e ʃɛʁ || > okɶ̃ de ʁestoʁɑ̃ u nu sɔm ale (♀ ale) n‿etɛ ʃɛʁ ||]

2440

EN We can go to either restaurant. I don't care.

FR Nous pouvons aller à l'un ou l'autre de ces restaurants. Ça ne m'importe pas.

IPA [nu puvɔ̃ ale a lœ̃ n‿u l‿otʁ dø se ʁestoʁã || sa nø m‿ɛ̃poʁt pa ||]

2441

EN I haven't been to either of those restaurants.

FR Je ne suis pas allé (♀allée) à ni l'un ni l'autre de ces restaurants.

IPA [ʒø nø sɥi pa z‿ale (♀ale) a ni lœ̃ ni l‿otʁ dø se ʁestoʁã ||]

2442

EN I asked two (2) people the way to the station, but neither of them knew.

FR J'ai demandé le chemin de la gare à deux personnes, mais aucune d'elles ne le connaissait.

IPA [ʒ‿ɛ dᵊmãde lø ʃᵊmɛ̃ dø la gaʁ a dø peʁsɔn | me okyn d‿el nø lø konese ||]

2443

EN Both of us were very tired.

FR Nous étions tous (♀toutes) deux très fatigués (♀fatiguées).

IPA [nu z‿etjɔ̃ tu (♀tut) dø tʁe fatige (♀fatige) ||]

2444

EN Neither of them want to have children.

FR Ni l'un ni l'autre ne veut avoir d'enfants.
IPA [ni lœ̃ ni l̩otʁ nø vø avwaʁ d̩ɑ̃fɑ̃ ‖]

2445

EN I couldn't decide which of the two (2) shirts to buy. I liked both.

FR Je ne pouvais pas décider quelle des deux chemises acheter. J'aimais bien les deux.
IPA [ʒø nø puvɛ pa deside kɛl de dø ʃᵊmiz aʃᵊte ‖ ʒ̩emɛ bjɛ̃ le dø ‖]

2446

EN I was both tired and hungry when I got home.

FR J'étais à la fois fatigué et affamé (♀ fatiguée et affamée) quand je suis rentré (♀ rentrée).
IPA [ʒ̩ete a la fwa fatige e afame (♀ fatige e afame) kɑ̃ ʒø sɥi ʁɑ̃tʁe (♀ ʁɑ̃tʁe) ‖]

2447

EN She said she would contact me, but she neither wrote nor called.

FR Elle a dit qu'elle communiquerait avec moi, mais elle n'a ni écrit, ni appelé.
IPA [ɛ l̩a di k̩ɛl komynikᵊʁɛ avɛk mwa | me ɛl n̩a ni ekʁi | ni apᵊle ‖]

2448

EN Either you apologize, or I'll never speak to you again.

FR Soit tu t'excuses, soit je ne te reparlerai plus jamais.
IPA [swa ty t‿ɛkskyz | swa ʒø nø tø ʁ°paʁl°ʁɛ plys ʒamɛ ‖]

2449

EN You could stay at either of these hotels. (2) > You could stay at any of these hotels. (many)

FR Vous pouvez séjourner dans un de ces deux hôtels. > Vous pouvez séjourner dans un de ces hôtels.
IPA [vu puve seʒuʁne dɑ̃ z‿œ̃ dø se dø otɛl ‖ > vu puve seʒuʁne dɑ̃ z‿œ̃ dø se otɛl ‖]

2450

EN We couldn't open the door, because neither of us had our key.

FR Nous ne pouvions pas ouvrir la porte, car aucun d'entre nous n'avait sa clé.
IPA [nu nø puvjɔ̃ pa z‿uvʁiʁ la pɔʁt | kaʁ okœ̃ d‿ɑ̃tʁ nu n‿avɛ sa kle ‖]

2451

EN All of us enjoyed the party.

FR Nous avons tous aimé la fête.
IPA [nu z‿avɔ̃ tu z‿eme la fɛt ‖]

2452

EN I'll do all I can to help. > I'll do everything I can to help.

FR Je ferai tout ce que je peux pour aider. > Je ferai tout mon possible pour aider.

IPA [ʒø fᵊʀɛ tu sø kø ʒø pø pu ʀ‿ede || > ʒø fᵊʀɛ tu mɔ̃ posibl pu ʀ‿ede ||]

2453

EN He thinks he knows everything.

FR Il pense qu'il sait tout.

IPA [il pɑ̃s k‿il sɛ tu ||]

2454

EN Our summer vacation was such a disaster. Everything that could go wrong went wrong.

FR Nos vacances d'été ont été un tel désastre. Tout ce qui pouvait aller mal a mal tourné.

IPA [no vakɑ̃s d‿ete ɔ̃ ete œ̃ tɛl dezastʀ || tu sø ki puvɛ ale ma l‿a mal tuʀne ||]

2455

EN All I've eaten today is a sandwich.

FR Tout ce que j'ai mangé aujourd'hui, c'est un sandwich.

IPA [tu sø kø ʒ‿ɛ mɑ̃ʒe oʒuʀdɥi | sɛ t‿œ̃ sɑ̃dwitʃ ||]

2456

EN Did you read the whole book?

FR As-tu lu le livre en entier?
IPA [a ty ly lø livʁ ɑ̃ n̪ɑ̃tje ‖]

2457

EN Lakshmi has lived her whole life in India.

FR Lakshmi a vécu toute sa vie en Inde.
IPA [(...) a veky tut sa vi ɑ̃ n̪ɛ̃d ‖]

2458

EN I've spent all the money you gave me.

FR J'ai dépensé tout l'argent que tu m'as donné.
IPA [ʒ̪ɛ depɑ̃se tu l̪aʁʒɑ̃ kø ty m̪a done ‖]

2459

EN When we were on vacation, we went to the beach every day.

FR Lorsque nous étions en vacances, nous sommes allés (♀allées) à la plage tous les jours.
IPA [lɔʁskə nu z̪etjɔ̃ z̪ɑ̃ vakɑ̃s | nu sɔm ale (♀ale) a la plaʒ tu le ʒuʁ ‖]

2460

EN The bus service is very good. There's a bus every ten (10) minutes.

FR Le service de bus est très bon. Il y a un bus toutes les dix minutes.

IPA [lø sɛʁvis dø bys e tʁɛ bɔ̃ || i l i a œ̃ bys tut le dis minyt ||]

2461

EN We don't see each other very often. About every six (6) months.

FR Nous ne nous voyons pas très souvent. Environ tous les six mois.

IPA [nu nø nu vwajɔ̃ pa tʁɛ suvɑ̃ || ɑ̃viʁɔ̃ tu le sis mwa ||]

2462

EN We spent all day at the beach.

FR Nous avons passé toute la journée à la plage.

IPA [nu z avɔ̃ pase tut la ʒuʁne a la plaʒ ||]

2463

EN He didn't say a word all night long.

FR Il n'a pas dit un mot de toute la nuit.

IPA [il n a pa di t œ̃ mo dø tut la nɥi ||]

2464

EN I've been looking for you all morning long. Where have you been?

FR Je t'ai cherché durant toute la matinée. Où étais-tu?
IPA [ʒø t‿ɛ ʃɛʀʃe dyʀɑ̃ tut la matine || u ete ty ||]

2465

EN They never go out. They're at home all the time.

FR Ils (♀elles) ne sortent jamais. Ils (♀elles) sont tout le temps à la maison.
IPA [il (♀ɛl) nø sɔʀt ʒamɛ || il (♀ɛl) sɔ̃ tu lø tɑ̃ a la mɛzɔ̃ ||]

2466

EN Every time I see you, you look different.

FR Chaque fois que je te vois, tu as l'air différent.
IPA [ʃak fwa kø ʒø tø vwa | ty a l‿ɛʀ difeʀɑ̃ ||]

2467

EN It was a terrible fire. The whole building got destroyed.

FR C'était un terrible incendie. Le bâtiment au complet a été détruit.
IPA [se etɛ œ̃ tɛʀibl ɛ̃sɑ̃di || lø batimɑ̃ o kɔ̃plɛ t‿a ete detʀɥi ||]

2468

EN I've read every one (1) of those books.

FR J'ai lu chacun de ces livres.

IPA [ʒ‿ɛ ly ʃakœ̃ dø se livʁ ‖]

2469

EN None of the rooms was the same. Each was different.

FR Aucune des chambres n'était la même. Chacune était différente.

IPA [okyn de ʃɑ̃bʁ n‿ete la mɛm ‖ ʃakyn ete difeʁɑ̃t ‖]

2470

EN Read each of these sentences carefully.

FR Lis chacune de ces phrases soigneusement.

IPA [lis ʃakyn dø se fʁaz swaɲøzᵊmɑ̃ ‖]

2471

EN The students were each given a book.

FR Les élèves ont reçu un livre chacun.

IPA [le z‿elɛv ɔ̃ ʁᵊsy œ̃ livʁ ʃakœ̃ ‖]

2472

EN There's a train to the city every hour.

FR Il y a un train qui va en ville toutes les heures.

IPA [i l‿i a œ̃ tʁɛ̃ ki va ɑ̃ vil tut le z‿œʁ ‖]

2473

EN Seat belts in cars save lives. Each driver should wear one.

FR Les ceintures de sécurité dans les voitures sauvent des vies. Chaque conducteur doit en porter une.

IPA [le sɛ̃tyʁ də sekyʁite dã le vwatyʁ sov de vi || ʃak kɔ̃dyktœʁ dwa ã poʁte ʁ‿yn ||]

2474

EN Write your answer to each question on a separate sheet of paper.

FR Donnez votre réponse à chaque question sur une feuille de papier séparée.

IPA [done vɔtʁ ʁepɔ̃s a ʃak kɛstjɔ̃ sy ʁ‿yn fœj də papje sepaʁe ||]

2475

EN The woman who lives next door is a doctor.

FR La femme qui habite à côté est médecin.

IPA [la fam ki abit a kote e mɛdsɛ̃ ||]

2476

EN We know a lot of people who live in the country.

FR Nous connaissons beaucoup de gens qui vivent à la campagne.

IPA [nu konɛsɔ̃ boku də ʒã ki viv a la kãpaɲ ||]

2477

EN Anyone who wants to apply for the job must do so by Friday.

FR Quiconque souhaitant postuler pour l'emploi doit le faire d'ici vendredi.

IPA [kikɔ̃k swɛtɑ̃ pɔstyle puʁ l‿ɑ̃plwa dwa lø fɛʁ d‿isi vɑ̃dʁ°di ‖]

2478

EN I don't like stories that have unhappy endings.

FR Je n'aime pas les histoires qui se terminent mal.

IPA [ʒø n‿ɛm pa le istwaʁ ki sø tɛʁmin mal ‖]

2479

EN The printer that broke down is working again now.

FR L'imprimante qui est tombée en panne fonctionne à nouveau maintenant.

IPA [l‿ɛ̃pʁimɑ̃t ki e tɔ̃be ɑ̃ pan fɔksjɔn a nuvo mɛ̃t°nɑ̃ ‖]

2480

EN Everything that happened was my fault.

FR Tout ce qui s'est passé est de ma faute.

IPA [tu sø ki s‿e pase e dø ma fot ‖]

164

ENFR

2481

EN I've never spoken to the woman who lives next door.

FR Je n'ai jamais parlé à la femme qui habite à côté.
IPA [ʒø n‿ɛ ʒamɛ paʁle a la fam ki abit a kote ‖]

2482

EN The building destroyed in the fire has now been rebuilt.

FR Le bâtiment détruit dans l'incendie a maintenant été reconstruit.
IPA [lø batimɑ̃ detʁɥi dɑ̃ l‿ɛ̃sɑ̃di a mɛ̃t°nɑ̃ t‿ete ʁ°kɔ̃stʁɥi ‖]

2483

EN The shuttle that goes to the airport runs every half hour.

FR La navette qui va à l'aéroport passe toutes les demi-heures.
IPA [la navɛt ki va a l‿aeʁopɔʁ pas tut le d°miœʁ ‖]

2484

EN A mystery is something that cannot be explained.

FR Un mystère est quelque chose qui ne peut pas être expliqué.
IPA [œ̃ mistɛʁ e kɛlk ʃoz ki nø pø pa z‿etʁ ɛksplike ‖]

2485

EN It seems that Earth is the only planet that can support life.

FR Il semble que la Terre soit la seule planète à pouvoir accueillir la vie.

IPA [il sãbl kø la tɛʁ swa la sœl planɛt a puvwaʁ akœjiʁ la vi ||]

2486

EN The driver who caused the accident was fined five hundred dollars ($500). > The driver who caused the accident was fined four hundred euros (€400).

FR Le conducteur qui a causé l'accident a été condamné à une amende de quatre cents euros.

IPA [lø kɔ̃dyktœʁ ki a koze l‿aksidã a ete kɔ̃dane a yn amãd dø katʁ sã z‿øʁo ||]

2487

EN We live in a world that is changing all the time.

FR Nous vivons dans un monde qui change tout le temps.

IPA [nu vivɔ̃ dã z‿œ̃ mɔ̃d ki ʃãʒ tu lø tã ||]

2488

EN A woman lives next door. She's a doctor. > The woman who lives next door is a doctor.

FR Une femme habite à côté. Elle est médecin. > La femme qui habite à côté est médecin.

IPA [yn fam abit a kote || ɛ l̩e mɛdsɛ̃ || > la fam ki abit a kote e mɛdsɛ̃ ||]

2489

EN The woman next door is a doctor.

FR La femme d'à côté est médecin.

IPA [la fam d a kote e mɛdsɛ̃ ||]

2490

EN There was cheese in the refrigerator. Where is it? > Where's the cheese that was in the refrigerator?

FR Il y avait du fromage dans le réfrigérateur. Où est-il? > Où est le fromage qui était dans le réfrigérateur?

IPA [i l̩i avɛ dy fʁomaʒ dɑ̃ lø ʁefʁiʒeʁatœʁ || u e t̩il || > u e lø fʁomaʒ ki etɛ dɑ̃ lø ʁefʁiʒeʁatœʁ ||]

2491

EN I wanted to see a woman. She was away on vacation.
> The woman whom I wanted to see was away on
vacation.

FR Je voulais voir une femme. Elle était en vacances. >
La femme que je voulais voir était en vacances.

IPA [ʒø vulɛ vwa ʁ‿yn fam || ɛ l‿etɛ t‿ã vakãs || > la
fam kø ʒø vulɛ vwaʁ etɛ t‿ã vakãs ||]

2492

EN The woman I wanted to see was away on vacation.

FR La femme que je voulais voir était en vacances.

IPA [la fam kø ʒø vulɛ vwaʁ etɛ t‿ã vakãs ||]

2493

EN Have you found the keys that you lost? > Have you
found the keys you lost?

FR As-tu trouvé les clés que tu as perdues?

IPA [a ty tʁuve le kle kø ty a pɛʁdy ||]

2494

EN The dress that Yuliana bought doesn't fit her very
well. > The dress that she bought doesn't fit her very
well.

FR La robe que Yuliana acheté ne lui va pas très bien. >
La robe qu'elle a achetée ne lui va pas très bien.

IPA [la ʁɔb kø (...) aʃºte nø lɥi va pa tʁɛ bjɛ̃ || > la ʁɔb
k‿ɛl a aʃºte nø lɥi va pa tʁɛ bjɛ̃ ||]

2495

EN Are these the books that you were looking for? > Are these the books you were looking for?

FR S'agit-il des livres que vous recherchiez?
IPA [s‿aʒi t‿il de livʁ kø vu ʁ°ʃeʁʃje ‖]

2496

EN The woman with whom he fell in love left him after a month. > The woman he fell in love with left him after a month.

FR La femme dont il est tombé amoureux l'a quitté après un mois. > La femme avec qui il est tombé en amour l'a quitté après un mois.
IPA [la fam dɔ̃ t‿i l‿e tɔ̃be amuʁø l‿a kite apʁɛ z‿œ̃ mwa ‖ > la fam avɛk ki i l‿e tɔ̃be ã n‿amuʁ l‿a kite apʁɛ z‿œ̃ mwa ‖]

2497

EN The man that I was sitting next to on the plane talked the whole time. > The man I was sitting next to on the plane talked the whole time.

FR L'homme à côté duquel j'étais assis dans l'avion a parlé tout le temps.
IPA [l‿ɔm a kote dykɛl ʒ‿ete asi dã l‿avjɔ̃ a paʁle tu lø tã ‖]

2498

EN Everything that they said was true. > Everything
they said was true.

FR Tout ce qu'ils ont dit était vrai.
IPA [tu sø k̺il ɔ̃ di etɛ vʁɛ ‖]

2499

EN I gave her all the money that I had. > I gave her all
the money I had.

FR Je lui ai donné tout l'argent que j'avais.
IPA [ʒø lɥi ɛ dɔne tu l̺aʁʒɑ̃ kø ʒ̺avɛ ‖]

2500

EN Did you hear the things that they said? > Did you
hear what they said?

FR As-tu entendu les choses qu'ils ont dit? > As-tu
entendu ce qu'ils ont dit?
IPA [a ty ɑ̃tɑ̃dy le ʃoz k̺il ɔ̃ di ‖ > a ty ɑ̃tɑ̃dy sø k̺il ɔ̃ di
‖]

GMS #2501 - 2600

2501

EN A friend is wearing a dress. You like it. > I like the dress you're wearing.

FR Une amie est vêtue d'une robe. Tu l'aimes. > J'aime la robe que tu portes.

IPA [yn ami e vety d‿yn ʁɔb || ty l‿ɛm || > ʒ‿ɛm la ʁɔb kø ty pɔʁt ||]

2502

EN A friend is going to see a movie. You want to know the name. > What's the name of the movie you're going to see?

FR Un ami va voir un film. Tu veux connaître le nom du film. > Quel est le nom du film que tu vas voir?

IPA [œ̃ n‿ami va vwa ʁ‿œ̃ film || ty vø konɛtʁ lø nõ dy film || > kɛ l‿e lø nõ dy film kø ty va vwaʁ ||]

2503

EN You wanted to visit a museum. It was closed when you got there. > The museum we were going to visit was closed when we got there.

FR Tu voulais visiter un musée. Il était fermé quand tu y es arrivé. > Le musée que nous allions visiter était fermé quand nous y sommes arrivés.

IPA [ty vulɛ vizite ʁ‿œ̃ myze || i l‿etɛ fɛʁme kɑ̃ ty i ɛ aʁive || > lø myze kø nu z‿aljɔ̃ vizite etɛ fɛʁme kɑ̃ nu z‿i sɔm aʁive ||]

2504

EN Your friend had to do some work. You want to know if she's finished. > Have you finished the work you had to do?

FR Ton amie avait du travail à faire. Tu veux savoir si elle a terminé. > As-tu fini le travail que tu avais à faire?

IPA [tɔ̃ n‿ami avɛ dy tʁavaj a fɛʁ || ty vø savwaʁ si ɛ l‿a tɛʁmine || > a ty fini lø tʁavaj kø ty avɛ a fɛʁ ||]

2505

EN You stayed at a hotel. Pavel recommended it to you. > We stayed at a hotel that Pavel recommended to us.

FR Tu as séjourné à l'hôtel. Pavel te l'a recommandé. > Nous avons séjourné à l'hôtel que Pavel nous a recommandé.

IPA [ty a seʒuʁne a l‿otɛl || (...) tø l‿a ʁ°komɑ̃de || > nu z‿avɔ̃ seʒuʁne a l‿otɛl kø (...) nu z‿a ʁ°komɑ̃de ||]

2506

EN I like the people I work with.

FR J'aime les gens avec qui je travaille.

IPA [ʒ‿ɛm le ʒɑ̃ avɛk ki ʒø tʁavaj ‖]

2507

EN What's the name of that hotel you told me about?

FR Quel est le nom de cet hôtel dont tu m'as parlé?

IPA [kɛ l‿e lø nɔ̃ dø sɛ t‿otɛl dɔ̃ ty m‿a paʁle ‖]

2508

EN I didn't get the job I applied for.

FR Je n'ai pas eu l'emploi pour lequel j'ai postulé.

IPA [ʒø n‿ɛ pa z‿y l‿ɑ̃plwa puʁ l°kɛl ʒ‿ɛ pɔstyle ‖]

2509

EN Julius is someone you can rely on.

FR Jules est quelqu'un sur qui tu peux compter.

IPA [ʒyl e kɛlkœ̃ syʁ ki ty pø kɔ̃te ‖]

2510

EN Who was that man I saw you with in the restaurant?

FR Qui était cet homme avec qui je t'ai vu au restaurant?

IPA [ki ete sɛ t‿ɔm avɛk ki ʒø t‿ɛ vy o ʁestoʁɑ̃ ‖]

2511

EN They give their children everything they want.

FR Ils donnent à leurs enfants tout ce qu'ils veulent.
IPA [il dɔn a lœ ʁ‿ɑ̃fɑ̃ tu sø k‿il vœl ‖]

2512

EN Tell me what you want, and I'll try to get it for you.

FR Dis-moi ce que tu veux, et je vais essayer de l'obtenir pour toi.
IPA [di mwa sø kø ty vø | e ʒø vɛ eseje dø l‿ɔpt°niʁ puʁ twa ‖]

2513

EN Why do you blame me for everything that goes wrong?

FR Pourquoi me blâmes-tu pour tout ce qui va mal?
IPA [puʁkwa mø blam ty puʁ tu sø ki va mal ‖]

2514

EN A widow is a woman whose husband has already passed away.

FR Une veuve est une femme dont le mari est déjà décédé.
IPA [yn vœv e t‿yn fam dɔ̃ lø maʁi e deʒa desede ‖]

2515

EN What's the name of the man whose car you borrowed?

FR Quel est le nom de l'homme à qui tu as emprunté la voiture?

IPA [kɛ le lø nɔ̃ dø lɔm a ki ty a ɑ̃pʁœ̃te la vwatyʁ ||]

2516

EN I met someone whose brother I went to school with.

FR J'ai rencontré quelqu'un dont je suis allé à l'école avec le frère.

IPA [ʒ e ʁɑ̃kɔ̃tʁe kɛlkœ̃ dɔ̃ ʒø sɥi ale a lekɔl avɛk lø fʁɛʁ ||]

2517

EN I met a man who knows you.

FR J'ai rencontré un homme qui te connaît.

IPA [ʒ e ʁɑ̃kɔ̃tʁe œ̃ nɔm ki tø kɔnɛ ||]

2518

EN I met a man whose sister knows you.

FR J'ai rencontré un homme dont la sœur te connaît.

IPA [ʒ e ʁɑ̃kɔ̃tʁe œ̃ nɔm dɔ̃ la sœʁ tø kɔnɛ ||]

2519

EN The woman I wanted to see was away on business.

FR La femme que je voulais voir était en voyage d'affaires.

IPA [la fam kø ʒø vulɛ vwaʁ etɛ t‿ã vwajaʒ d‿afɛʁ ‖]

2520

EN The people I work with are very nice.

FR Les gens avec qui je travaille sont très gentils.

IPA [le ʒã avɛk ki ʒø tʁavaj sõ tʁɛ ʒãti ‖]

2521

EN I recently went back to the town where I grew up.

FR Je suis récemment allé dans la ville où j'ai grandi.

IPA [ʒø sɥi ʁesamã t‿ale dã la vil u ʒ‿ɛ gʁãdi ‖]

2522

EN I'd like to live in a place where there's plenty of sunshine.

FR J'aimerais vivre dans un endroit où il y a beaucoup de soleil.

IPA [ʒ‿ɛmᵊʁɛ vivʁ dã z‿œ̃ n‿ãdʁwa u i l‿i a boku dø solɛj ‖]

2523

EN Do you remember the day we went to the zoo?

FR Te souviens-tu du jour où nous sommes allés au zoo?
IPA [tø suvjɛ̃ ty dy ʒuʁ u nu sɔm ale o zoo ‖]

2524

EN I haven't seen them since the year they got married.

FR Je ne les ai pas vus depuis l'année où ils se sont mariés.
IPA [ʒø nø le zˌɛ pa vy dᵊpɥi lˌane u il sø sɔ̃ maʁje ‖]

2525

EN The reason I'm calling you is to ask your advice.

FR La raison pour laquelle je t'appelle est pour te demander ton avis.
IPA [la ʁɛzɔ̃ puʁ lakɛl ʒø tˌapɛl e puʁ tø dᵊmɑ̃de tɔ̃ nˌavi ‖]

2526

EN A cemetery is a place where people are buried.

FR Un cimetière est un endroit où les gens sont enterrés.
IPA [œ̃ simᵊtjɛʁ e tˌœ̃ nˌɑ̃dʁwa u le ʒɑ̃ sɔ̃ ɑ̃teʁe ‖]

2527

EN I went to see the doctor, who told me to rest for a few days.

FR Je suis allé voir le médecin, qui m'a dit de me reposer pendant quelques jours.

IPA [ʒø sɥi ale vwaʁ lø mɛdsɛ̃ | ki m‿a di dø mø ʁəpoze pɑ̃dɑ̃ kɛlk ʒuʁ ‖]

2528

EN Do you know anyone who speaks French and Italian?

FR Connais-tu quelqu'un qui parle français et italien?

IPA [konɛ ty kɛlkœ̃ ki paʁl fʁɑ̃sɛ e italjɛ̃ ‖]

2529

EN Valerio, who speaks French and Italian, works as a tour guide.

FR Valerio, qui parle français et italien, travaille comme guide touristique.

IPA [(...) | ki paʁl fʁɑ̃sɛ e italjɛ̃ | tʁavaj kɔm gid tuʁistik ‖]

2530

EN Wilma works for a company that makes furniture.

FR Wilma travaille pour une entreprise qui fabrique des meubles.

IPA [(...) tʁavaj pu ʁ‿yn ɑ̃tʁəpʁiz ki fabʁik de mœbl ‖]

2531

EN This morning I met somebody I hadn't seen in ages.

FR Ce matin, j'ai rencontré quelqu'un que je n'avais pas vu depuis très longtemps.

IPA [sø matɛ̃ | ʒ‿ɛ ʁɑ̃kɔ̃tʁe kɛlkœ̃ kø ʒø n‿avɛ pa vy dᵊpɥi tʁɛ lɔ̃tɑ̃ ||]

2532

EN The population of London, which was once the largest city in the world, is now decreasing.

FR La population de Londres, qui était autrefois la plus grande ville du monde, est maintenant en baisse.

IPA [la popylasjɔ̃ dø lɔ̃dʁᵊ | ki ete t‿otʁᵊfwa la plys gʁɑ̃d vil dy mɔ̃d | e mɛ̃tᵊnɑ̃ t‿ɑ̃ bɛs ||]

2533

EN Few of the people who applied for the job had the necessary qualifications.

FR Peu de personnes qui ont postulé pour cet emploi avaient les qualifications nécessaires.

IPA [pø dø pɛʁsɔn ki ɔ̃ pɔstyle puʁ sɛ t‿ɑ̃plwa avɛ le kalifikasjɔ̃ nesesɛʁ ||]

2534

EN Camila showed me a picture of her son, who is a police officer.

FR Camila m'a montré une photo de son fils, qui est un agent de police.

IPA [(...) m‿a mɔ̃tʁe yn foto də sɔ̃ fis | ki e t‿œ̃ n‿aʒɑ̃ də polis ‖]

2535

EN The doctor who examined me couldn't find anything wrong.

FR Le médecin qui m'a examiné ne pouvait pas trouver quoi que ce soit qui cloche.

IPA [lø medsɛ̃ ki m‿a ɛgzamine nø puvɛ pa tʁuve kwa kø sø swa ki klɔʃ ‖]

2536

EN The sun, which is one (1) of millions of stars in the universe, provides us with heat and light.

FR Le Soleil, qui est l'une des millions d'étoiles de l'univers, nous fournit chaleur et lumière.

IPA [lø solɛj | ki e lyn de miljɔ̃ d‿etwal də l‿ynivɛʁ | nu fuʁni ʃalœʁ e lymjɛʁ ‖]

2537

EN Mr. Lopez, whom I spoke with at the meeting, is very interested in our plan.

FR Monsieur Lopez, à qui j'ai parlé lors de la réunion, est très intéressé par notre plan.

IPA [mᵊsjø (...) | a ki ʒ‿ɛ paʁle lɔʁ dø la ʁeynjɔ̃ | e tʁɛ z‿ɛ̃teʁese paʁ nɔtʁ plɑ̃ ‖]

2538

EN Fortunately, we had a map that we would have gotten lost without.

FR Heureusement, nous avions une carte sans laquelle nous nous serions perdus.

IPA [øʁøzᵊmɑ̃ | nu z‿avjɔ̃ z‿yn kaʁt sɑ̃ lakɛl nu nu sᵊʁjɔ̃ pɛʁdy ‖]

2539

EN This is my friend from Italy that I was telling you about.

FR Ceci est mon ami (♀ amie) d'Italie de qui je te parlais.

IPA [sᵊsi e mɔ̃ n‿ami (ami) italie dø ki ʒø tø paʁlɛ ‖]

2540

EN Ten people applied for the job, none of whom were suitable.

FR Dix personnes ont postulé pour l'emploi et aucune d'elles ne convenait.

IPA [dis pɛʁsɔn ɔ̃ pɔstyle puʁ l‿ɑ̃plwa e okyn d‿ɛl nø kɔ̃v°nɛ ‖]

2541

EN Priscilla has two (2) sisters, both of whom were teachers.

FR Priscilla a deux sœurs qui étaient toutes deux enseignantes.

IPA [(...) a dø sœʁ ki etɛ tut dø z‿ɑ̃sɛɲɑ̃t ‖]

2542

EN We drove along the road, the sides of which were lined with trees.

FR Nous avons roulé le long de la route, dont les côtés étaient bordés d'arbres.

IPA [nu z‿avɔ̃ ʁule lø lɔ̃ dø la ʁut | dɔ̃ le kote etɛ bɔʁde d‿aʁbʁ ‖]

2543

EN The company has a new business plan, the aim of which is to save money.

FR La société dispose d'un nouveau plan d'affaires dont le but est d'économiser de l'argent.

IPA [la sosjete dispoz d̯œ̃ nuvo plɑ̃ d̯afɛʁ dɔ̃ lø byt e d̯ekonomize dø l̯aʁʒɑ̃ ||]

2544

EN Yijuan doesn't have a phone, which makes it difficult to contact her.

FR Yijuan n'a pas de téléphone, ce qui complique le fait de communiquer avec elle.

IPA [(...) n̯a pa dø telefɔn | sø ki kɔ̃plik lø fɛ dø komynike avɛk ɛl ||]

2545

EN Police investigating the crime are looking for three (3) men.

FR La police qui enquête sur le crime est à la recherche de trois hommes.

IPA [la polis ki ɑ̃kɛt syʁ lø kʁim e a la ʁ°ʃɛʁʃ dø tʁwa ɔm ||]

2546

EN The road connecting the two (2) towns is very narrow.

FR La route reliant les deux villes est très étroite.

IPA [la ʁut ʁəljã le dø vil e tʁɛ z‿etʁwat ‖]

2547

EN I have a large bedroom overlooking the garden.

FR J'ai une grande chambre donnant sur le jardin.

IPA [ʒ‿ɛ yn gʁãd ʃãbʁ donã syʁ lø ʒaʁdɛ̃ ‖]

2548

EN The boy injured in the accident was taken to the hospital.

FR Le garçon blessé dans l'accident a été transporté à l'hôpital.

IPA [lø gaʁsɔ̃ blese dã l‿aksidã a ete tʁãspɔʁte a l‿opital ‖]

2549

EN The police never found the money stolen in the robbery.

FR La police n'a jamais trouvé l'argent volé lors du cambriolage.

IPA [la polis n‿a ʒamɛ tʁuve l‿aʁʒã vole lɔʁ dy kãbʁijolaʒ ‖]

2550

EN Most of the goods made in this factory are exported.

FR La plupart des produits fabriqués dans cette usine sont exportés.

IPA [la plypaʁ de pʁodɥi fabʁike dɑ̃ sɛt yzin sɔ̃ ɛkspɔʁte ‖]

2551

EN There are only a few chocolates left.

FR Il n'y a seulement que quelques chocolats restants.

IPA [il n̪ i a sœl°mɑ̃ kø kɛlk ʃokola ʁɛstɑ̃ ‖]

2552

EN I didn't talk much to the man sitting next to me on the plane.

FR Je n'ai pas beaucoup parlé à l'homme assis à côté de moi dans l'avion.

IPA [ʒø n̪ ɛ pa boku paʁle a l̪ɔm asi a kote dø mwa dɑ̃ l̪avjɔ̃ ‖]

2553

EN The taxi taking us to the airport broke down.

FR Le taxi nous emmenant à l'aéroport est tombé en panne.

IPA [lø taksi nu z̪ɑ̃m°nɑ̃ a l̪aeʁopɔʁ e tɔ̃be ɑ̃ pan ‖]

2554

EN The road damaged in the storm has now been repaired.

FR La route endommagée lors de la tempête a maintenant été réparée.

IPA [la ʁut ɑ̃domaʒe lɔʁ də la tɑ̃pɛt a mɛ̃t°nɑ̃ t‿ete ʁepaʁe ‖]

2555

EN Most of the suggestions made at the meeting weren't very reasonable.

FR La plupart des suggestions faites à la réunion n'étaient pas très raisonnables.

IPA [la plypaʁ de syɡʒɛstjɔ̃ fɛt a la ʁeynjɔ̃ n‿ete pa tʁɛ ʁezonabl ‖]

2556

EN What was the name of the man arrested by the police?

FR Quel était le nom de l'homme arrêté par la police?

IPA [kɛl ete lø nɔ̃ də l‿ɔm aʁete paʁ la polis ‖]

2557

EN I don't have anything to do. I'm bored.

FR Je n'ai rien à faire. Je m'ennuie.

IPA [ʒø n‿ɛ ʁjɛ̃ a fɛʁ ‖ ʒø m‿ɑ̃nɥi ‖]

2558

EN The teacher's explanation was confusing. Most of the students didn't understand it.

FR L'explication de l'enseignant (♀ enseignante) était mélangeante. La plupart des étudiants ne l'ont pas comprise.

IPA [l̩eksplikasjɔ̃ dø l̩ɑ̃sɛɲɑ̃ (♀ ɑ̃sɛɲɑ̃t) ete melɑ̃ʒɑ̃t || la plypaʁ de z̩etydjɑ̃ nø l̩ɔ̃ pa kɔ̃pʁiz ||]

2559

EN The kitchen hadn't been cleaned in ages. It was really disgusting.

FR La cuisine n'avait pas été nettoyée depuis des lunes. C'était vraiment dégoûtant.

IPA [la kɥizin n̩avɛ pa z̩ete netwaje dᵊpɥi de lyn || se etɛ vʁemɑ̃ degutɑ̃ ||]

2560

EN You don't have to get annoyed just because I'm a few minutes late.

FR Tu n'as pas besoin de t'énerver juste parce que je suis en retard de quelques minutes.

IPA [ty n̩a pa bøzwɛ̃ dø t̩enɛʁve ʒyst paʁs kø ʒø sɥi z̩ɑ̃ ʁᵊtaʁ dø kɛlk minyt ||]

2561

EN I've been working very hard all day, and now I'm exhausted.

FR J'ai travaillé très fort toute la journée et maintenant je suis épuisé (♀ épuisée).

IPA [ʒ‿ɛ tʁavaje tʁɛ fɔʁ tut la ʒuʁne e mɛ̃t°nɑ̃ ʒø sɥi epɥize (♀ epɥize) ‖]

2562

EN Vitale is very good at telling funny stories. He can be very amusing.

FR Vitale est très bon pour raconter des histoires drôles. Il peut être très amusant.

IPA [(...) e tʁɛ bɔ̃ puʁ ʁakɔ̃te de istwaʁ dʁol ‖ il pø etʁ tʁɛ z‿amyzɑ̃ ‖]

2563

EN He's one of the most boring people I've ever met. He never stops talking, and he never says anything interesting.

FR C'est une des personnes les plus ennuyantes que j'ai jamais rencontrées. Il n'arrête jamais de parler et il ne dit jamais rien d'intéressant.

IPA [sɛ t‿yn de pɛʁsɔn le ply ennuyantes kø ʒ‿ɛ ʒamɛ ʁɑ̃kɔ̃tʁe ‖ il n‿aʁɛt ʒamɛ dø paʁle e il nø di ʒamɛ ʁjɛ̃ d‿ɛ̃teʁɛsɑ̃ ‖]

2564

EN As the movie went on, it became more and more boring.

FR Au fur et à mesure que le film progressait, il devenait de plus en plus ennuyant.

IPA [o fyʁ e a mᵊzyʁ kø lø film pʁogʁɛsɛ | il dᵊvᵊnɛ dø ply s̬ã ply s̬ãnɥijã ‖]

2565

EN The dinner smells good.

FR Le dîner sent bon.

IPA [lø dine sã bɔ̃ ‖]

2566

EN This milk tastes a little strange.

FR Ce lait goûte un peu étrange.

IPA [sø lɛ gut œ̃ pø etʁãʒ ‖]

2567

EN I can't eat this. I just tried it and it tastes awful!

FR Je ne peux pas manger ça. Je viens tout juste de l'essayer et c'est horrible!

IPA [ʒø nø pø pa mãʒe sa ‖ ʒø vjɛ̃ tu ʒyst dø l̬eseje e sɛ t̬oʁibl ‖]

2568

EN Why do you look all wet? Have you been out in the rain?

FR Pourquoi as-tu l'air tout mouillé (♀toute mouillée)? Es-tu sorti (♀sortie) sous la pluie?

IPA [puʁkwa a ty lɛʁ tu muje (♀tut muje) || ɛ ty sɔʁti (♀sɔʁti) su la plɥi ||]

2569

EN There's no point in doing a job if you don't do it properly.

FR Il ne sert à rien de faire un travail si tu ne le fais pas correctement.

IPA [il nø sɛʁ a ʁjɛ̃ dø fɛʁ œ̃ tʁavaj si ty nø lø fɛ pa kɔʁɛktᵊmã ||]

2570

EN They'll be away for the next few weeks.

FR Ils seront partis pour les prochaines semaines.

IPA [il sᵊʁɔ̃ paʁti puʁ le pʁoʃen sᵊmen ||]

2571

EN Two people were seriously injured in the accident.

FR Deux personnes ont été grièvement blessées dans l'accident.

IPA [dø pɛʁsɔn ɔ̃ ete gʁijɛvᵊmã blese dã lˌaksidã ||]

2572

EN We didn't go out because it was raining heavily.

FR Nous ne sommes pas sortis (♀ sorties), car il pleuvait beaucoup.

IPA [nu nø sɔm pa sɔʁti (♀ sɔʁti) | kaʁ il pløvɛ boku |||]

2573

EN Even though Rosetta still makes mistakes, her English is already very fluent.

FR Même si Rosetta fait encore des erreurs, son anglais est déjà très fluide.

IPA [mɛm si (...) fɛ ɑ̃kɔʁ de z‿ɛʁœʁ | sɔ̃ n‿ɑ̃glɛ z‿e deʒa tʁɛ flɥid |||]

2574

EN The shoes I tried on fit me perfectly.

FR Les chaussures que j'ai essayées me vont parfaitement.

IPA [le ʃosyʁ kø ʒ‿ɛ esɛje mø vɔ̃ paʁfɛtᵊmɑ̃ |||]

2575

EN We know how to learn languages incredibly quickly.

FR Nous savons comment apprendre des langues incroyablement rapidement.

IPA [nu savɔ̃ kɔmɑ̃ t‿apʁɑ̃dʁ de lɑ̃g ɛ̃kʁwajablᵊmɑ̃ ʁapidᵊmɑ̃ |||]

2576

EN Two people got seriously injured in the accident.

FR Deux personnes ont été grièvement blessées dans l'accident.

IPA [dø pɛʁsɔn ɔ̃ ete gʁijɛv°mã blese dã l̩aksidã ||]

2577

EN The conference was badly organized.

FR La conférence était mal organisée.

IPA [la kɔ̃feʁɑ̃s etɛ ma l̩ɔʁganize ||]

2578

EN The movie was unnecessarily long. It could have been much shorter.

FR Le film est inutilement long. Il aurait pu être beaucoup plus court.

IPA [lø film e inytil°mã lɔ̃ || i l̩oʁe py ɛtʁ boku plys kuʁ ||]

2579

EN Esteban always wears nice clothes. He's always well dressed.

FR Esteban porte toujours de beaux vêtements. Il est toujours bien habillé.

IPA [(...) pɔʁt tuʒuʁ dø bo vɛt°mã || i l̩e tuʒuʁ bjɛ̃ abije ||]

2580

EN Elisa has a lot of responsibility in her job, but she isn't very well paid.

FR Elisa a beaucoup de responsabilités à son travail, mais elle n'est pas très bien payée.

IPA [(...) a boku dø ʁɛspɔ̃sabilite a sɔ̃ tʁavaj | mɛ ɛl n̪e pa tʁɛ bjɛ̃ peje ‖]

2581

EN You're speaking too quietly, I can hardly hear you.

FR Tu parles trop doucement, je peux à peine t'entendre.

IPA [ty paʁl tʁo dusᵊmã | ʒø pø a pɛn t̪ɑ̃tɑ̃dʁ ‖]

2582

EN You look the same now as you looked fifteen (15) years ago. You've hardly changed!

FR Tu as l'air du même (♀ de la même) maintenant qu'il y a quinze ans. Tu as à peine changé!

IPA [ty a l̪ɛʁ dy mɛm (♀ dø la mɛm) mɛ̃tᵊnã k̪il i a kɛ̃z ã ‖ ty a a pɛn ʃɑ̃ʒe ‖]

2583

EN Our new boss is not very popular. Hardly anyone likes her.

FR Notre nouveau patron n'est pas très populaire. Presque personne ne l'aime.

IPA [nɔtʁ nuvo patʁɔ̃ n̪e pa tʁɛ popylɛʁ ‖ pʁesk pɛʁsɔn nø l̪em ‖]

2584

EN It was very crowded in the room. There was hardly anywhere to sit.

FR C'était très achalandé dans la chambre. Il n'y avait pratiquement nulle part où s'asseoir.

IPA [se etɛ tʁɛ z‿aʃalɑ̃de dɑ̃ la ʃɑ̃bʁ ‖ il n‿i avɛ pʁatik°mɑ̃ nyl pa ʁ‿u s‿aswaʁ ‖]

2585

EN I hate this town. There's hardly anything to do and hardly anywhere to go for fun.

FR Je déteste cette ville. Il n'y a pratiquement rien à faire et pratiquement nulle part où s'amuser.

IPA [ʒø detɛst sɛt vil ‖ il n‿i a pʁatik°mɑ̃ ʁjɛ̃ a fɛʁ e pʁatik°mɑ̃ nyl pa ʁ‿u s‿amyze ‖]

2586

EN The story was so stupid. > It was such a stupid story.

FR L'histoire était si stupide. > C'était une histoire si stupide.

IPA [l‿istwaʁ etɛ si stypid ‖ > se etɛ yn istwaʁ si stypid ‖]

2587

EN They are so nice. > They are such nice people.

FR Ils sont tellement gentils. > Ils sont des gens tellement gentils.

IPA [il sɔ̃ tɛlˀmɑ̃ ʒɑ̃ti ‖ > il sɔ̃ de ʒɑ̃ tɛlˀmɑ̃ ʒɑ̃ti ‖|]

2588

EN We had such a good time on vacation that we didn't want to come home.

FR Nous avons tellement passé du bon temps en vacances que nous ne voulions pas rentrer à la maison.

IPA [nu z‿avɔ̃ tɛlˀmɑ̃ pase dy bɔ̃ tɑ̃ ɑ̃ vakɑ̃s kø nu nø vuljɔ̃ pa ʁɑ̃tʁe a la mɛzɔ̃ ‖|]

2589

EN She speaks English so well you would think it was her native language.

FR Elle parle si bien anglais que tu croirais que c'est sa langue maternelle.

IPA [ɛl paʁl si bjɛ̃ n‿ɑ̃glɛ kø ty kʁwaʁɛ kø sɛ sa lɑ̃g matɛʁnɛl ‖|]

2590

EN The music was so loud that you could hear it from miles away.

FR La musique était si forte qu'on pouvait l'entendre à des kilomètres.

IPA [la myzik etɛ si fɔʁt k‿ɔ̃ puvɛ l‿ɑ̃tɑ̃dʁ a de kilomɛtʁ ‖]

2591

EN I haven't seen her for such a long time.

FR Je ne l'ai pas vu depuis si longtemps.

IPA [ʒø nø l‿ɛ pa vy dᵊpɥi si lɔ̃tɑ̃ ‖]

2592

EN I didn't know it was such a long way.

FR Je ne savais pas que c'était un si long chemin.

IPA [ʒø nø savɛ pa kø se etɛ œ̃ si lɔ̃ ʃᵊmɛ̃ ‖]

2593

EN You're lazy. You don't work hard enough.

FR Tu es paresseux (♀paresseuse). Tu ne travailles pas assez fort.

IPA [ty ɛ paʁɛsø (♀paʁɛsøz) ‖ ty nø tʁavaj pa z‿ase fɔʁ ‖]

2594

EN Is Raj going to apply for the job? Does he have enough experience? > Is he experienced enough for the job?

FR Est-ce que Raj va postuler pour le poste? A-t-il assez d'expérience? > Est-il assez expérimenté pour le poste?

IPA [ɛsᵊ kø (...) va pɔstyle puʁ lø pɔst || a t‿il ase d‿ɛkspeʁjãs || > e t‿il ase z‿ɛkspeʁimãte puʁ lø pɔst ||]

2595

EN They're too young to get married. > They're not old enough to get married.

FR Ils sont trop jeunes pour se marier. > Ils ne sont pas assez vieux pour se marier.

IPA [il sɔ̃ tʁo ʒœn puʁ sø maʁje || > il nø sɔ̃ pa z‿ase vjø puʁ sø maʁje ||]

2596

EN It's too far to walk home from here.

FR C'est trop loin d'ici pour rentrer à la maison à pied.

IPA [sɛ tʁo lwɛ̃ d‿isi puʁ ʁɑ̃tʁe a la mɛzɔ̃ a pje ||]

2597

EN These apples aren't ripe enough to eat.

FR Ces pommes ne sont pas assez mûres pour être mangées.

IPA [se pɔm nø sɔ̃ pa z‿ase myʁ pu ʁ‿ɛtʁ mɑ̃ʒe ||]

2598

EN The situation is too complicated to explain.

FR La situation est trop compliquée à expliquer.

IPA [la sitɥasjɔ̃ e tʁo kɔ̃plike a ɛksplike ||]

2599

EN You're standing too close to the camera. Can you move a little farther away?

FR Tu es trop près de l'appareil. Peux-tu t'éloigner un peu?

IPA [ty ɛ tʁo pʁɛ dø l‿apaʁɛj || pø ty t‿elwaɲe œ̃ pø ||]

2600

EN The instructions were very complicated. They could have been simpler.

FR Les instructions étaient très compliquées. Elles auraient pu être plus simples.

IPA [le z‿ɛ̃stʁyksjɔ̃ etɛ tʁɛ kɔ̃plike || ɛ l‿oʁɛ py ɛtʁ plys sɛ̃pl ||]

GMS #2601 - 2700

2601

EN It takes longer by train than car.

FR Ça prend plus de temps en train qu'en voiture.
IPA [sa pʁɑ̃ plys də tɑ̃ ɑ̃ tʁɛ̃ k‿ɑ̃ vwatyʁ ||]

2602

EN Walter did worse than I did on the test.

FR Walter a fait pire que moi lors de l'examen.
IPA [(...) a fɛ piʁ kø mwa lɔʁ də l‿ɛgzamɛ̃ ||]

2603

EN My friends arrived earlier than I expected.

FR Mes amis sont arrivés plus tôt que prévu.
IPA [me z‿ami sɔ̃ aʁive plys to kø pʁevy ||]

2604

EN The buses run more often than the trains.

FR Les bus passent plus souvent que les trains.
IPA [le bys pas plys suvɑ̃ kø le tʁɛ̃ ||]

2605

EN There were a lot of people on the bus. It was more crowded than usual.

FR Il y avait beaucoup de gens dans le bus. C'était plus achalandé que d'habitude.

IPA [i l‿i avɛ boku dø ʒɑ̃ dɑ̃ lø bys ‖ se etɛ ply s‿aʃalɑ̃de kø d‿abityd ‖]

2606

EN Could you speak a bit more slowly?

FR Pourrais-tu parler un peu plus lentement?

IPA [puʁɛ ty paʁle ʁ‿œ̃ pø plys lɑ̃tᵊmɑ̃ ‖]

2607

EN This bag is slightly heavier than the other one.

FR Ce sac est légèrement plus lourd que l'autre.

IPA [sø sak e leʒɛʁᵊmɑ̃ plys luʁ kø l‿otʁ ‖]

2608

EN Her illness was far more serious than we thought at first.

FR Sa maladie était beaucoup plus grave que nous ne le pensions au début.

IPA [sa maladi etɛ boku plys gʁav kø nu nø lø pɑ̃sjɔ̃ o deby ‖]

2609

EN I've waited long enough and I'm not waiting any longer.

FR J'ai attendu assez longtemps et je n'attendrai pas plus longtemps.

IPA [ʒ‿ɛ atɑ̃dy ase lɔ̃tɑ̃ z‿e ʒø n‿atɑ̃dʁe pa plys lɔ̃tɑ̃ ‖]

2610

EN We expected their house to be very big, but it's no bigger than ours.

FR Nous nous attendions à ce que leur maison soit très grande, mais elle n'est pas plus grande que la nôtre.

IPA [nu nu z‿atɑ̃djɔ̃ a sø kø lœʁ mɛzɔ̃ swa tʁɛ gʁɑ̃d | mɛ ɛl n‿e pa plys gʁɑ̃d kø la notʁ ‖]

2611

EN This hotel is better than the other one, and it's no more expensive.

FR Cet hôtel est mieux que l'autre, et il n'est pas plus cher.

IPA [sɛ t‿otɛl e mjø kø l‿otʁ | e il n‿e pa plys ʃɛʁ ‖]

2612

EN What time should we leave? — The sooner the better.

FR À quelle heure devrions-nous partir? — Le plus tôt serait le mieux.

IPA [a kɛ l‿œʁ d°vʁijɔ̃ nu paʁtiʁ ‖ — lø plys to s°ʁɛ lø mjø ‖]

2613

EN When you're traveling, the less luggage you have the better.

FR Lorsque tu voyages, moins de bagages tu as, mieux c'est.

IPA [lɔʁskᵊ ty vwajaʒ | mwɛ̃ dø bagaʒ ty a | mjø sɛ ||]

2614

EN The sooner we leave, the earlier we'll arrive.

FR Plus nous partons tôt, plus nous arriverons tôt.

IPA [plys nu paʁtɔ̃ to | plys nu z̽aʁivᵊʁɔ̃ to ||]

2615

EN The more I thought about the plan, the less I liked it.

FR Plus je pensais au plan, moins je l'aimais.

IPA [plys ʒø pɑ̃sɛ o plɑ̃ | mwɛ̃ ʒø l̩emɛ ||]

2616

EN The shopping mall wasn't as crowded as usual. >
The shopping mall was less crowded than usual.

FR Le centre commercial n'est pas aussi achalandé que d'habitude. > Le centre commercial était moins bondé que d'habitude.

IPA [lø sɑ̃tʁ komɛʁsjal n̩e pa z̽osi aʃalɑ̃de kø d̥abityd ||
> lø sɑ̃tʁ komɛʁsjal ete mwɛ̃ bɔ̃de kø d̥abityd ||]

2617

EN I don't know as many people as you do. > I know fewer people than you do.

FR Je ne connais pas autant de gens que toi. > Je connais moins de gens que toi.

IPA [ʒø nø konɛ pa zˌotɑ̃ dø ʒɑ̃ kø twa ‖ > ʒø konɛ mwɛ̃ dø ʒɑ̃ kø twa ‖‖]

2618

EN I'm sorry I'm late. I got here as fast as I could.

FR Je suis désolé d'être en retard. Je suis venu aussi vite que j'ai pu.

IPA [ʒø sɥi dezole dˌetʁ ɑ̃ ʁˁtaʁ ‖ ʒø sɥi vˁny osi vit kø ʒˌɛ py ‖‖]

2619

EN You're free to have as much food as you want.

FR Tu es libre de manger autant de nourriture que tu le veux.

IPA [ty ɛ libʁ dø mɑ̃ʒe otɑ̃ dø nuʁityʁ kø ty lø vø ‖‖]

2620

EN Could you send me the money as soon as possible?

FR Pourrais-tu m'envoyer l'argent dès que possible?

IPA [puʁɛ ty mˌɑ̃vwaje lˌaʁʒɑ̃ dɛ kø posibl ‖‖]

2621

EN Gas is twice as expensive as it was a few years ago.

FR Le gaz est deux fois plus cher qu'il y a quelques années.

IPA [lø gaz e dø fwa plys ʃɛʁ k‿il i a kɛl k‿ane ‖]

2622

EN Satomi's salary is the same as mine. > Satomi gets the same salary as me.

FR Le salaire de Satomi est le même que le mien. > Satomi reçoit le même salaire que moi.

IPA [lø salɛʁ dø (...) e lø mɛm kø lø mjɛ̃ ‖ > (...) ʁ°swa lø mɛm salɛʁ kø mwa ‖]

2623

EN They have more money than we do. > They have more money than us.

FR Ils ont plus d'argent que nous en avons. > Ils ont plus d'argent que nous.

IPA [i l‿ɔ̃ plys d‿aʁʒɑ̃ kø nu z‿ɑ̃ n‿avɔ̃ ‖ > i l‿ɔ̃ plys d‿aʁʒɑ̃ kø nu ‖]

2624

EN I can't run as fast as he can. > I can't run as fast as him.

FR Je ne peux pas courir aussi vite qu'il ne le peut. > Je ne peux pas courir aussi vite que lui.

IPA [ʒø nø pø pa kuʁiʁ osi vit k‿il nø lø pø ‖ > ʒø nø pø pa kuʁiʁ osi vit kø lɥi ‖]

2625

EN The movie we just watched was the most boring movie I've ever seen.

FR Le film que nous venons de voir est le film le plus ennuyeux que j'aie jamais vu.

IPA [lø film kø nu v°nɔ̃ dø vwaʁ e lø film lø ply s‿ɑ̃nɥijø kø ʒ‿ɛ ʒamɛ vy ‖]

2626

EN Why does she always come to see me at the worst possible time?

FR Pourquoi vient-elle toujours me voir au pire moment possible?

IPA [puʁkwa vjɛ̃ t‿ɛl tuʒuʁ mø vwaʁ o piʁ momɑ̃ posibl ‖]

2627

EN He's the most patient person I've ever met.

FR Il est la personne la plus patiente que j'aie jamais rencontrée.

IPA [i l‿e la pɛʁsɔn la plys pasjɑ̃t kø ʒ‿ɛ ʒamɛ ʁɑ̃kɔ̃tʁe ‖]

2628

EN His eldest son is sixteen (16) years old.

FR Son fils aîné est âgé de seize ans.

IPA [sɔ̃ fis ene e aʒe dø sɛz ɑ̃ ‖]

2629

EN What's the most important decision you've ever had to make? — It was moving to another country.

FR Quelle est la décision la plus importante que tu aies déjà eu à prendre? — C'était : déménager dans un autre pays.

IPA [kɛ l‿e la desizjɔ̃ la ply s‿ɛpɔʁtɑ̃t kø ty ɛ deʒa y a pʁɑ̃dʁ ‖ — se etɛ | demenaʒe dɑ̃ z‿œ̃ n‿otʁ pei ‖]

2630

EN When we went to Munich, our guide spoke English fluently.

FR Quand nous sommes allés (♀allées) à Munich, notre guide parlait couramment l'anglais.

IPA [kɑ̃ nu sɔm ale (♀ale) a (...) | nɔtʁ gid paʁlɛ kuʁamɑ̃ l‿ɑ̃glɛ ‖]

2631

EN I met a friend of mine on my way home.

FR J'ai rencontré un (♀une) de mes amis (♀amies) en rentrant à la maison.

IPA [ʒ‿ɛ ʁɑ̃kɔ̃tʁe œ̃ (♀yn) də me z‿ami (♀ami) ɑ̃ ʁɑ̃tʁɑ̃ a la mɛzɔ̃ ‖]

2632

EN Walter hardly ever watches TV, and rarely reads newspapers.

FR Walter regarde à peine la télévision et lit rarement les journaux.

IPA [(...) ʁ°gaʁd a pɛn la televizjɔ̃ e li ʁaʁ°mɑ̃ le ʒuʁno ‖]

2633

EN The traffic isn't usually as bad as it was this morning.

FR La circulation n'est généralement pas aussi mauvaise qu'elle l'était ce matin.

IPA [la siʁkylasjɔ̃ n‿e ʒeneʁal°mɑ̃ pa z‿osi movɛz k‿el l‿etɛ sø matɛ̃ ‖]

2634

EN I'll be there next week, but I probably won't see you.

FR Je serai là la semaine prochaine, mais je ne vais probablement pas te voir.

IPA [ʒø s°ʁe la la s°mɛn pʁoʃɛn | me ʒø nø vɛ pʁobabl°mɑ̃ pa tø vwaʁ ‖]

2635

EN Gerardo and Feliciana have both applied for the job.

FR Gerardo et Feliciana ont tous deux postulé pour le poste.

IPA [(...) e (...) ɔ̃ tu dø pɔstyle puʁ lø pɔst ‖]

2636

EN He always says he won't be late, but he always is.

FR Il dit toujours qu'il ne sera pas en retard, mais il finit toujours par l'être.

IPA [il di tuʒuʁ k‿il nø s°ʁa pa z‿ɑ̃ ʁ°taʁ | mɛ il fini tuʒuʁ paʁ l‿ɛtʁ ‖]

2637

EN Yevgeniy doesn't work here anymore. He left last month. But Alan still works here.

FR Yevgeniy ne travaille plus ici. Il est parti le mois dernier, mais Alan travaille encore ici.

IPA [(...) nø tʁavaj ply s‿isi ‖ i l‿e paʁti lø mwa dɛʁnje | mɛ (...) tʁavaj ɑ̃kɔʁ isi ‖]

2638

EN We used to be good friends, but we aren't anymore.
> We're no longer friends.

FR Nous étions de bons amis (♀bonnes amies), mais
nous ne le sommes plus. > Nous ne sommes plus
amis (♀amies).

IPA [nu z‿etjɔ̃ də bɔ̃ z‿ami (♀bɔ n‿ami) | mɛ nu nə lø
sɔm plys || > nu nø sɔm ply s‿ami (♀ami) ||]]

2639

EN Have you gone to the bank yet? > Not yet.

FR Es-tu allé à la banque? > Pas encore.

IPA [ɛ ty ale a la bɑ̃k || > pa z‿ɑ̃kɔʁ ||]]

2640

EN Violetta lost her job six (6) months ago and hasn't
found another job yet.

FR Violetta a perdu son emploi il y a six mois et n'a pas
encore trouvé un autre emploi.

IPA [(...) a pɛʁdy sɔ̃ n‿ɑ̃plwa i l‿i a sis mwa e n‿a pa
z‿ɑ̃kɔʁ tʁuve œ̃ n‿otʁ ɑ̃plwa ||]]

2641

EN She said she would be here an hour ago, and she still hasn't arrived.

FR Elle a dit qu'elle serait là il y a une heure, et elle n'est toujours pas arrivée.

IPA [ɛ l̪a di k̪ɛl sˤʁɛ la i l̪i a yn œʁ | e ɛl n̪e tuʒuʁ pa z̪aʁive ‖]

2642

EN Have you written him yet? — Yes, and he still hasn't replied.

FR Lui as-tu écrit? — Oui, et il n'a toujours pas répondu.

IPA [lɥi a ty ekʁi ‖ — wi | e il n̪a tuʒuʁ pa ʁepɔ̃dy ‖]

2643

EN Should I tell him what happened, or does he already know?

FR Devrais-je lui dire ce qui s'est passé, ou le sait-il déjà?

IPA [dˤvʁɛ ʒø lɥi diʁ sø ki s̪e pase | u lø sɛ t̪il deʒa ‖]

2644

EN I've just had lunch, and I'm already hungry.

FR Je viens de déjeuner, et j'ai déjà faim.

IPA [ʒø vjɛ̃ dø deʒˤœne | e ʒ̪ɛ deʒa fɛ̃ ‖]

2645

EN Would you like to eat with us, or have you already eaten?

FR Voudrais-tu manger avec nous, ou as-tu déjà mangé?

IPA [vudʁɛ ty mɑ̃ʒe avɛk nu | u a ty deʒa mɑ̃ʒe ‖]

2646

EN The plane is still waiting on the runway and hasn't taken off yet.

FR L'avion attend toujours sur la piste et n'a pas encore décollé.

IPA [l̩ avjɔ̃ atɑ̃ tuʒuʁ syʁ la pist e n̩ a pa z ɑ̃kɔʁ dekole ‖]

2647

EN Has his flight landed yet? > Not yet, it should land in about thirty (30) minutes.

FR Son vol est-il atterri? > Pas encore, il devrait atterrir dans une trentaine de minutes.

IPA [sɔ̃ vɔl e t̩ il atɛʁi ‖ > pa z ɑ̃kɔʁ | il dᵊvʁɛ atɛʁiʁ dɑ̃ z̩ yn tʁɑ̃ten dø minyt ‖]

2648

EN He always wears a coat, even in hot weather.

FR Il porte toujours un manteau, même par temps chaud.

IPA [il pɔʁt tuʒu ʁ̩ œ̃ mɑ̃to | mɛm paʁ tɑ̃ ʃo ‖]

2649

EN They weren't very friendly to us. They didn't even say hello.

FR Ils n'étaient pas très sympa avec nous. Ils n'ont même pas dit bonjour.

IPA [il n‿ete pa tʁɛ sɛpa avɛk nu ‖ il n‿ɔ̃ mɛm pa di bɔ̃ʒuʁ ‖]

2650

EN I got up very early, but my teacher got up even earlier.

FR Je me suis levé (♀levée) très tôt, mais mon professeur s'est levé encore plus tôt.

IPA [ʒø mø sɥi lᵊve (♀lᵊve) tʁɛ to ǀ me mɔ̃ pʁofɛsœʁ s‿e lᵊve ãkɔʁ plys to ‖]

2651

EN I knew I didn't have much money, but I have even less than I thought.

FR Je savais que je n'avais pas beaucoup d'argent, mais j'en ai encore moins que je pensais.

IPA [ʒø savɛ kø ʒø n‿avɛ pa boku d‿aʁʒã ǀ me ʒã ɛ ãkɔʁ mwɛ̃ kø ʒø pãsɛ ‖]

ENFR

2652

EN Even though she can't drive, she still bought a car.

FR Même si elle ne peut pas conduire, elle a tout de même acheté une voiture.

IPA [mɛm si ɛl nø pø pa kɔ̃dɥiʁ | ɛ l‿a tu dø mɛm aʃᵊte yn vwatyʁ ‖]

2653

EN I'll probably see you tomorrow. But even if I don't see you tomorrow, I'm sure we'll see each other before the weekend.

FR Je vais sans doute te revoir demain, mais même si je ne te vois pas demain, je suis sûr que nous nous reverrons avant le week-end.

IPA [ʒø vɛ sɑ̃ dut tø ʁᵊvwaʁ dᵊmɛ̃ | me mɛm si ʒø nø tø vwa pa dᵊmɛ̃ | ʒø sɥi syʁ kø nu nu ʁᵊveʁɔ̃ avɑ̃ lø wikɛnd ‖]

2654

EN We're going to the beach tomorrow, even if it's raining.

FR Nous allons à la plage demain, même s'il pleut.

IPA [nu z‿alɔ̃ a la plaʒ dᵊmɛ̃ | mɛm s'il plø ‖]

2655

EN I didn't get the job, although I was well qualified. > I didn't get the job in spite of being well qualified.

FR Je n'ai pas eu le poste, même si j'étais bien qualifié (♀ qualifiée). > Je n'ai pas eu le poste en dépit d'être qualifié (♀ qualifiée).

IPA [ʒø n‿ɛ pa z‿y lø pɔst | mɛm si ʒ‿etɛ bjɛ̃ kalifje (♀ kalifje) || > ʒø n‿ɛ pa z‿y lø pɔst ɑ̃ depi d‿etʁ kalifje (♀ kalifje) ||]

2656

EN Although she wasn't feeling well, she still went to work. > In spite of not feeling well, she still went to work.

FR Bien qu'elle ne se sentait pas bien, elle est tout de même allée au travail. > En dépit de se sentir mal, elle est tout de même allée au travail.

IPA [bjɛ̃ k‿ɛl nø sø sɑ̃tɛ pa bjɛ̃ | ɛ l‿e tu dø mɛm ale o tʁavaj || > ɑ̃ depi dø sø sɑ̃tiʁ mal | ɛ l‿e tu dø mɛm ale o tʁavaj ||]

2657

EN I didn't get the job despite the fact that I was extremely qualified.

FR Je n'ai pas eu l'emploi en dépit d'être extrêmement qualifié (♀ qualifiée).

IPA [ʒø n‿ɛ pa z‿y l‿ɑ̃plwa ɑ̃ depi d‿etʁ ɛkstʁɛm°mɑ̃ kalifje (♀ kalifje) ||]

2658

EN I couldn't sleep despite being very tired. > Even though I was really tired, I couldn't sleep.

FR Je ne pouvais pas dormir en dépit d'être très fatigué (♀ fatiguée). > Bien que j'étais vraiment fatigué (♀ fatiguée), je ne pouvais pas dormir.

IPA [ʒø nø puvɛ pa dɔʁmi ʁ‿ɑ̃ depi d‿etʁ tʁɛ fatige (♀ fatige) ‖ > bjɛ̃ kø ʒ‿ete vʁɛmɑ̃ fatige (♀ fatige) | ʒø nø puvɛ pa dɔʁmiʁ ‖]

2659

EN I didn't get the job though I had all the necessary qualifications.

FR Je n'ai pas eu le poste bien que j'aie toutes les qualifications nécessaires.

IPA [ʒø n‿ɛ pa z‿y lø pɔst bjɛ̃ kø ʒ‿ɛ tut le kalifikasjɔ̃ nesesɛʁ ‖]

2660

EN She only accepted the job because of the salary, which was very high.

FR Elle n'a accepté le poste qu'à cause du salaire, qui était très élevé.

IPA [ɛl n‿a aksɛpte lø pɔst k a koz dy salɛʁ | ki ete tʁɛ z‿elᵉve ‖]

2661

EN She accepted the job in spite of the salary, which was rather low.

FR Elle a accepté le poste en dépit du salaire, qui était plutôt bas.

IPA [ɛ l a aksɛpte lø pɔst ɑ̃ depi dy salɛʁ | ki ete plyto ba ‖]

2662

EN I'll send you a map and directions in case you can't find our house.

FR Je t'enverrai une carte et le chemin à suivre au cas où tu ne puisses pas trouver notre maison.

IPA [ʒø t ɑ̃vɛʁɛ yn kaʁt e lø ʃ°mɛ̃ a sɥivʁ o ka u ty nø pɥis pa tʁuve nɔtʁ mɛzɔ̃ ‖]

2663

EN I'll remind him of the meeting in case he's forgotten.

FR Je lui reparlerai de la réunion au cas où il aurait oublié.

IPA [ʒø lɥi ʁ°paʁl°ʁɛ dø la ʁeynjɔ̃ o ka u i l oʁɛ ublije ‖]

2664

EN I'll leave my phone on just in case my mother calls.

FR Je vais laisser mon portable allumé au cas où ma mère appellerait.

IPA [ʒø vɛ lese mɔ̃ pɔʁtabl alyme o ka u ma mɛʁ apɛl°ʁɛ ‖]

2665

EN I'll give you my phone number in case you need to contact me.

FR Je te donnerai mon numéro de téléphone au cas où tu aies besoin de communiquer avec moi.

IPA [ʒø tø dɔnəʁe mɔ̃ nymeʁo dø telefɔn o ka u ty ɛ bøzwɛ̃ dø komynike avɛk mwa ‖]

2666

EN You should register your bike in case it's stolen.

FR Tu devrais enregistrer ton vélo au cas où il se ferait voler.

IPA [ty dəvʁɛ ɑ̃ʁəʒistʁe tɔ̃ velo o ka u il sø fəʁɛ vole ‖]

2667

EN You should tell the police if you have any information about the crime.

FR Tu devrais parler à la police si tu as de l'information à propos du crime.

IPA [ty dəvʁɛ paʁle a la polis si ty a dø l ɛ̃fɔʁmasjɔ̃ a pʁopo dy kʁim ‖]

2668

EN The club is for members only. You can't go in unless you're a member.

FR Le club est pour membres seulement. Tu ne peux pas y aller à moins d'être membre.

IPA [lø klœb e puʁ mãbʁ sœl°mã ‖ ty nø pø pa z̯i ale a mwɛ̃ d̯ɛtʁ mãbʁ ‖]

2669

EN I'll see you tomorrow unless I have to work late.

FR Je te vois demain à moins que je doive travailler tard.

IPA [ʒø tø vwa d°mɛ̃ a mwɛ̃ kø ʒø dwav tʁavaje taʁ ‖]

2670

EN You can borrow my car as long as you promise not to drive too fast. > You can borrow my car provided that you don't drive too fast.

FR Tu peux emprunter ma voiture pourvu que tu promettes de ne pas conduire trop rapidement. > Tu peux emprunter ma voiture pourvu que tu ne conduises pas trop vite.

IPA [ty pø ãpʁœ̃te ma vwatyʁ puʁvy kø ty pʁomɛt dø nø pa kɔ̃dɥiʁ tʁo ʁapid°mã ‖ > ty pø ãpʁœ̃te ma vwatyʁ puʁvy kø ty nø kɔ̃dɥiz pa tʁo vit ‖]

2671

EN I don't care which hotel we stay at as long as the room is clean. > Provided that the room's clean, I don't really care which hotel we stay at.

FR Je me fiche dans quel hôtel on séjourne, pourvu que la chambre soit propre. > À condition que la chambre soit propre, je me fiche vraiment de l'hôtel où on séjourne.

IPA [ʒø mø fiʃ dɑ̃ kɛ lˌotɛl ɔ̃ seʒuʁn | puʁvy kø la ʃɑ̃bʁ swa pʁɔpʁ || > a kɔ̃disjɔ̃ kø la ʃɑ̃bʁ swa pʁɔpʁ | ʒø mø fiʃ vʁɛmɑ̃ dø lˌotɛl u ɔ̃ seʒuʁn |||]

2672

EN I'm not going unless it stops raining.

FR Je n'y vais pas, à moins que la pluie cesse.

IPA [ʒø nˌi vɛ pa | a mwɛ̃ kø la plɥi sɛs |||]

2673

EN Ayman slipped as he was getting off the bus.

FR Ayman a glissé alors qu'il descendait du bus.

IPA [(...) a glise alɔʁ kˌil desɑ̃dɛ dy bys |||]

2674

EN We met Yuko as we were leaving the hotel.

FR Nous avons rencontré Yuko alors que nous partions de l'hôtel.

IPA [nu zˌavɔ̃ ʁɑ̃kɔ̃tʁe (...) alɔʁ kø nu paʁtjɔ̃ dø lˌotɛl |||]

2675

EN I had to leave just as the meeting was getting started.

FR J'ai dû partir alors que la réunion commençait.

IPA [ʒ‿ɛ dy paʁtiʁ alɔʁ kø la ʁeynjɔ̃ komɑ̃sɛ ‖]

2676

EN The phone rang just as I sat down.

FR Le téléphone a sonné comme je me suis assis.

IPA [lø telefɔn a sone kɔm ʒø mø sɥi asi ‖]

2677

EN The thief was difficult to identify, as he was wearing a mask.

FR Le voleur était difficile à identifier parce qu'il portait un masque.

IPA [lø volœʁ ete difisil a idɑ̃tifje paʁs k‿il pɔʁte t‿œ̃ mask ‖]

2678

EN I couldn't contact David as he was on a business trip in Japan and his cellphone doesn't work there.

FR Je ne pouvais pas communiquer avec David parce qu'il était en voyage d'affaires au Japon et que son téléphone portable ne fonctionne pas là-bas.

IPA [ʒø nø puvɛ pa komynike avɛk (...) paʁs k‿il ete t‿ɑ̃ vwajaʒ d‿afɛʁ o ʒapɔ̃ e kø sɔ̃ telefɔn pɔʁtabl nø fɔ̃ksjɔn pa laba ‖]

2679

EN Some sports, like motorcycle racing, can be dangerous.

FR Certains sports, comme la course de moto, peuvent être très dangereux.

IPA [sɛʁtɛ̃ spɔʁ | kɔm la kuʁs dø moto | pœv etʁ tʁɛ dɑ̃ʒ°ʁø ||]

2680

EN You should have done it as I showed you. > You should have done it like this.

FR Tu aurais dû faire comme je t'ai montré. > Tu aurais dû le faire comme ça.

IPA [ty oʁɛ dy fɛʁ kɔm ʒø t̪ɛ mõtʁe || > ty oʁɛ dy lø fɛʁ kɔm sa ||]

2681

EN As always, you're late to class. > You're late to class, as usual.

FR Comme toujours, tu es en retard en classe. > Tu es en retard en classe, comme d'habitude.

IPA [kɔm tuʒuʁ | ty ɛ ɑ̃ ʁ°taʁ ɑ̃ klas || > ty ɛ ɑ̃ ʁ°taʁ ɑ̃ klas | kɔm d̪abityd ||]

2682

EN Jiyeong works as the manager in his company.

FR Jiyeong travaille comme manageur au sein de son entreprise.

IPA [(...) tʁavaj kɔm manaʒœʁ o sɛ̃ də sɔ̃ n‿ɑ̃tʁᵊpʁiz ‖]

2683

EN Euna has to make important decisions, just like the manager.

FR Euna doit prendre des décisions importantes, tout comme le manageur.

IPA [(...) dwa pʁɑ̃dʁ de desizjɔ̃ ɛ̃pɔʁtɑ̃t | tu kɔm lə manaʒœʁ ‖]

2684

EN That house looks like it's going to fall down. > That house looks as if it's going to fall down.

FR Cette maison semble vouloir tomber. > Cette maison a l'air de vouloir tomber.

IPA [sɛt mɛzɔ̃ sɑ̃bl vulwaʁ tɔ̃be ‖ > sɛt mɛzɔ̃ a l‿ɛʁ də vulwaʁ tɔ̃be ‖]

2685

EN Iris is very late, isn't she? It looks like she isn't coming. > It looks as if she isn't coming. > It looks as though she isn't coming.

FR Iris est très en retard, n'est-ce pas? Il semble qu'elle ne viendra pas. > Il semble qu'elle ne viendra pas. > On dirait qu'elle ne viendra pas.

IPA [(...) e tʁɛ z‿ɑ̃ ʁ°taʁ | n‿e sø pa || il sɑ̃bl k‿ɛl nø vjɛ̃dʁa pa || > il sɑ̃bl k‿ɛl nø vjɛ̃dʁa pa || > ɔ̃ diʁɛ k‿ɛl nø vjɛ̃dʁa pa ||]

2686

EN We took an umbrella because it looked like it was going to rain.

FR Nous avons pris un parapluie, car il semblait qu'il allait pleuvoir.

IPA [nu z‿avɔ̃ pʁi z‿œ̃ paʁaplɥi | kaʁ il sɑ̃blɛ k‿il alɛ pløvwaʁ ||]

2687

EN Do you hear music coming from next door? It sounds like they're having a party.

FR Entendez-vous la musique venant d'à côté? On dirait qu'ils font une fête.

IPA [ɑ̃tɑ̃de vu la myzik v°nɑ̃ d a kote || ɔ̃ diʁɛ k‿il fɔ̃ t‿yn fɛt ||]

2688

EN After the interruption, the speaker went on talking as if nothing had happened.

FR Après l'interruption, l'orateur continua de parler comme si rien ne s'était passé.

IPA [apʁɛ l‿ɛ̃tɛʁypsjɔ̃ | l‿oʁatœʁ kɔ̃tinɥa dø paʁle kɔm si ʁjɛ̃ nø s‿etɛ pase ‖]

2689

EN When I told them my plan, they looked at me as though I was crazy.

FR Quand je leur ai dit mon plan, ils m'ont regardé comme si j'étais fou (folle).

IPA [kɑ̃ ʒø lœʁ ‿ɛ di mɔ̃ plɑ̃ | il m‿ɔ̃ ʁ°gaʁde kɔm si ʒ‿etɛ fu (fɔl) ‖]

2690

EN She's always asking me to do things for her, as if I didn't have enough to do already.

FR Elle me demande toujours de faire des choses pour elle, comme si je n'avais pas déjà assez de choses à faire.

IPA [ɛl mø d°mɑ̃d tuʒuʁ dø fɛʁ de ʃoz pu ʁ‿ɛl | kɔm si ʒø n‿avɛ pa deʒa ase dø ʃoz a fɛʁ ‖]

2691

EN   Sachiko is going away for a week in September.

FR   Sachiko part pour une semaine en septembre.
IPA   [(...) paʁ pu ʁ‿yn sᵊmɛn ɑ̃ sɛptɑ̃bʁ ‖]

2692

EN   Where have you been? I've been waiting for ages.

FR   Où étais-tu? J'attends depuis des siècles.
IPA   [u etɛ ty ‖ ʒ‿atɑ̃ dᵊpɥi de sjɛkl ‖]

2693

EN   I fell asleep during the movie. > I fell asleep while I
      was watching the movie.

FR   Je me suis endormi (♀endormie) pendant le film. >
      Je me suis endormi (♀endormie) pendant que je
      regardais le film.
IPA   [ʒø mø sɥi ɑ̃dɔʁmi (♀ɑ̃dɔʁmi) pɑ̃dɑ̃ lø film ‖ > ʒø
      mø sɥi ɑ̃dɔʁmi (♀ɑ̃dɔʁmi) pɑ̃dɑ̃ kø ʒø ʁᵊgaʁdɛ lø
      film ‖]

2694

EN   We met some really nice people during our vacation.

FR   Nous avons rencontré des gens très sympa pendant
      nos vacances.
IPA   [nu z‿avɔ̃ ʁɑ̃kɔ̃tʁe de ʒɑ̃ tʁɛ sɛ̃pa pɑ̃dɑ̃ no vakɑ̃s ‖]

2695

EN I'll call you sometime during the afternoon.

FR Je t'appellerai au cours de l'après-midi.

IPA [ʒø t‿apɛlˤʁɛ o kuʁ dø l apʁɛ midi ‖]

2696

EN It rained for three (3) days without stopping.

FR Il a plu pendant trois jours sans arrêt.

IPA [i l‿a ply pãdã tʁwa ʒuʁ sã z‿aʁɛ ‖]

2697

EN There was a phone call for you while you were out.

FR Il y a eu un appel téléphonique pour toi pendant que tu étais sorti (♀ sortie).

IPA [i l‿i a y œ̃ n‿apɛl telefonik puʁ twa pãdã kø ty ete sɔʁti (♀ sɔʁti) ‖]

2698

EN I'll be in London next week, and I hope to see John while I'm there.

FR Je serai à Londres la semaine prochaine, et j'espère voir John pendant que j'y serai.

IPA [ʒø sˤʁɛ a lõdʁˤ la sˤmɛn pʁoʃɛn | e ʒ‿ɛspɛʁ vwaʁ john pãdã kø ʒ‿i sˤʁɛ ‖]

2699

EN I sent the package to them today, so they should receive it by Monday. > They should receive it no later than Monday.

FR Je leur ai envoyé le paquet aujourd'hui, alors ils devraient le recevoir d'ici lundi. > Ils devraient le recevoir au plus tard lundi.

IPA [ʒø lœ ʁ‿ɛ ɑ̃vwaje lø pakɛ oʒuʁdɥi | alɔ ʁ‿il dᵊvʁɛ lø ʁᵊsᵊvwaʁ d‿isi lœ̃di || > il dᵊvʁɛ lø ʁᵊsᵊvwaʁ o plys taʁ lœ̃di ||]

2700

EN I have to be home by five [o'clock] (5:00). > I have to be home no later than five [o'clock] (5:00).

FR Je dois être à la maison à cinq heures. > Je dois être à la maison au plus tard à cinq heures.

IPA [ʒø dwa ɛtʁ a la mɛzɔ̃ a sɛ̃ k‿œʁ || > ʒø dwa ɛtʁ a la mɛzɔ̃ o plys taʁ a sɛ̃ k‿œʁ ||]

GMS #2701 - 2800

2701

EN I slept until noon this morning. > I didn't get up until noon this morning.

FR J'ai dormi jusqu'à midi ce matin. > Je ne me suis pas levé avant midi ce matin.

IPA [ʒ‿ɛ dɔʁmi ʒyska midi sø matɛ̃ || > ʒø nø mø sɥi pa lᵊve avɑ̃ midi sø matɛ̃ ||]

2702

EN Pablo will be away until Saturday. > Pablo will be back by Saturday.

FR Pablo sera absent jusqu'à samedi. > Pablo sera de retour samedi.

IPA [(...) sᵊʁa apsɑ̃ ʒyska samᵊdi || > (...) sᵊʁa dø ʁᵊtuʁ samᵊdi ||]

2703

EN I have to work until eleven pm (11:00) > I'll have finished my work by eleven pm (11:00).

FR Je dois travailler jusqu'à vingt-trois heures (23 h). > J'aurai fini mon travail d'ici vingt-trois heures (23 h).

IPA [ʒø dwa tʁavaje ʒyska vɛ̃ttʁwa z‿œʁ (23 h) || > ʒ‿oʁɛ fini mɔ̃ tʁavaj d‿isi vɛ̃ttʁwa z‿œʁ (23 h) ||]

2704

EN It's too late to go to the bank now. By the time we get there, it'll be closed.

FR Il est trop tard pour aller à la banque aujourd'hui. D'ici à ce que nous arrivions, elle sera fermée.

IPA [i l̩e tʁo taʁ pu ʁ‿ale a la bɑ̃k oʒuʁdɥi ‖ d̩isi a sø kø nu z‿aʁivjɔ̃ | ɛl s°ʁa fɛʁme ‖]

2705

EN By the time we get to the movies, it'll have already started.

FR D'ici à ce que nous arrivions au cinéma, le film aura déjà commencé.

IPA [d̩isi a sø kø nu z‿aʁivjɔ̃ o sinema | lø film oʁa deʒa komɑ̃se ‖]

2706

EN Silvio's car broke down on his way to his friend's house. By the time he arrived, everybody had left.

FR La voiture de Silvio est tombée en panne sur le chemin de la maison de son ami. Quand il est arrivé, tout le monde était parti.

IPA [la vwatyʁ dø (…) e tɔ̃be ɑ̃ pan syʁ lø ʃ°mɛ̃ dø la mɛzɔ̃ dø sɔ̃ n‿ami ‖ kɑ̃ d̩i l̩e t‿aʁive | tu lø mɔ̃d etɛ paʁti ‖]

2707

EN I'll see you AT noon, ON Wednesday, ON the twenty-fifth, IN December.

FR Je te verrai à midi, le mercredi vingt-cinq (25) décembre.

IPA [ʒø tø veʁe a midi | lø meʁkʁ°di vɛ̃tsɛ̃k (25) desɑ̃bʁ ‖]

2708

EN I'll see you IN the morning, ON May thirty-first (31st), twenty-fourteen (2014).

FR Je te verrai le trente et un (31) mai deux mille quatorze (2014) au matin.

IPA [ʒø tø veʁe lø tʁɑ̃t e œ̃ (31) me dø mil katɔʁz (2014) o matɛ̃ ‖]

2709

EN I have to work IN the afternoons.

FR Je dois travailler les après-midi.

IPA [ʒø dwa tʁavaje le ‿zapʁe midi ‖]

2710

EN The train will be leaving IN a few minutes.

FR Le train va partir dans quelques minutes.

IPA [lø tʁɛ̃ va paʁtiʁ dɑ̃ kɛlk minyt ‖]

2711

EN I'll be back IN a week.

FR Je reviens dans une semaine.
IPA [ʒø ʁ°vjɛ̃ dã z‿yn s°mɛn ‖]

2712

EN They're getting married in six (6) months' time.

FR Ils vont se marier dans six mois.
IPA [il vɔ̃ sø maʁje dã sis mwa ‖]

2713

EN Everything began and ended ON time.

FR Tout a commencé et s'est terminé à temps.
IPA [tu t‿a komãse e s‿e teʁmine a tã ‖]

2714

EN If I say ten o'clock (10:00), then I mean, be ON time.

FR Si je dis dix heures (10 h), alors que je veux dire
« sois à l'heure ».
IPA [si ʒø di di z‿œʁ (10 h) | alɔʁ kø ʒø vø diʁswa a l‿œʁ
‖]

2715

EN Will you be home IN time for dinner? > No, I'll be late.

FR Seras-tu à la maison à temps pour dîner? > Non, je vais être en retard.

IPA [s°ʁa ty a la mɛzɔ̃ a tɑ̃ puʁ dine || > nɔ̃ | ʒø vɛ ɛtʁ ɑ̃ ʁ°taʁ ||]

2716

EN We got on the train just IN time.

FR Nous sommes montés à bord du train juste à temps.

IPA [nu sɔm mɔ̃te a bɔʁ dy tʁɛ̃ ʒyst a tɑ̃ ||]

2717

EN I hit the brakes just IN time and didn't hit the child.

FR J'ai freiné juste à temps et je n'ai pas touché l'enfant.

IPA [ʒ‿ɛ fʁene ʒyst a tɑ̃ e ʒø n‿ɛ pa tuʃe l‿ɑ̃fɑ̃ ||]

2718

EN At first we didn't get along very well, but in the end we became good friends.

FR Au début, nous ne nous entendions pas très bien, mais à la fin nous sommes devenus de bons amis (♀bonnes amies).

IPA [o deby | nu nø nu z‿ɑ̃tɑ̃djɔ̃ pa tʁɛ bjɛ̃ | mɛ a la fɛ̃ nu sɔm d°v°ny dø bɔ̃ z‿ami (♀bɔ n‿ami) ||]

2719

EN I'm going away at the beginning of January. > I'm going away at the beginning of the year.

FR Je pars au début de janvier. > Je pars au début de l'année.

IPA [ʒø paʁ o deby dø ʒɑ̃vje || > ʒø paʁ o deby dø l̩ane ||]

2720

EN I'm coming back at the end of December. > I'm coming back at the end of the year.

FR Je reviens à la fin de décembre. > Je reviens à la fin de l'année.

IPA [ʒø ʁəvjɛ̃ a la fɛ̃ dø desɑ̃bʁ || > ʒø vɛ ʁəvjɛ̃ a la fɛ̃ dø l̩ane ||]

2721

EN The hotel we're going to is on a small island in the middle of a lake.

FR L'hôtel où nous allons est sur une petite île au milieu d'un lac.

IPA [l̩otɛl u nu z̩alɔ̃ e syʁ une pətit il o miljø d̩œ̃ lak ||]

2722

EN There's somebody at the door, could you please answer it?

FR Il y a quelqu'un à la porte, pourrais-tu s'il te plaît répondre?

IPA [i l‿i a kɛlkœ̃ a la pɔʁt | puʁɛ ty s‿il tø plɛ ʁepɔ̃dʁ ||]

2723

EN I like to sit in the back row at the movies.

FR J'aime m'asseoir dans la rangée arrière au cinéma.

IPA [ʒ‿ɛm m‿aswaʁ dɑ̃ la ʁɑ̃ʒe aʁjɛʁ o sinema ||]

2724

EN I just started working in the sales department.

FR Je viens tout juste de commencer à travailler dans le département des ventes.

IPA [ʒø vjɛ̃ tu ʒyst dø komɑ̃se a tʁavaje dɑ̃ lø depaʁt°mɑ̃ de vɑ̃t ||]

2725

EN Our apartment is on the second floor of the building.

FR Notre appartement est situé au deuxième étage de l'immeuble.

IPA [nɔtʁ apaʁt°mɑ̃ e sitɥe o døzjɛm etaʒ dø l‿imœbl ||]

2726

EN They drive on the left in Britain, Japan, and
Singapore.

FR Ils roulent à gauche en Grande-Bretagne, au Japon et
à Singapour.

IPA [il ʁul a goʃ ɑ̃ gʁɑ̃d bʁ°taɲ | o ʒapɔ̃ e a singapuʁ ‖]

2727

EN I stopped to get gas on the way home from work.

FR Je me suis arrêté pour prendre de l'essence en
rentrant à la maison du travail.

IPA [ʒø mø sɥi aʁete puʁ pʁɑ̃dʁ dø l̩esɑ̃s ɑ̃ ʁɑ̃tʁɑ̃ a la
mɛzɔ̃ dy tʁavaj ‖]

2728

EN The plant is in the corner of the room.

FR La plante est dans le coin de la pièce.

IPA [la plɑ̃t e dɑ̃ lø kwɛ̃ dø la pjɛs ‖]

2729

EN The mailbox is on the corner of the street.

FR La boîte aux lettres est au coin de la rue.

IPA [la bwat o lɛtʁ e o kwɛ̃ dø la ʁy ‖]

2730

EN Have you ever been in the hospital?

FR As-tu déjà été à l'hôpital?
IPA [a ty deʒa ete a l̩opital ‖]

2731

EN Have you ever been in prison? > Have you ever been in jail?

FR As-tu déjà été en prison?
IPA [a ty deʒa ete ɑ̃ pʁizɔ̃ ‖]

2732

EN My brother's in college, and I'm still in high school. > He's in medical school, but I want to go to law school.

FR Mon frère est à l'université et je suis toujours au lycée. > Il fait l'école de médecine, mais je veux faire l'école de droit.
IPA [mɔ̃ fʁɛʁ e a l̩ynivɛʁsite e ʒø sɥi tuʒuʁ o lise ‖ > il fɛ l̩ekɔl dø medsin | me ʒø vø fɛʁ l̩ekɔl dø dʁwa ‖]

2733

EN We went ON a cruise last week, and there weren't many people ON the ship.

FR Nous avons fait une croisière la semaine dernière et il n'y avait pas beaucoup de gens sur le bateau.
IPA [nu z̩avɔ̃ fɛ t̩yn kʁwazjɛʁ la sᵊmɛn dɛʁnjɛʁ e il n̩i avɛ pa boku dø ʒɑ̃ syʁ lø bato ‖]

2734

EN There were no seats left when we got ON the train.

FR Il n'y avait plus de sièges quand nous sommes montés
(♀montées) dans le train.

IPA [il n‿i avɛ plys də sjɛʒ kɑ̃ nu som mɔ̃te (♀mɔ̃te) dɑ̃ lø
tʁɛ̃ ‖]

2735

EN The bus was very crowded when we got ON.

FR Le bus était très bondé lorsque nous sommes montés
(♀montées).

IPA [lø bys etɛ tʁɛ bɔ̃de lɔʁskᵊ nu som mɔ̃te (♀mɔ̃te) ‖]

2736

EN I had an aisle seat ON the plane. > I had an aisle
seat ON the flight.

FR J'ai eu un siège côté couloir dans l'avion. > J'ai eu
un siège côté couloir sur le vol.

IPA [ʒ‿ɛ y œ̃ sjɛʒ kote kulwaʁ dɑ̃ l‿avjɔ̃ ‖ > ʒ‿ɛ y œ̃ sjɛʒ
kote kulwaʁ syʁ lø vɔl ‖]

2737

EN Nuria passed me ON her bike yesterday.

FR Nuria m'a dépassé (♀dépassée) sur son vélo hier.

IPA [(...) m‿a depase (♀depase) syʁ sɔ̃ velo jɛʁ ‖]

2738

EN My friends are IN China. They'll be going back TO Italy next week.

FR Mes amis sont en Chine. Ils vont retourner en Italie la semaine prochaine.

IPA [me z‿ami sɔ̃ t‿ɑ̃ ʃin ‖ il vɔ̃ ʁᵊtuʁne ʁ‿ɑ̃ italie la sᵊmɛn pʁoʃɛn ‖]

2739

EN My parents are AT the zoo. My aunt is going TO the zoo to meet them there.

FR Mes parents sont au zoo. Ma tante va au zoo pour les rencontrer là-bas.

IPA [me paʁɑ̃ sɔ̃ o zoo ‖ ma tɑ̃t va o zoo puʁ le ʁɑ̃kɔ̃tʁe laba ‖]

2740

EN Sir, I'm in a hurry to catch my flight ON time. When will we arrive AT the airport?

FR Monsieur, je suis pressé de prendre l'avion à temps. Quand allons-nous arriver à l'aéroport?

IPA [mᵊsjø | ʒø sɥi pʁese dø pʁɑ̃dʁ l‿avjɔ̃ a tɑ̃ ‖ kɑ̃ alɔ̃ nu aʁive a l‿aeʁopɔʁ ‖]

2741

EN Four of us got INTO a car and the others got ONTO
a bus.

FR Quatre d'entre nous sont montés (♀montées) dans
une voiture et les autres sont monté (♀montées) dans
un bus.

IPA [katʁ d‿ɑ̃tʁ nu sɔ̃ mɔ̃te (♀mɔ̃te) dɑ̃ z‿yn vwatyʁ e le
z‿otʁ sɔ̃ mɔ̃te (♀mɔ̃te) dɑ̃ z‿œ̃ bys ‖]

2742

EN Since it was too hot to sit in the sun, we found a table
IN the shade.

FR Comme il faisait trop chaud pour s'asseoir au soleil,
nous avons trouvé une table à l'ombre.

IPA [kɔm il fᵊzɛ tʁo ʃo puʁ s‿aswaʁ o solɛj | nu z‿avɔ̃
tʁuve yn tabl a l‿ɔ̃bʁ ‖]

2743

EN Don't go out IN the rain, or else you'll get all wet.

FR Ne sors pas sous la pluie, ou bien tu seras tout
mouillé (♀toute mouillée).

IPA [nø sɔʁ pa su la plɥi | u bjɛ̃ ty sᵊʁa tu muje (♀tut
muje) ‖]

2744

EN When filling out forms, be sure to print your name IN capital letters so it's legible.

FR Lors du remplissage de formulaires, assure-toi d'imprimer ton nom en lettres capitales pour que ce soit lisible.

IPA [lɔʁ dy ʁãplisaʒ dø fɔʁmylɛʁ | asyʁ twa d‿ɛ̃pʁime tɔ̃ nɔ̃ ã lɛtʁ kapital puʁ kø sø swa lizibl ||]

2745

EN Have you ever been IN love with somebody?

FR As-tu déjà été en amour avec quelqu'un?

IPA [a ty deʒa ete ã n‿amuʁ avɛk kɛlkœ̃ ||]

2746

EN IN my opinion, the movie wasn't that great.

FR Selon moi, le film n'était pas terrible.

IPA [sᵊlɔ̃ mwa | lø film n‿ete pa tɛʁibl ||]

2747

EN IN my mother's opinion, the food AT this restaurant is the best.

FR Selon ma mère, la nourriture dans ce restaurant est la meilleure.

IPA [sᵊlɔ̃ ma mɛʁ | la nuʁityʁ dã sø ʁestoʁã e la mɛjœʁ ||]

2748

EN Latifa left school AT the age OF seventeen (17). > She left school AT seventeen (17).

FR Latifa a quitté l'école à l'âge de dix-sept ans. > Elle a quitté l'école à dix-sept (17) ans.

IPA [(...) a kite l‿ekɔl a l‿aʒ dø disɛ t‿ã || > ɛ l‿a kite l‿ekɔl a disɛt (17) ã ||]

2749

EN We took off an hour ago, and now we're flying AT a speed OF nine hundred (900) kilometers per hour AT an altitude OF ten thousand (10,000) meters.

FR Nous avons décollé il y a une heure et nous volons maintenant à une vitesse de neuf cents kilomètres à l'heure à une altitude de dix mille mètres.

IPA [nu z‿avõ dekole i l‿i a yn œʁ e nu volõ mɛ̃tᵊnã a yn vitɛs dø nœf sã kilomɛtʁ a l‿œʁ a yn altityd dø dis mil mɛtʁ ||]

2750

EN The train was traveling AT a speed OF one hundred twenty (120) miles per hour when the driver lost control. > The train was traveling AT a speed OF two hundred (200) kilometers per hour when the driver lost control.

FR Le train roulait à une vitesse de deux cents kilomètres-heure lorsque le conducteur a perdu le contrôle.

IPA [lø tʁɛ̃ ʁulɛ a yn vitɛs dø dø sã kilomɛtʁœʁ lɔʁskᵊ lø kõdyktœ ʁ‿a pɛʁdy lø kõtʁol ||]

2751

EN Water boils AT a temperature OF one hundred degrees (100º) Celsius.

FR L'eau bout à une température de cent degrés Celsius.

IPA [l̞o bu a yn tãpeʁatyʁ dø sã d°gʁe (...) ‖]

2752

EN Some singers go ON a world tour every year.

FR Certains chanteurs font une tournée mondiale chaque année.

IPA [seʁtẽ ʃãtœʁ fɔ̃ t̞yn tuʁne mɔ̃djal ʃak ane ‖]

2753

EN I didn't hear the news ON the radio, nor ON the television; I saw it ON the internet.

FR Je n'ai pas entendu les nouvelles à la radio ni à la télévision, je l'ai vu sur Internet.

IPA [ʒø n̞ɛ pa z̞ãtãdy le nuvɛl a la ʁadjo ni a la televizjɔ̃ | ʒø l̞ɛ vy sy ʁ̞ẽteʁnet ‖]

2754

EN I've never met the woman IN charge OF marketing, but I've spoken to her ON the phone a few times.

FR Je n'ai jamais rencontré la femme responsable du marketing, mais je lui ai parlé au téléphone à quelques reprises.

IPA [ʒø n̞ɛ ʒamɛ ʁãkɔ̃tʁe la fam ʁespɔ̃sabl dy maʁketiŋ | mɛ ʒø lɥi ɛ paʁle o telefɔn a kɛlk ʁ°pʁiz ‖]

2755

EN There's no train service today because all the railroad workers are ON strike.

FR Il n'y a pas de service de train aujourd'hui, parce que tous les travailleurs de chemin de fer sont en grève.

IPA [il n‿i a pa də sɛʁvis də tʁɛ̃ oʒuʁdɥi | paʁs kə tu le tʁavajœʁ də ʃ°mɛ̃ də fɛʁ sɔ̃ t‿ɑ̃ gʁɛv ‖]

2756

EN She's put ON a lot of weight this year, so she wants to go ON a diet.

FR Elle a pris beaucoup de poids cette année, alors elle veut faire un régime.

IPA [ɛ l‿a pʁi boku də pwa sɛt ane | alɔʁ ɛl vø fɛʁ œ̃ ʁeʒim ‖]

2757

EN While I was watching F1 racing yesterday, I saw one of the cars catch ON fire.

FR Alors que je regardais la course de F1 hier, j'ai vu une des voitures prendre feu.

IPA [alɔʁ kə ʒə ʁ°gaʁdɛ la kuʁs də (...) jɛʁ | ʒ‿ɛ vy yn de vwatyʁ pʁɑ̃dʁ fø ‖]

2758

EN Sometimes my job can be really stressful, but ON the whole I like the people and enjoy the job.

FR Parfois, mon travail peut être très stressant, mais dans l'ensemble j'aime les gens et j'apprécie le travail.

IPA [paʁfwa | mɔ̃ tʁavaj pø ɛtʁ tʁɛ stʁɛsɑ̃ | mɛ dɑ̃ l̩ɑ̃sɑ̃bl ʒ̩ɛm le ʒɑ̃ e ʒ̩apʁesi lø tʁavaj ‖]

2759

EN I didn't mean to annoy you, I didn't do it ON purpose.

FR Je ne voulais pas t'importuner, je ne l'ai pas fait exprès.

IPA [ʒø nø vulɛ pa t̩ɛ̃pɔʁtyne | ʒø nø l̩ɛ pa fɛ t̩ɛkspʁɛ ‖]

2760

EN He bumped INTO me ON accident.

FR Il se heurta à moi par accident.

IPA [il sø œʁta a mwa pa ʁ̩aksidɑ̃ ‖]

2761

EN He bumped INTO me BY mistake.

FR Il se heurta à moi par erreur.

IPA [il sø œʁta a mwa pa ʁ̩ɛʁœʁ ‖]

2762

EN All of my contact information is ON my business card, but it's easiest to get ahold of me BY email or cellphone.

FR Toutes mes informations de contact sont sur ma carte de visite, mais c'est plus facile de me rejoindre par courriel ou par téléphone portable.

IPA [tut me z‿ɛ̃fɔʁmasjɔ̃ də kɔ̃takt sɔ̃ syʁ ma kaʁt də vizit | mɛ sɛ plys fasil də mø ʁ°ʒwɛ̃dʁ paʁ kuʁjɛl u paʁ telefɔn pɔʁtabl ||]

2763

EN I didn't bring enough cash, so could I pay BY credit card?

FR Je n'ai pas apporté assez d'argent, alors pourrais-je payer par carte de crédit?

IPA [ʒø n‿ɛ pa z‿apɔʁte ase d‿aʁʒɑ̃ | alɔʁ puʁɛ ʒø peje paʁ kaʁt də kʁedi ||]

2764

EN You don't need to fix that BY hand, I can write a computer program to help you. > You don't need to fix that manually.

FR Tu n'as pas besoin de résoudre ce problème à la main, je peux écrire un programme informatique pour t'aider. > Tu n'as pas besoin de corriger cela manuellement.

IPA [ty n‿a pa bøzwɛ̃ də ʁezudʁ sø pʁɔblɛm a la mɛ̃ | ʒø pø ekʁiʁ œ̃ pʁɔgʁam ɛ̃fɔʁmatik puʁ t‿ede || > ty n‿a pa bøzwɛ̃ də kɔʁiʒe s°la manɥɛl°mɑ̃ ||]

2765

EN My father sometimes goes to work by taxi, and I go to work by bus.

FR Mon père va parfois travailler en taxi et je vais travailler en bus.

IPA [mɔ̃ pɛʁ va paʁfwa tʁavaje ʁ‿ɑ̃ taksi e ʒø vɛ tʁavaje ʁ‿ɑ̃ bys ‖]

2766

EN Olga's father is an oil tycoon, and goes to work BY helicopter and BY plane.

FR Le père d'Olga est un magnat du pétrole et il va travailler en hélicoptère et en avion.

IPA [lø pɛʁ d‿(...) e t‿œ̃ magna dy petʁɔl e il va tʁavaje ʁ‿ɑ̃ n‿elikɔptɛʁ e ɑ̃ n‿avjɔ̃ ‖]

2767

EN It's a two-hour drive to the airport BY car, but it's only forty (40) minutes by high-speed rail.

FR L'aéroport est à deux heures de route en voiture, mais il est à seulement quarante (40) minutes en train à grande vitesse.

IPA [l‿aeʁɔpɔʁ e a dø z‿œʁ dø ʁut ɑ̃ vwatyʁ | mɛ i l‿e a sœlᵊmɑ̃ kaʁɑ̃t (40) miny t‿ɑ̃ tʁɛ̃ a gʁɑ̃d vitɛs ‖]

2768

EN   I arrived ON the seven-o'clock (7:00) train.

FR   Je suis arrivé dans le train de sept heures (7 h).
IPA [ʒø sɥi aʁive dɑ̃ lø tʁɛ̃ dø sɛ t‿œʁ (7 h) ||]

2769

EN   The door's not broken, so it must have been opened
     by somebody with a key.

FR   La porte n'est pas cassée, alors elle doit avoir été
     ouverte par quelqu'un avec une clé.
IPA [la pɔʁt n‿e pa kase | alɔʁ ɛl dwa avwaʁ ete uvɛʁt
     paʁ kɛlkœ̃ avɛk yn kle ||]

2770

EN   My salary has increased from two thousand dollars
     ($2000) a month to twenty-five hundred ($2500). >
     My salary's increased BY five hundred dollars
     ($500). > My salary has increased from fifteen
     hundred fifty euros (€1550) a month to nineteen
     hundred (€1900). > My salary's increased BY three
     hundred fifty euro (€350).

FR   Mon salaire a augmenté de mille cinq cents cinquante
     euros (1550 euros) à mille neuf cents euros (1900
     euros) par mois. > Mon salaire a augmenté de trois
     cents cinquante euros (350 euros).
IPA [mɔ̃ salɛʁ a ogmɑ̃te dø mil sɛ̃k sɑ̃ sɛ̃kɑ̃t øʁo (1550
     øʁo) a mil nœf sɑ̃ z‿øʁo (1900 øʁo) paʁ mwa || >
     mɔ̃ salɛʁ a ogmɑ̃te dø tʁwa sɑ̃ sɛ̃kɑ̃t øʁo (350 øʁo)
     ||]

2771

EN I finished the race three (3) meters ahead of you. > I won the race BY three (3) meters.

FR J'ai terminé la course trois mètres devant toi. > J'ai gagné la course de trois mètres.

IPA [ʒ‿ɛ tɛʁmine la kuʁs tʁwa mɛtʁ dᵊvɑ̃ twa ‖ > ʒ‿ɛ gaɲe la kuʁs də tʁwa mɛtʁ ‖]

2772

EN Some American companies give college graduates a check FOR five thousand dollars ($5000) AS a signing bonus.

FR Certaines entreprises américaines donnent aux diplômés universitaires un chèque de cinq mille (5000) dollars à titre de prime de signature.

IPA [sɛʁtɛ n‿ɑ̃tʁᵊpʁiz ameʁiken dɔn o diplome z‿ynivɛʁsitɛʁ ɶ̃ ʃek də sɛ̃k mil (5000) dolaʁ a titʁ də pʁim də siɲatyʁ ‖]

2773

EN I wrote a check FOR five hundred dollars ($500) to the insurance company. > I wrote a check FOR four hundred euros (€400) to the insurance company.

FR J'ai écrit un chèque de quatre cents euros à la compagnie d'assurance.

IPA [ʒ‿ɛ ekʁi t‿ɶ̃ ʃek də katʁ sɑ̃ z‿øʁo a la kɔ̃paɲi d‿asyʁɑ̃s ‖]

2774

EN The company grew quickly due to a strong demand FOR its products.

FR La société s'est rapidement développée en raison d'une forte demande pour ses produits.

IPA [la sosjete s‿e ʁapid°mã dev°lope ã ʁɛzɔ̃ d‿yn fɔʁt d°mãd puʁ se pʁodɥi ‖]

2775

EN There's no need FOR impolite behavior.

FR Il n'y a pas besoin de se comporter impoliment.

IPA [il n‿i a pa bøzwɛ̃ dø sø kɔ̃pɔʁte ɛ̃polimã ‖]

2776

EN The advantage OF living alone is that you have more freedom.

FR L'avantage de vivre seul, c'est que tu as plus de liberté.

IPA [l‿avãtaʒ dø vivʁ sœl | sɛ kø ty a plys dø libɛʁte ‖]

2777

EN In fact, there are many advantages TO living alone.

FR En fait, il y a de nombreux avantages à vivre seul.

IPA [ã fɛ | i l‿i a dø nɔ̃bʁø z‿avãtaʒ a vivʁ sœl ‖]

2778

EN The authorities are still baffled by the cause of the explosion.

FR Les autorités sont toujours déconcertées par la cause de l'explosion.

IPA [le z‿otoʁite sɔ̃ tuʒuʁ dekɔ̃sɛʁte paʁ la koz dø l‿ɛksplozjɔ̃ ‖]

2779

EN I have all the photos OF my family in my cellphone.

FR J'ai toutes les photos de ma famille dans mon téléphone portable.

IPA [ʒ‿ɛ tut le foto dø ma famij dã mɔ̃ telefɔn pɔʁtabl ‖]

2780

EN I think we're lost. We need to get a map OF this city. — I'll search FOR an app.

FR Je pense que nous sommes perdus. Nous devons obtenir une carte de la ville. — Je vais rechercher une application.

IPA [ʒø pɑ̃s kø nu sɔm pɛʁdy ‖ nu dᵊvɔ̃ ɔptᵊni ʁ‿yn kaʁt dø la vil ‖ — ʒø vɛ ʁᵊʃɛʁʃe ʁ‿yn aplikasjɔ̃ ‖]

2781

EN There's always an increase IN the number OF traffic accidents around New Year's.

FR Il y a toujours une augmentation du nombre d'accidents de la route autour de la nouvelle année.

IPA [i l̩ i a tuʒu ʁ‿yn ogmãtasjɔ̃ dy nɔ̃bʁ d‿aksidã dø la ʁut otuʁ dø la nuvɛ l̩ane ‖]

2782

EN The last twenty (20) years has seen a tremendous decrease IN crime.

FR Les vingt dernières années ont vu une diminution considérable de la criminalité.

IPA [le vɛ̃ dɛʁnjɛ ʁ‿ane ɔ̃ vy yn diminysjɔ̃ kɔ̃sideʁabl dø la kʁiminalite ‖]

2783

EN It was a bad year for the company as it faced a huge drop IN sales.

FR Ce fut une mauvaise année pour l'entreprise, car elle a fait face à une énorme baisse des ventes.

IPA [sø fy t‿yn movɛz ane puʁ l̩ ãtʁ°pʁiz | kaʁ ɛ l̩a fe fas a yn enɔʁm bɛs de vãt ‖]

2784

EN Since the accident was my fault, I had to pay for the damage to the other car.

FR Comme l'accident était de ma faute, j'ai dû payer pour les dommages causés à l'autre voiture.

IPA [kɔm l̩aksidɑ̃ etɛ dø ma fot | ʒ̩ɛ dy peje puʁ le domaʒ koze a l̩otʁ vwatyʁ ‖]

2785

EN A lot of my friends are getting married this year. I've been getting lots of invitations TO wedding banquets.

FR Beaucoup de mes amis se marient cette année. Je reçois beaucoup d'invitations à des réceptions de mariage.

IPA [boku dø me z̩ami sø maʁi sɛt ane ‖ ʒø ʁ°swa boku d̩ẽvitasjɔ̃ a de ʁesɛpsjɔ̃ dø maʁjaʒ ‖]

2786

EN The scientists have been working ON a solution TO the problem FOR many years.

FR Les scientifiques travaillent sur une solution au problème depuis de nombreuses années.

IPA [le sjɑ̃tifik tʁavaj sy ʁ̩yn solysjɔ̃ o pʁoblɛm d°pɥi dø nɔ̃bʁø z̩ane ‖]

2787

EN I was very surprised BY her reaction TO my simple suggestion.

FR J'ai été très surpris (♀ surprise) par sa réaction à ma simple suggestion.

IPA [ʒ‿ɛ ete tʁɛ syʁpʁi (♀ syʁpʁiz) paʁ sa ʁeaksjɔ̃ a ma sɛ̃pl sygʒestjɔ̃ ‖]

2788

EN His attitude toward his job is so positive that he increases his sales every month.

FR Son attitude envers son travail est tellement positive qu'il augmente ses ventes chaque mois.

IPA [sɔ̃ n‿atityd ɑ̃vɛʁ sɔ̃ tʁavaj e tɛl°mɑ̃ pozitiv k‿il ogmɑ̃t se vɑ̃t ʃak mwa ‖]

2789

EN Do you have a good relationship WITH your parents?

FR As-tu une bonne relation avec tes parents?

IPA [a ty yn bɔn ʁ°lasjɔ̃ avɛk te paʁɑ̃ ‖]

2790

EN The police want to question a suspect in connection with the murder.

FR La police veut interroger un suspect dans le cadre de l'assassinat.

IPA [la polis vø ɛ̃teʁoʒe ʁ‿œ̃ syspɛ dɑ̃ lø kadʁ dø l‿asasina ‖]

2791

EN The police believe there's a connection between the two (2) murders, based on DNA evidence.

FR La police croit qu'il y a un lien entre les deux meurtres, basé sur des preuves d'ADN.

IPA [la polis kʁwa k‿il i a œ̃ ljɛ̃ ɑ̃tʁ le dø mœʁtʁ | baze syʁ de pʁœv (...) ‖]

2792

EN There are minor differences between many European languages.

FR Il existe des différences mineures entre de nombreuses langues européennes.

IPA [i l‿ɛgzist de difeʁɑ̃s minœʁ ɑ̃tʁ dø nɔ̃bʁøz lɑ̃g øʁopeɛn ‖]

2793

EN It was really kind of you to help me. I really appreciate it.

FR C'était vraiment gentil de ta part de m'aider. Je l'apprécie vraiment.

IPA [se ete vʁɛmɑ̃ ʒɑ̃ti dø ta paʁ dø m‿ede ‖ ʒø l‿apʁesi vʁɛmɑ̃ ‖]

2794

EN He donated half his wealth to charity, which was very generous of him.

FR Il a fait don de la moitié de sa fortune à la charité, ce qui était très généreux de sa part.

IPA [i l̩a fɛ dɔ̃ dø la mwatje dø sa fɔʁtyn a la ʃaʁite | sø ki etɛ tʁɛ ʒeneʁø dø sa paʁ ‖]

2795

EN Always be polite and nice to strangers. They might be the boss at your next job.

FR Sois toujours poli et gentil (♀polie et gentille) envers les étrangers. Ils pourraient être le patron à ton prochain travail.

IPA [swa tuʒuʁ poli e ʒãti (♀poli e ʒãtij) ãvɛʁ le z̩etʁãʒe ‖ il puʁe ɛtʁ lø patʁɔ̃ a tɔ̃ pʁoʃẽ tʁavaj ‖]

2796

EN Rashid is really angry about what his brother said.

FR Rashid est vraiment en colère à propos de ce que son frère a dit.

IPA [(...) e vʁemã t̩ã kolɛʁ a pʁopo dø sø kø sɔ̃ fʁɛʁ a di ‖]

2797

EN He's upset with him because he wants to put their parents in a nursing home.

FR Il est en colère contre lui parce qu'il veut mettre leurs parents dans une maison pour personnes âgées.

IPA [i le t ̪ɑ̃ kolɛʁ kɔ̃tʁ lɥi paʁs k il və mɛtʁ lœʁ paʁɑ̃ dɑ̃ z yn mɛzɔ̃ puʁ pɛʁsɔn aʒe ‖]

2798

EN In fact, his sister was even more furious when she heard it.

FR En fait, sa sœur était encore plus furieuse quand elle l'a appris.

IPA [ɑ̃ fɛ | sa sœʁ ete ɑ̃kɔʁ plys fyʁjøz kɑ̃ d ɛl l a apʁi ‖]

2799

EN Are you excited about going to Europe next week?

FR As-tu hâte d'aller en Europe la semaine prochaine?

IPA [a ty at d ale ɑ̃ øʁop la sᵊmɛn pʁɔʃɛn ‖]

2800

EN Actually, I'm upset about not getting invited to the most important conference.

FR En fait, je suis en colère de ne pas être invité (♀invitée) à la conférence la plus importante.

IPA [ɑ̃ fɛ | ʒø sɥi z ɑ̃ kolɛʁ dø nø pa z ɛtʁ ɛ̃vite (♀ɛ̃vite) a la kɔ̃feʁɑ̃s la ply s ɛ̃pɔʁtɑ̃t ‖]

GMS #2801 - 2900

2801

EN I'm sorry to hear that.

FR Je suis désolé d'entendre cela.

IPA [ʒø sɥi dezole d‿ɑ̃tɑ̃dʁ s°la ‖]

2802

EN Were you nervous about giving a speech in a foreign language?

FR Es-tu nerveux (♀nerveuse) à l'idée de donner un discours dans une langue étrangère?

IPA [ɛ ty nɛʁvø (♀nɛʁvøz) a l‿ide dø done ʁ‿œ̃ diskuʁ dɑ̃ z‿yn lɑ̃g etʁɑ̃ʒɛʁ ‖]

2803

EN I was very pleased with the audience's reception of my speech.

FR J'ai été très heureux de la réception de mon discours par l'audience.

IPA [ʒ‿ɛ ete tʁɛ z‿øʁø dø la ʁesɛpsjɔ̃ dø mɔ̃ diskuʁ paʁ l‿odjɑ̃s ‖]

2804

EN Everybody was shocked by the news on September eleventh (11th), two thousand one (2001).

FR Tout le monde a été choqué par les nouvelles du onze (11) septembre deux mille un (2001).

IPA [tu lø mɔ̃d a ete ʃoke paʁ le nuvɛl dy ɔ̃z (11) sɛptɑ̃bʁ dø mil œ̃ (2001) ‖]

2805

EN I was very impressed with his speech. He's an eloquent speaker.

FR J'ai été très impressionné par son discours. Il est un orateur éloquent.

IPA [ʒ‿ɛ ete tʁɛ z‿ɛ̃pʁesjone paʁ sɔ̃ diskuʁ ‖ i l‿e t‿œ̃ n‿oʁatœʁ elokɑ̃ ‖]

2806

EN I didn't enjoy my last job. When I got fed up with it, I asked to resign.

FR Je n'ai pas aimé mon dernier emploi. Quand j'en ai eu marre, j'ai demandé de démissionner.

IPA [ʒø n‿ɛ pa z‿eme mɔ̃ dɛʁnje ʁ‿ɑ̃plwa ‖ kɑ̃ ʒ‿ɑ̃ ɛ y maʁ | ʒ‿ɛ dᵊmɑ̃de dø demisjone ‖]

2807

EN I'm sorry about the mess. I'll clean it up later.

FR Je suis désolé pour le désordre. Je vais le nettoyer plus tard.

IPA [ʒø sɥi dezole puʁ lø dezɔʁdʁ || ʒø vɛ lø netwaje plys taʁ ||]

2808

EN I'm sorry for shouting at you yesterday. > I'm sorry I shouted at you yesterday. — Thank you for apologizing to me.

FR Je suis désolé d'avoir crié contre toi hier. > Je suis désolé d'avoir crié contre toi hier. — Merci de t'excuser.

IPA [ʒø sɥi dezole d‿avwaʁ kʁije kɔ̃tʁ twa jɛʁ || > ʒø sɥi dezole d‿avwaʁ kʁije kɔ̃tʁ twa jɛʁ || — mɛʁsi dø t‿ekskyze ||]

2809

EN I feel sorry for the loser. > I pity the loser.

FR Je me sens désolé pour le perdant. > J'ai pitié pour le perdant.

IPA [ʒø mø sɑ̃s dezole puʁ lø pɛʁdɑ̃ || > ʒ‿e pitje puʁ lø pɛʁdɑ̃ ||]

2810

EN Are you scared of spiders? > Are you afraid of spiders? > Are spiders scary? > Are spiders frightening?

FR As-tu peur des araignées? > As-tu peur des araignées? > Les araignées t'effraient-elles? > Les araignées sont-elles effrayantes?

IPA [a ty pøʁ de z‿aʁɛɲe ‖ > a ty pøʁ de z‿aʁɛɲe ‖ > le z‿aʁɛɲe t‿efʁɛ t‿el ‖ > le z‿aʁɛɲe sɔ̃ t‿el efʁɛjɑ̃t ‖]

2811

EN Do you fear spiders? > Do spiders scare you? > Do spiders frighten you?

FR Crains-tu les araignées? > Les araignées t'effraient-elles? > Est-ce que les araignées te font peur?

IPA [kʁɛ̃ ty le z‿aʁɛɲe ‖ > le z‿aʁɛɲe t‿efʁɛ t‿el ‖ > ɛsᵊ kø le z‿aʁɛɲe tø fɔ̃ pøʁ ‖]

2812

EN I'm terrified of spiders. > Spiders terrify me.

FR Je suis terrifié (♀terrifiée) des araignées. > Les araignées me terrifient.

IPA [ʒø sɥi teʁifje (♀teʁifje) de z‿aʁɛɲe ‖ > le z‿aʁɛɲe mø teʁifi ‖]

2813

EN The giant spider in The Hobbit scared me to death!

FR L'araignée géante dans Le Hobbit m'a effrayé à mort!
IPA [l‿aʁɛɲe ʒeãt dã lø hobbit m‿a efʁɛje a mɔʁ ‖]

2814

EN Some children feel proud of their parents, while others are ashamed of them.

FR Certains enfants se sentent fiers de leurs parents tandis que d'autres ont honte d'eux.
IPA [sɛʁtɛ̃ z‿ãfã sø sãt fjeʁ dø lœʁ paʁã tandis kø dot ʁ‿ɔ̃ ɔ̃t d‿ø ‖]

2815

EN Many children make their parents proud, while some make their parents ashamed.

FR Beaucoup d'enfants rendent leurs parents fiers, tandis que d'autres rendent leurs parents honteux.
IPA [boku d‿ãfã ʁãd lœʁ paʁã fjeʁ | tandis kø dotʁ ʁãd lœʁ paʁã ɔ̃tø ‖]

2816

EN Don't be jealous or envious of that popular girl in school.

FR Ne sois pas jalouse ou envieuse de cette fille populaire à l'école.
IPA [nø swa pa ʒaluz u ãvjøz dø sɛt fij popyleʁ a l‿ekɔl ‖]

2817

EN The police remained suspicious of the suspect's motives.

FR La police demeurait méfiante quant aux motifs du suspect.

IPA [la polis dᵊmœʁɛ mefjɑ̃t kɑ̃ o motif dy syspɛ ‖]

2818

EN The audience was critical of the music performance.

FR Le public a critiqué la performance musicale.

IPA [lø pyblik a kʁitike la pɛʁfɔʁmɑ̃s myzikal ‖]

2819

EN Many countries are not tolerant of foreigners.

FR Beaucoup de pays ne sont pas tolérants envers les étrangers.

IPA [boku dø pei nø sɔ̃ pa toleʁɑ̃ z‿ɑ̃vɛʁ le z‿etʁɑ̃ʒe ‖]

2820

EN Are you aware of the seriousness of this crime?

FR Es-tu conscient de la gravité de ce crime?

IPA [ɛ ty kɔ̃sjɑ̃ dø la gʁavite dø sø kʁim ‖]

2821

EN I wasn't conscious during the operation. The doctors had given me anesthesia.

FR Je n'étais pas conscient (♀consciente) pendant l'opération. Les médecins m'ont anesthésié (♀anesthésiée).

IPA [ʒø n‿etɛ pa kɔ̃sjɑ̃ (♀kɔ̃sjɑ̃t) pɑ̃dɑ̃ l‿opeʁasjɔ̃ || le mɛdsɛ̃ m‿ɔ̃ anɛstezje (♀anɛstezje) ||]

2822

EN I'm fully confident that you're capable of passing the exam.

FR Je suis pleinement confiant (♀confiante) du fait que tu sois capable de passer l'examen.

IPA [ʒø sɥi plɛnᵊmɑ̃ kɔ̃fjɑ̃ (kɔ̃fjɑ̃t) dy fɛ kø ty swa kapabl dø pase l‿ɛgzamɛ̃ ||]

2823

EN The paper I wrote for class was full of obvious mistakes.

FR L'article que j'ai écrit pour la classe était plein d'erreurs évidentes.

IPA [l‿aʁtikl kø ʒ‿ɛ ekʁi puʁ la klas etɛ plɛ̃ d‿ɛʁœʁ evidɑ̃t ||]

2824

EN He's late again. It's typical of him to keep everybody waiting.

FR Il est encore en retard. C'est typique de lui de faire attendre tout le monde.

IPA [i l̩e ɑ̃kɔʁ ɑ̃ ʁ°taʁ || sɛ tipik dø lɥi dø fɛʁ atɑ̃dʁ tu lø mɔ̃d ||]

2825

EN I'm tired of eating the same food every day. Let's try something different.

FR Je suis fatigué (♀ fatiguée) de manger la même nourriture tous les jours. Essayons quelque chose de différent.

IPA [ʒø sɥi fatige (♀ fatige) dø mɑ̃ʒe la mɛm nuʁityʁ tu le ʒuʁ || esejɔ̃ kɛlk ʃoz dø difeʁɑ̃ ||]

2826

EN She told me she's arriving tonight. — Are you sure of it?

FR Elle m'a dit qu'elle arrivait ce soir. — En es-tu bien sûr?

IPA [ɛl m̩a di k̩ɛl aʁive sø swaʁ || — ɑ̃ ɛ ty bjɛ̃ syʁ ||]

2827

EN Shakira got married to an American, and now she's married with two (2) children.

FR Shakira s'est mariée à un Américain, et maintenant elle est mariée et a deux enfants.

IPA [(...) s̬e maʁje a œ̃ n̪ameʁikɛ̃ | e mɛ̃t°nã t̬ɛ l̪e maʁje e a dø z̬ãfã ||]

2828

EN The customs in their country are similar to ours.

FR Les coutumes de leur pays sont semblables aux nôtres.

IPA [le kutym dø lœʁ pei sɔ̃ sãblabl o notʁ ||]

2829

EN The film was completely different from what I'd been expecting.

FR Le film était complètement différent de ce à quoi je m'attendais.

IPA [lø film ete kɔ̃plɛt°mã difeʁã dø sø a kwa ʒø m̪atãdɛ ||]

2830

EN If you're dependent on your parents, it means you still need them for money. If not, then you're financially independent.

FR Si tu es dépendant (♀ dépendante) de tes parents, cela signifie que tu as encore besoin d'eux pour de l'argent. Sinon, tu es financièrement indépendant (♀ indépendante).

IPA [si ty ɛ depɑ̃dɑ̃ (♀ depɑ̃dɑ̃t) dø te paʁɑ̃ | sᵊla siɲifi kø ty a ɑ̃kɔʁ bøzwɛ̃ d̪ø puʁ dø l̪aʁʒɑ̃ || sinɔ̃ | ty ɛ finɑ̃sjɛʁᵊmɑ̃ t̪ɛ̃depɑ̃dɑ̃ (♀ ɛ̃depɑ̃dɑ̃t) ||]

2831

EN When we got to the Eiffel Tower, it was crowded with tourists.

FR Quand nous sommes arrivés à la Tour Eiffel, elle était envahie par les touristes.

IPA [kɑ̃ nu sɔm aʁive a la tuʁ eiffel | ɛ l̪ete ɑ̃vai paʁ le tuʁist ||]

2832

EN Italy is famous for its art, cuisine, architecture, history, and fashion. It's rich in culture.

FR L'Italie est célèbre pour son art, sa cuisine, son architecture, son histoire, et sa mode. Elle est riche en culture.

IPA [l italie e selɛbʁ puʁ sɔ̃ n̪aʁ | sa kɥizin | sɔ̃ n̪aʁʃitɛktyʁ | sɔ̃ n̪istwaʁ | e sa mɔd || ɛ l̪e ʁiʃ ɑ̃ kyltyʁ ||]

2827

EN Shakira got married to an American, and now she's married with two (2) children.

FR Shakira s'est mariée à un Américain, et maintenant elle est mariée et a deux enfants.

IPA [(...) s‿e maʁje a œ̃ n‿ameʁikɛ̃ | e mɛ̃t°nɑ̃ t‿ɛ l‿e maʁje e a dø z‿ɑ̃fɑ̃ ‖]

2828

EN The customs in their country are similar to ours.

FR Les coutumes de leur pays sont semblables aux nôtres.

IPA [le kutym dø lœʁ pei sɔ̃ sɑ̃blabl o notʁ ‖]

2829

EN The film was completely different from what I'd been expecting.

FR Le film était complètement différent de ce à quoi je m'attendais.

IPA [lø film ete kɔ̃plɛt°mɑ̃ difeʁɑ̃ dø sø a kwa ʒø m‿atɑ̃dɛ ‖]

2830

EN If you're dependent on your parents, it means you still need them for money. If not, then you're financially independent.

FR Si tu es dépendant (♀dépendante) de tes parents, cela signifie que tu as encore besoin d'eux pour de l'argent. Sinon, tu es financièrement indépendant (♀indépendante).

IPA [si ty ɛ depãdã (♀depãdãt) dø te paʁã | sᵊla siɲifi kø ty a ãkɔʁ bøzwɛ̃ d̪ø puʁ dø l̪aʁʒã || sinɔ̃ | ty ɛ finãsjɛʁᵊmã t̪ɛ̃depãdã (♀ɛ̃depãdãt) ||]

2831

EN When we got to the Eiffel Tower, it was crowded with tourists.

FR Quand nous sommes arrivés à la Tour Eiffel, elle était envahie par les touristes.

IPA [kã nu sɔm aʁive a la tuʁ eiffel | ɛ l̪ete ãvai paʁ le tuʁist ||]

2832

EN Italy is famous for its art, cuisine, architecture, history, and fashion. It's rich in culture.

FR L'Italie est célèbre pour son art, sa cuisine, son architecture, son histoire, et sa mode. Elle est riche en culture.

IPA [l italie e selɛbʁ puʁ sɔ̃ n̪aʁ | sa kɥizin | sɔ̃ n̪aʁʃitɛktyʁ | sɔ̃ n̪istwaʁ | e sa mɔd || ɛ l̪e ʁiʃ ã kyltyʁ ||]

2833

EN The police are still trying to determine who was responsible for the murders.

FR La police tente toujours de déterminer qui a été responsable de ces meurtres.

IPA [la polis tɑ̃t tuʒuʁ də detɛʁmine ki a ete ʁɛspɔ̃sabl də se mœʁtʁ ‖]

2834

EN Have you responded to your boss's email?

FR As-tu répondu au courriel de ton patron?

IPA [a ty ʁepɔ̃dy o kuʁjɛl də tɔ̃ patʁɔ̃ ‖]

2835

EN I can't understand this, can you explain it to me?

FR Je ne comprends pas ça, peux-tu me l'expliquer?

IPA [ʒø nø kɔ̃pʁɑ̃ pa sa | pø ty mø l‿eksplike ‖]

2836

EN Let me describe to you how it happened.

FR Permets-moi de te décrire ce qui s'est passé.

IPA [pɛʁmɛ mwa də tø dekʁiʁ sø ki s‿e pase ‖]

2837

EN His lawyer refused to answer the policeman's question.

FR Son avocat a refusé de répondre à la question du policier.

IPA [sɔ̃ n‿avoka a ʁ°fyze dø ʁepɔ̃dʁ a la kɛstjɔ̃ dy polisje ‖]

2838

EN Don't worry, they think you're funny. They weren't laughing at you, they were laughing at your joke.

FR Ne t'inquiète pas, ils pensent que tu es drôle. Ils ne riaient pas de toi, ils riaient de ta blague.

IPA [nø t‿ɛ̃kjɛt pa | il pɑ̃s kø ty ɛ dʁol ‖ il nø ʁjɛ pa dø twa | il ʁjɛ dø ta blag ‖]

2839

EN The suspect was shouting at the police very loudly.

FR Le suspect criait très fort contre la police.

IPA [lø syspɛ kʁijɛ tʁɛ fɔʁ kɔ̃tʁ la polis ‖]

2840

EN The police pointed their guns at the suspect and told him to lie on the ground.

FR Les policiers ont pointé leurs armes sur le suspect et lui ont dit de s'allonger sur le sol.

IPA [le polisje ɔ̃ pwɛ̃te lœ ʁ‿aʁm syʁ lø syspɛ e lɥi ɔ̃ di dø s‿alɔ̃ʒe syʁ lø sɔl ‖]

2841

EN But the man reached for his pockets, and that's when the police started shooting at him.

FR Mais l'homme a mis la main dans ses poches, et c'est à ce moment que la police a commencé à tirer sur lui.

IPA [mɛ lˌɔm a mi la mɛ̃ dɑ̃ se pɔʃ | e sɛ a sø momɑ̃ kø la polis a komɑ̃se a tiʁe syʁ lɥi ‖]

2842

EN And then onlookers started shouting to each other.

FR Puis les spectateurs ont commencé à s'engueuler.

IPA [pɥi le spɛktatœʁ ɔ̃ komɑ̃se a sˌɑ̃gøle ‖]

2843

EN Somebody threw a shoe at the politician.

FR Quelqu'un a jeté une chaussure au politicien.

IPA [kɛlkœ̃ nˌa ʒˀte yn ʃosyʁ o politisjɛ̃ ‖]

2844

EN I asked her to throw the keys to me from the window, but when they hit the ground, they fell down a drain.

FR Je lui ai demandé de me lancer les clés par la fenêtre, mais quand elles ont touché le sol, elles sont tombées dans un égout.

IPA [ʒø lɥi ɛ dˀmɑ̃de dø mø lɑ̃se le kle paʁ la fˀnɛtʁ | mɛ kɑ̃ dˌɛ lˌɔ̃ tuʃe lø sɔl | ɛl sɔ̃ tɔ̃be dɑ̃ zˌœ̃ nˌegu ‖]

2845

EN We had a morning meeting and a discussion about what we should do.

FR Nous avons eu une réunion matinale et une discussion à propos de ce que nous devrions faire.

IPA [nu z‿avɔ̃ y yn ʁeynjɔ̃ matinal e yn diskysjɔ̃ a pʁopo dø sø kø nu dᵊvʁijɔ̃ fɛʁ ‖]

2846

EN If you're worried about it, don't just sit there, do something about it.

FR Si tu es inquiet (♀inquiète) à ce sujet, ne restes pas là, fais quelque chose à ce sujet.

IPA [si ty ɛ ɛ̃kjɛ (♀ɛ̃kjɛt) a sø syʒɛ | nø ʁɛst pa la | fɛ kɛlk ʃoz a sø syʒɛ ‖]

2847

EN He's so selfish that he doesn't care about anybody else.

FR Il est tellement égoïste qu'il ne se soucie pas de personne d'autre.

IPA [i l‿e tɛlᵊmɑ̃ t‿egoist k‿il nø sø susi pa dø pɛʁsɔn d‿otʁ ‖]

2848

EN You're an independent person and can make your own decisions. I don't care what you do.

FR Tu es une personne indépendante et tu peux prendre tes propres décisions. Je me fiche de ce que tu fais.

IPA [ty ɛ yn pɛʁsɔn ɛ̃depɑ̃dɑ̃t e ty pø pʁɑ̃dʁ te pʁɔpʁ desizjɔ̃ || ʒə mø fiʃ dø sø kø ty fɛ ||]

2849

EN Would you care for a hot drink or some hot soup?

FR Voudrais-tu une boisson chaude ou de la soupe chaude?

IPA [vudʁɛ ty yn bwasɔ̃ ʃod u dø la sup ʃod ||]

2850

EN My grandfather is already ninety (90) years old and needs somebody to care for him, so we take turns looking after him.

FR Mon grand-père a déjà quatre-vingt-dix ans et a besoin de quelqu'un pour s'occuper de lui. Donc, nous nous relayons pour prendre soin de lui.

IPA [mɔ̃ gʁɑ̃pɛʁ a deʒa katʁᵊvɛ̃di z̩ɑ̃ e a bøzwɛ̃ dø kɛlkœ̃ puʁ s̩okype dø lɥi || dɔ̃k | nu nu ʁᵊlejɔ̃ puʁ pʁɑ̃dʁ swɛ̃ dø lɥi ||]

2851

EN Vikram and Lakshmi both take turns taking care of their elderly parents.

FR Vikram et Lakshmi prennent tous deux soin de leurs parents âgés à tour de rôle.

IPA [(...) e (...) pʁɛn tu dø swɛ̃ dø lœʁ paʁɑ̃ aʒe a tuʁ dø ʁol ||]

2852

EN I'll take care of all the travel arrangements so you don't need to worry about anything.

FR Je vais m'occuper de tous les arrangements de voyage pour que tu n'aies à te soucier de rien.

IPA [ʒø vɛ m‿okype dø tu le z‿aʁɑ̃ʒ°mɑ̃ dø vwajaʒ puʁ kø ty n‿ɛ a tø susje dø ʁjɛ̃ ||]

2853

EN Why don't you apply FOR this job? — I'd like to apply TO university instead.

FR Pourquoi ne postules-tu pas pour ce poste? — Je préférerais plutôt postuler à l'université.

IPA [puʁkwa nø pɔstyl ty pa puʁ sø pɔst || — ʒø pʁefeʁ°ʁɛ plyto pɔstyle a l‿ynivɛʁsite ||]

2854

EN You should leave FOR work earlier so you get there on time.

FR Tu devrais partir pour le travail plus tôt afin d'y être à temps.

IPA [ty dᵊvʁɛ paʁtiʁ puʁ lø tʁavaj plys to t̯afɛ̃ d̯i ɛtʁ a tɑ̃ ‖]

2855

EN What kind of person have you dreamed of becoming?

FR Quel genre de personne as-tu déjà rêvé de devenir?

IPA [kɛl ʒɑ̃ʁ dø pɛʁsɔn a ty deʒa ʁeve dø dᵊvᵊniʁ ‖]

2856

EN My father heard from an old friend in high school last night.

FR Mon père a eu des nouvelles d'un vieil ami de l'école secondaire la nuit dernière. > Mon père a eu des nouvelles d'un vieil ami du lycée la nuit dernière.

IPA [mɔ̃ pɛʁ a y de nuvɛl d̯œ̃ vjɛj l̩ami dø l̩ekɔl sᵊgɔ̃dɛʁ la nɥi dɛʁnjɛʁ > mɔ̃ pɛʁ a y de nuvɛl d̯œ̃ vjɛj l̩ami dø lise la nɥi dɛʁnjɛʁ ‖]

2857

EN You remind me of my mother's kindness.

FR Tu me rappelles la bonté de ma mère.

IPA [ty mø ʁapɛl la bɔ̃te dø ma mɛʁ ‖]

2858

EN   That's a good idea. Why didn't I think of that?

FR   C'est une bonne idée. Pourquoi n'y ai-je pas pensé?

IPA [sɛ t‿yn bɔn ide || puʁkwa n‿i ɛ ʒø pa pɑ̃se ||]

2859

EN   I'm glad you reminded me about the meeting,
     because I'd totally forgotten about it.

FR   Je suis heureux que tu m'aies parlé de la réunion
     parce que j'avais totalement oublié.

IPA [ʒø sɥi øʁø kø ty m‿ɛ paʁle dø la ʁeynjɔ̃ paʁs kø
     ʒ‿avɛ totalᵊmɑ̃ t‿ublije ||]

2860

EN   I'd like to complain to the manager about your
     service.

FR   J'aimerais porter plainte auprès du directeur de ton
     service.

IPA [ʒ‿emᵊʁɛ pɔʁte plɛ̃t opʁɛ dy diʁektœʁ dø tɔ̃ sɛʁvis ||]

2861

EN   Samiya was complaining of a pain in her tummy, so
     we advised her to see a doctor as soon as possible.

FR   Samiya se plaignait d'une douleur au ventre, alors
     nous lui avons conseillé de consulter un médecin dès
     que possible.

IPA [samija sø plɛɲɛ d‿yn dulœʁ o vɑ̃tʁ | alɔʁ nu lɥi avɔ̃
     kɔ̃seje dø kɔ̃sylte ʁ‿œ̃ medsɛ̃ dɛ kø posibl ||]

2862

EN I knew he was strange because everybody had warned me about him.

FR Je savais qu'il était étrange, car tout le monde m'avait mis en garde contre lui.

IPA [ʒø savɛ k‿il etɛ etʁɑ̃ʒ | kaʁ tu lø mɔ̃d m‿avɛ mi z‿ɑ̃ gaʁd kɔ̃tʁ lɥi ‖]

2863

EN Scientists continue to warn us about the effects of global warming.

FR Les scientifiques continuent de nous avertir des effets du réchauffement climatique.

IPA [le sjɑ̃tifik kɔ̃tiny dø nu z‿avɛʁtiʁ de z‿efɛ dy ʁeʃofmɑ̃ klimatik ‖]

2864

EN She accused me of being selfish.

FR Elle m'a accusé d'être égoïste.

IPA [ɛl m‿a akyze d‿ɛtʁ egoist ‖]

2865

EN After discovering he had been wrongly accused of murder, the authorities let him out of prison.

FR Après avoir découvert qu'il avait été injustement accusé de meurtre, les autorités lui ont permis de sortir de prison.

IPA [apʁɛ z‿avwaʁ dekuveʁ k‿il avɛ ete ɛ̃ʒystˢmɑ̃ t‿akyze də mœʁtʁ | le z‿otoʁite lɥi ɔ̃ pɛʁmi də sɔʁtiʁ də pʁizɔ̃ ||]

2866

EN Some students were suspected of cheating on the exam.

FR On soupçonne certains élèves d'avoir triché durant l'examen.

IPA [ɔ̃ supsɔn sɛʁtɛ̃ z‿elɛv d‿avwaʁ tʁiʃe dyʁɑ̃ l‿ɛgzamɛ̃ ||]

2867

EN His parents don't approve of what he does, but they can't stop him.

FR Ses parents n'approuvent pas ce qu'il fait, mais ils ne peuvent pas l'arrêter.

IPA [se paʁɑ̃ n‿apʁuv pa sø k‿il fɛ | mɛ il nø pœv pa l‿aʁete ||]

2868

EN The famous actor died OF a heart attack when he was only fifty-one (51).

FR Le célèbre acteur est mort d'une crise cardiaque alors qu'il n'avait que cinquante et un (51) ans.

IPA [lø selɛbʁ aktœʁ e mɔʁ d‿yn kʁiz kaʁdjak alɔʁ k‿il n‿avɛ kø sɛ̃kɑ̃t e œ̃ (51) ɑ̃ ||]

2869

EN He died FROM heart disease.

FR Il est mort d'une maladie cardiaque.

IPA [i l‿e mɔʁ d‿yn maladi kaʁdjak ||]

2870

EN Our meal consisted of seven (7) courses.

FR Notre repas était composé de sept services.

IPA [nɔtʁ ʁ°pa ete kɔ̃poze dø sɛt sɛʁvis ||]

2871

EN Water consists of hydrogen oxide.

FR L'eau est constituée de oxyde d'hydrogène.

IPA [l‿o e kɔ̃stitɥe dø ɔksid d‿idʁoʒɛn ||]

2872

EN   Cake consists mainly of sugar, flour, and butter.

FR   Le gâteau se compose principalement de sucre, de farine et de beurre.

IPA   [lø gato sø kɔ̃poz pʁɛsipalˀmɑ̃ dø sykʁ | dø faʁin e dø bœʁ ||]

2873

EN   I didn't have enough money to pay for the meal.

FR   Je n'avais pas assez d'argent pour payer le repas.

IPA   [ʒø n‿avɛ pa z‿ase d‿aʁʒɑ̃ puʁ peje lø ʁˀpa ||]

2874

EN   I didn't have enough money to pay the rent.

FR   Je n'avais pas assez d'argent pour payer le loyer.

IPA   [ʒø n‿avɛ pa z‿ase d‿aʁʒɑ̃ puʁ peje lø lwaje ||]

2875

EN   When you went to the movies with your boyfriend, did he pay for the tickets?

FR   Quand tu es allée au cinéma avec ton copain, a-t-il payé pour les billets?

IPA   [kɑ̃ ty ɛ ale o sinema avɛk tɔ̃ kopɛ̃ | a t‿il peje puʁ le bijɛ ||]

FR Quand tu es allée au cinéma avec ton copain, a-t-il
    payé pour les billets?
IPA [kã ty ɛ ale o sinema avɛk tɔ̃ kopɛ̃ | a t‿il peje puʁ le
    bijɛ ||]

2876

EN I couldn't pay the minimum amount on my credit card bill.

FR Je ne pouvais pas payer le montant minimum sur la facture de ma carte de crédit.

IPA [ʒø nø puvɛ pa peje lø mɔ̃tɑ̃ minimɔm syʁ la faktyʁ dø ma kaʁt dø kʁedi ‖]

2877

EN After doing a homestay in England, I thanked my hosts for their kind hospitality.

FR Après avoir fait un séjour en Angleterre, j'ai remercié mes hôtes pour leur généreuse hospitalité.

IPA [apʁɛ z‿avwaʁ fɛ t‿œ̃ seʒuʁ ɑ̃ n‿ɑ̃gløtɛʁ | ʒ‿ɛ ʁᵊmɛʁsje me z‿ot puʁ lœʁ ʒeneʁøz ɔspitalite ‖]

2878

EN It's difficult to forgive a murderer for his crimes.

FR Il est difficile de pardonner à un meurtrier pour ses crimes.

IPA [i l‿e difisil dø paʁdone a œ̃ mœʁtʁije puʁ se kʁim ‖]

2879

EN No matter how much a murderer apologizes for what he's done, it doesn't bring the victims back.

FR Peu importe combien de fois un meurtrier s'excuse pour ce qu'il a fait, ça ne ramène pas les victimes à la vie.

IPA [pø ɛ̃pɔʁt kɔ̃bjɛ̃ də fwa œ̃ mœʁtʁije s‿ɛkskyz puʁ sø k‿il a fɛ | sa nø ʁamɛn pa le viktim a la vi ‖]

2880

EN The misunderstanding was my fault, so I apologized. > I apologized for the misunderstanding.

FR Le malentendu était de ma faute, alors je me suis excusé (♀excusée). > Je me suis excusé (♀excusée) pour le malentendu.

IPA [lø malɑ̃tɑ̃dy etɛ də ma fot | alɔʁ ʒø mø sɥi ɛkskyze (♀ɛkskyze) ‖ > ʒø mø sɥi ɛkskyze (♀ɛkskyze) puʁ lø malɑ̃tɑ̃dy ‖]

2881

EN Don't blame your behavior on your sister. You owe her an apology.

FR Ne blâme pas ta soeur pour ton comportement. Tu lui dois des excuses.

IPA [nø blam pa ta sœʁ puʁ tɔ̃ kɔ̃pɔʁt°mɑ̃ ‖ ty lɥi dwa de z‿ɛkskyz ‖]

2882

EN She always says everything is my fault. > She always blames me for everything.

FR Elle dit toujours que tout est de ma faute. > Elle me reproche toujours tout.

IPA [ɛl di tuʒuʁ kə tu t̪e dø ma fot ‖ > ɛl mø ʁᵊpʁɔʃ tuʒuʁ tu ‖]

2883

EN Do you blame the government for the economic crisis? > I think everybody wants to blame the government for the economic crisis.

FR Blâmes-tu le gouvernement pour la crise économique? > Je pense que tout le monde veut blâmer le gouvernement pour la crise économique.

IPA [blam ty lø guvɛʁnᵊmã puʁ la kʁiz ekonomik ‖ > ʒø pãs kø tu lø mɔ̃d vø blame lø guvɛʁnᵊmã puʁ la kʁiz ekonomik ‖]

2884

EN The number of people suffering from heart disease has increased. > The number of heart disease sufferers has increased.

FR Le nombre de personnes souffrant d'une maladie cardiaque a augmenté. > Le nombre de personnes souffrant de maladies du cœur a augmenté.

IPA [lø nɔ̃bʁ dø pɛʁsɔn sufʁã d̪yn maladi kaʁdjak a ogmãte ‖ > lø nɔ̃bʁ dø pɛʁsɔn sufʁã dø maladi dy kœʁ a ogmãte ‖]

2885

EN I think the increase in violent crime is the fault of television. > I blame the increase in violent crime on television.

FR Je pense que l'augmentation de crimes violents est la faute de la télévision. > Je blâme la télévision pour l'augmentation des crimes violents.

IPA [ʒø pɑ̃s kø l‿oɡmɑ̃tasjɔ̃ dø kʁim vjolɑ̃ z‿e la fot dø la televizjɔ̃ || > ʒø blam la televizjɔ̃ puʁ l‿oɡmɑ̃tasjɔ̃ de kʁim vjolɑ̃ ||]

2886

EN I think the increase in suicides recently is to be blamed on the economy.

FR Je pense que l'économie doit être blâmée pour l'augmentation récente des suicides.

IPA [ʒø pɑ̃s kø l‿ekonomi dwa ɛtʁ blame puʁ l‿oɡmɑ̃tasjɔ̃ ʁesɑ̃t de sɥisid ||]

2887

EN My mother suffers from bad headaches.

FR Ma mère souffre de terribles maux de tête.

IPA [ma mɛʁ sufʁ dø teʁibl mo dø tɛt ||]

2888

EN Sunblock protects the skin from the harmful effects of the sun's ultraviolet (UV) rays.

FR L'écran solaire protège la peau contre les effets nocifs des rayons ultraviolets du soleil.

IPA [l̩ekʁɑ̃ soleʁ pʁoteʒ la po kɔ̃tʁ le z̩ efɛ nosif de ʁejɔ̃ yl°tʁavjolɛ dy solɛj ||]

2889

EN The rock star needs a bodyguard to protect him from crazy fans.

FR L'étoile du rock a besoin d'un garde du corps pour la protéger des admirateurs fous.

IPA [l̩etwal dy ʁɔk a bøzwɛ̃ d̩œ̃ gaʁd dy kɔʁ puʁ la pʁoteʒe de z̩admiʁatœʁ fu ||]

2890

EN I don't know when I'll get home, as it depends on traffic conditions.

FR Je ne sais pas quand je vais rentrer à la maison, car ça dépend des conditions de route.

IPA [ʒø nø sɛ pa kɑ̃ ʒø vɛ ʁɑ̃tʁe a la mɛzɔ̃ | kaʁ sa depɑ̃ de kɔ̃disjɔ̃ dø ʁut ||]

2891

EN Everybody relies on her because she always keeps her promises.

FR Tout le monde se fie à elle parce qu'elle tient toujours ses promesses.

IPA [tu lø mɔ̃d sø fi a ɛl paʁs k‿ɛl tjɛ̃ tuʒuʁ se pʁomɛs ‖]

2892

EN His salary is so low that he doesn't have enough to live on.

FR Son salaire est si bas qu'il n'a pas assez pour vivre.

IPA [sɔ̃ salɛʁ e si ba k‿il n‿a pa z‿ase puʁ vivʁ ‖]

2893

EN She is a very simple woman, and lives on just bread and eggs.

FR Elle est une femme très simple et vit avec seulement du pain et des œufs.

IPA [ɛ l‿e t‿yn fam tʁɛ sɛ̃pl e vi avɛk seulement dy pɛ̃ e de z‿ø ‖]

2894

EN We held a party to congratulate my sister on being admitted to law school.

FR Nous avons organisé une fête pour féliciter ma sœur pour son admission à l'école de droit.

IPA [nu z‿avɔ̃ ɔʁganize yn fɛt puʁ felisite ma sœʁ puʁ sɔ̃ n‿admisjɔ̃ a l‿ekɔl dø dʁwa ‖]

2895

EN I congratulated my brother for winning the tennis tournament.

FR J'ai félicité mon frère pour avoir remporté le tournoi de tennis.

IPA [ʒ‿ɛ felisite mɔ̃ fʁɛʁ pu ʁ‿avwaʁ ʁɑ̃pɔʁte lø tuʁnwa dø tenis ‖]

2896

EN You know you can rely on me if you ever need any help.

FR Tu sais que tu peux compter sur moi si tu as besoin d'aide.

IPA [ty sɛ kø ty pø kɔ̃te syʁ mwa si ty a bøzwɛ̃ d‿ɛd ‖]

2897

EN It's terrible that some people are dying of hunger while others eat too much.

FR C'est terrible que certaines personnes meurent de faim tandis que d'autres mangent trop.

IPA [sɛ tɛʁibl kø sɛʁtɛn pɛʁsɔn mœʁ dø fɛ̃ tandis kø dotʁ mɑ̃ʒ tʁo ‖]

2898

EN The accident was my fault, so I had to pay for the repairs.

FR L'accident était de ma faute, alors j'ai dû payer pour les réparations.

IPA [l̩ aksidɑ̃ ete dø ma fot | alɔʁ ʒ ɛ dy peje puʁ le ʁepaʁasjɔ̃ ‖]

2899

EN Her speech in English was impeccable, so I complimented her afterwards.

FR Son discours en anglais était impeccable, alors je l'ai félicitée après.

IPA [sɔ̃ disku ʁ ɑ̃ n ɑ̃glɛ ete ɛ̃pekabl | alɔʁ ʒø l ɛ felisite apʁɛ ‖]

2900

EN Since she doesn't have a job, she depends on her parents for money.

FR Comme elle n'a pas de travail, elle dépend de ses parents côté argent.

IPA [kɔm ɛl n a pa dø tʁavaj | ɛl depɑ̃ dø se paʁɑ̃ kote aʁʒɑ̃ ‖]

GMS #2901 - 3000

2901

EN They wore warm clothes to protect themselves from the cold.

FR Ils portaient des vêtements chauds pour se protéger du froid.

IPA [il pɔʁtɛ de vɛt°mɑ̃ ʃo puʁ sø pʁoteʒe dy fʁwa ‖]

2902

EN All their sweaters and blankets were not enough to prevent them from getting sick though.

FR Tous les chandails et couvertures n'ont pas suffi à les empêcher de tomber malade.

IPA [tu le ʃɑ̃daj e kuvɛʁtyʁ n‿ɔ̃ pa syfi a le ɑ̃peʃe dø tɔ̃be malad ‖]

2903

EN I believe in saying what I think.

FR Je crois en l'idée de dire ce que je pense.

IPA [ʒø kʁwa z‿ɑ̃ l‿ide dø diʁ sø kø ʒø pɑ̃s ‖]

2904

EN Karim is a lawyer who specializes in company law.

FR Karim est un avocat spécialisé dans le droit des entreprises.

IPA [(...) e t‿œ̃ n‿avoka spesjalize dɑ̃ lø dʁwa de z‿ɑ̃tʁ°pʁiz ‖]

2905

EN I hope you succeed in finding the job you want.

FR J'espère que tu réussiras à trouver l'emploi que tu désires.

IPA [ʒ‿ɛspɛʁ kø ty ʁeysiʁa a tʁuve l‿ɑ̃plwa kø ty deziʁ ‖]

2906

EN He lost control of his car and crashed it into the highway barrier.

FR Il a perdu le contrôle de sa voiture et s'est écrasé contre la barrière de l'autoroute.

IPA [i l‿a pɛʁdy lø kɔ̃tʁol dø sa vwatyʁ e s‿e ekʁaze kɔ̃tʁ la baʁjɛʁ dø l‿otoʁut ‖]

2907

EN Megan and I ran into each other on the subway on Monday.

FR Megan et moi nous sommes rencontrés (♀rencontrées) par hasard dans le métro lundi.

IPA [(...) e mwa nu sɔm ʁɑ̃kɔ̃tʁe (♀ʁɑ̃kɔ̃tʁe) paʁ azaʁ dɑ̃ lø metʁo lœ̃di ‖]

2908

EN His novels have been translated from English into thirty (30) languages.

FR Ses romans ont été traduits de l'anglais en trente langues.

IPA [se ʁomã ɔ̃ ete tʁadɥi də l‿ãglɛ ã tʁãt lãg ‖]

2909

EN This book is divided into three (3) parts.

FR Ce livre est divisé en trois parties.

IPA [sø livʁ e divize ã tʁwa paʁti ‖]

2910

EN I threw the coconut onto the rock again, and it finally split open.

FR J'ai jeté la noix de coco sur la roche à nouveau et elle a finalement fendu.

IPA [ʒ‿ɛ ʒ°te la nwa də koko syʁ la ʁɔʃ a nuvo e ɛ l‿a final°mã fãdy ‖]

2911

EN A truck collided with a bus on the highway this morning, causing a five-car pile-up.

FR Un camion est entré en collision avec un bus sur l'autoroute ce matin, causant un carambolage de cinq voitures.

IPA [œ̃ kamjɔ̃ e ãtʁe ã kolizjɔ̃ avɛk œ̃ bys syʁ l‿otoʁut sø matɛ̃ | kozã t‿œ̃ kaʁãbolaʒ də sɛ̃k vwatyʁ ‖]

2912

EN Please fill this pot with water and put it on the stove to boil.

FR Remplis cette théière d'eau et mets-la sur la cuisinière pour la faire bouillir, s'il te plaît.

IPA [ʁɑ̃pli sɛt tejɛʁ d̥o e mɛ la syʁ la kɥizinjɛʁ puʁ la fɛʁ bujiʁ | s̝il tø plɛ ‖]

2913

EN Our parents provide us with food, clothing, education, healthcare and love.

FR Nos parents nous fournissent nourriture, vêtements, éducation, santé et amour.

IPA [no paʁɑ̃ nu fuʁnis nuʁityʁ | vɛt°mɑ̃ | edykasjɔ̃ | sɑ̃te e amuʁ ‖]

2914

EN Our teachers provide us with an education necessary for competing in the real world.

FR Nos professeurs nous inculquent l'éducation nécessaire pour être compétitif dans le monde réel.

IPA [no pʁofɛsœʁ nu z̝ɛ̃kylk l̝edykasjɔ̃ nesesɛʁ pu ʁ̝etʁ kɔ̃petitif dɑ̃ lø mɔ̃d ʁeɛl ‖]

2915

EN Whatever happened to that murder case? Did the police end up finding the killer?

FR Qu'est-il arrivé à ce cas de meurtre? La police a-t-elle fini par trouver le tueur?

IPA [k‿e t‿il aʁive a sø ka dø mœʁtʁ ‖ la polis a t‿ɛl fini paʁ tʁuve lø tɥœʁ ‖]

2916

EN They happened to come across an important piece of evidence, and now he's in prison.

FR Ils sont tombés sur une pièce à conviction très importante, et il est maintenant en prison.

IPA [il sɔ̃ tɔ̃be sy ʁ‿yn pjɛs a kɔ̃viksjɔ̃ tʁɛ z‿ɛ̃poʁtãt | e i l‿e mɛ̃t°nã t‿ã pʁizɔ̃ ‖]

2917

EN I wanted to stay home, but my friends insisted on my coming.

FR Je voulais rester à la maison, mais mes amis (♀amies) ont insisté pour que je vienne.

IPA [ʒø vulɛ ʁɛste a la mɛzɔ̃ | mɛ me z‿ami (♀ami) ɔ̃ ɛ̃siste puʁ kø ʒø vjɛn ‖]

2918

EN How much time do you spend on your English assignments every day?

FR Combien de temps passes-tu à faire tes devoirs d'anglais chaque jour?

IPA [kɔ̃bjɛ̃ dø tɑ̃ pas ty a fɛʁ te dᵊvwaʁ dᵊɑ̃glɛ ʃak ʒuʁ ‖]

2919

EN If you have trash that can be recycled, throw it away in the proper bins.

FR Si tu as des déchets qui peuvent être recyclés, jette-les dans les poubelles appropriées.

IPA [si ty a de deʃɛ ki pœv ɛtʁ ʁᵊsikle | ʒɛt le dɑ̃ le pubɛl apʁopʁije ‖]

2920

EN Take your shoes off before coming inside my house, and please don't wake the baby up.

FR Enlève tes chaussures avant d'entrer dans ma maison, et s'il te plaît ne réveille pas le bébé.

IPA [ɑ̃lɛv te ʃosy ʁᵊavɑ̃ dᵊɑ̃tʁe dɑ̃ ma mɛzɔ̃ | e sᵢil tø plɛ nø ʁevɛj pa lø bebe ‖]

2921

EN The fridge isn't working because you haven't plugged it in properly.

FR Le réfrigérateur ne fonctionne pas parce que tu ne l'as pas branché correctement.

IPA [lø ʁefʁiʒeʁatœʁ nø fɔ̃ksjɔn pa paʁs kø ty nø l‿a pa bʁɑ̃ʃe koʁɛkt°mɑ̃ ‖]

2922

EN Xavier went to college but dropped out after a couple semesters. He's what we call a college drop-out.

FR Xavier est allé à l'université, mais a abandonné après quelques semestres. C'est ce que nous appelons un décrocheur.

IPA [(...) e ale a l‿ynivɛʁsite | mɛ a abɑ̃dɔne apʁɛ kɛlk s°mɛstʁ ‖ sɛ sø kø nu z‿ap°lɔ̃ z‿œ̃ dekroʃœʁ ‖]

2923

EN What did you get out of your college education? — Besides a professional degree, I also made many friends for life.

FR Qu'as-tu tiré de tes études universitaires? — En plus d'un diplôme professionnel, je me suis aussi fait de nombreux amis pour la vie.

IPA [k‿a ty tiʁe dø te z‿etyd ynivɛʁsitɛʁ ‖ — ɑ̃ plys d‿œ̃ diplom pʁofɛsjonɛl | ʒø mø sɥi osi fɛ dø nɔ̃bʁø z‿ami puʁ la vi ‖]

2924

EN I'd promised I'd attend her wedding, now there's nothing I can do to get out of it.

FR J'avais promis d'être présent (♀présente) à son mariage, il n'y a maintenant rien que je puisse faire pour m'en sortir.

IPA [ʒ‿avɛ pʁomi d‿ɛtʁ pʁezɑ̃ (♀pʁezɑ̃t) a sɔ̃ maʁjaʒ | il n‿i a mɛ̃t°nɑ̃ ʁjɛ̃ kø ʒø pɥis fɛʁ puʁ m‿ɑ̃ sɔʁtiʁ ||]

2925

EN The police outsmarted the murderer; he simply couldn't get away with murder.

FR La police a déjoué le meurtrier; il ne pouvait tout simplement pas s'en tirer avec un meurtre.

IPA [la polis a deʒwe lø mœʁtʁije;il nø puvɛ tu sɛ̃pl°mɑ̃ pa s‿ɑ̃ tiʁe avɛk œ̃ mœʁtʁ ||]

2926

EN You can tell Tomoko works out at the gym every day because she looks great. She jogs, takes a yoga class, does aerobics, and lifts weights.

FR On peut voir que Tomoko travaille dans un gym tous les jours, car elle a l'air magnifique. Elle fait du jogging, prend un cours de yoga, fait de l'aérobie et soulève des poids.

IPA [ɔ̃ pø vwaʁ kø (...) tʁavaj dɑ̃ z‿œ̃ ʒim tu le ʒuʁ | kaʁ ɛ l‿a l‿ɛʁ maɲifik || ɛl fɛ dy dʒɔgiŋ | pʁɑ̃ d‿œ̃ kuʁ dø joga | fɛ dø l‿aeʁobi e sulɛv de pwa ||]

2927

EN It seems that Ludwig and Rita's relationship is having trouble, but we really hope they work it out.

FR Il semble que la relation de Ludwig et Rita souffre de problèmes, mais nous espérons vraiment qu'ils mettent les choses au point.

IPA [il sɑ̃bl kø la ʁ°lasjɔ̃ dø (...) e (...) sufʁ dø pʁoblɛm | mɛ nu z‿ɛspeʁɔ̃ vʁɛmɑ̃ k‿il mɛt le ʃoz o pwɛ̃ ||]

2928

EN The two (2) companies worked out a cooperation agreement.

FR Les deux entreprises ont convenu d'un accord de coopération.

IPA [le dø z‿ɑ̃tʁ°pʁiz ɔ̃ kɔ̃v°ny d‿œ̃ akɔʁ dø koopeʁasjɔ̃ ||]

2929

EN Nobody believed Sara at first, but she turned out to be right.

FR Personne ne croyait Sara au début, mais elle s'est avérée être juste.

IPA [pɛʁsɔn nø kʁwajɛ (...) o deby | mɛ ɛl s‿e aveʁe ɛtʁ ʒyst ||]

2930

EN Better find a gas station. We're running out of gas.

FR Mieux vaut trouver une station d'essence. Nous sommes à court d'essence.

IPA [mjø vo tʁuve ʁ‿yn stasjɔ̃ d‿esɑ̃s ‖ nu sɔm a kuʁ d‿esɑ̃s ‖]

2931

EN Please buy more toilet paper before you use it all up.

FR S'il te plaît, achète plus de papier hygiénique avant de tout l'utiliser.

IPA [s‿il tø plɛ | aʃɛt plys dø papje iʒjenik avɑ̃ dø tu l‿ytilize ‖]

2932

EN I'm sorry, the book you're looking for isn't in stock. It's all sold out.

FR Je suis désolé, le livre que tu cherches n'est pas en stock. Tout est vendu.

IPA [ʒø sɥi dezole | lø livʁ kø ty ʃɛʁʃ n‿e pa z‿ɑ̃ stɔk ‖ tu t‿e vɑ̃dy ‖]

2933

EN I've been handing out business cards all day, and now I'm all out of them.

FR J'ai distribué des cartes de visite toute la journée et maintenant je suis à court d'elles.

IPA [ʒ̟ɛ distʁibɥe de kaʁt dø vizit tut la ʒuʁne e mɛ̃t°nɑ̃ ʒø sɥi a kuʁ d̟ɛl ‖]

2934

EN Valentina found a beautiful dress at the department store, but she wanted to try it on before she bought it.

FR Valentina a trouvé une belle robe au magasin, mais elle voulait l'essayer avant de l'acheter.

IPA [(...) a tʁuve yn bɛl ʁɔb o magazɛ̃ | mɛ ɛl vulɛ l̟eseje avɑ̃ dø l̟aʃ°te ‖]

2935

EN Please don't stop telling your story, please go on.

FR S'il te plaît, n'arrête pas de raconter ton histoire, continue s'il te plaît.

IPA [s̟il tø plɛ | n̟aʁɛt pa dø ʁakɔ̃te tɔ̃ n̟istwaʁ | kɔ̃tiny s̟il tø plɛ ‖]

2936

EN The concert had to be called off because of the typhoon.

FR Le concert a dû être annulé en raison du typhon.

IPA [lø kɔ̃sɛʁ a dy ɛtʁ anyle ɑ̃ ʁɛzɔ̃ dy tifɔ̃ ‖]

2937

EN Tomorrow I'm off to Paris.

FR Demain, je pars pour Paris.
IPA [dᵊmɛ̃ | ʒø paʁ puʁ (...) ||]

2938

EN Oscar left home at the age of eighteen (18) and went off to Spain.

FR Oscar a quitté la maison à l'âge de dix-huit (18) ans et il est parti en Espagne.
IPA [(...) a kite la mɛzɔ̃ a l̪aʒ dø dizɥit (18) ɑ̃ e i l̪e paʁti ɑ̃ espagne ||]

2939

EN Our plane was delayed on the tarmac and we couldn't take off for an hour.

FR Notre avion a été retardé sur la piste et nous n'avons pas pu décoller pendant une heure.
IPA [nɔtʁ avjɔ̃ a ete ʁᵊtaʁde syʁ la pist e nu n̪avɔ̃ pa py dekole pɑ̃dɑ̃ t̪yn œʁ ||]

2940

EN My parents and friends saw me off at the airport
before I embarked on my adventure around the
world.

FR Mes parents et mes amis m'ont accompagné à
l'aéroport avant que je ne commence mon aventure
autour du monde.

IPA [me paʁɑ̃ e me z‿ami m‿ɔ̃ akɔ̃paɲe a l‿aeʁopɔʁ avɑ̃
kø ʒø nø komɑ̃s mɔ̃ n‿avɑ̃tyʁ otuʁ dy mɔ̃d ‖]

2941

EN I don't want to keep going on discussing marketing,
let's move on to the production issues.

FR Je ne veux pas continuer à discuter marketing,
passons aux questions de production.

IPA [ʒø nø vø pa kɔ̃tinɥe a diskyte maʁketiŋ | pasɔ̃ o
kɛstjɔ̃ dø pʁodyksjɔ̃ ‖]

2942

EN Mahmud always dozes off in economics class.

FR Mahmud somnole toujours en classe économique.

IPA [(...) sɔmnɔl tuʒu ʁ‿ɑ̃ klas ekonomik ‖]

2943

EN The food was lousy and the service sucked, then they charged us an arm and a leg! We totally got ripped off!

FR La nourriture était mauvaise et le service était nul, puis ça nous a coûté la peau des fesses! Nous nous sommes totalement fait arnaquer!

IPA [la nuʁityʁ ete movɛz e lø sɛʁvis ete nyl | pɥi sa nu z‿a kute la po de fɛs ‖ nu nu sɔm total°mã fɛ aʁnake ‖]

2944

EN He always buys expensive things to show off.

FR Il achète toujours des choses cher pour frimer.

IPA [i l‿aʃet tuʒuʁ de ʃoz ʃɛʁ puʁ fʁime ‖]

2945

EN Some old houses were torn down to make room for a new housing development. The owners of the houses tried to protest, but it was to no avail.

FR Certaines vieilles maisons ont été démolies pour faire place à un nouvel ensemble de logements. Les propriétaires des maisons ont essayé de protester, mais ce fut en vain.

IPA [sɛʁten vjɛj mɛzɔ̃ ɔ̃ ete demoli puʁ fɛʁ plas a œ̃ nuvɛ l‿ãsãbl dø lɔʒ°mã ‖ le pʁopʁijetɛʁ de mɛzɔ̃ ɔ̃ eseje dø pʁoteste | mɛ sø fy t‿ã vɛ̃ ‖]

2946

EN One man was so upset by the whole ordeal that he commited suicide.

FR Un homme a été tellement bouleversé par toute cette épreuve qu'il s'est suicidé.

IPA [œ̃ n‿ɔm a ete tɛlᵊmɑ̃ bulᵊvɛʁse paʁ tut sɛt epʁœv k‿il s‿e sɥiside ‖]

2947

EN The firefighters were able to put the fire out before the house burned down.

FR Les pompiers ont réussi à éteindre le feu avant que la maison ne brûle.

IPA [le pɔ̃pje ɔ̃ ʁeysi a etɛ̃dʁ lø fø avɑ̃ kø la mɛzɔ̃ nø bʁyl ‖]

2948

EN However, the firefighters had a hard time trying to calm a woman down. Apparently, her cat perished in the fire.

FR Toutefois, les pompiers ont eu du mal à calmer une femme. Apparemment, son chat aurait péri dans l'incendie.

IPA [tutᵊfwa | le pɔ̃pje ɔ̃ y dy mal a kalme ʁ‿yn fam ‖ apaʁamɑ̃ | sɔ̃ ʃa oʁɛ peʁi dɑ̃ l‿ɛ̃sɑ̃di ‖]

2949

EN Talks between Russia and the United States have broken down.

FR Les pourparlers entre la Russie et les États-Unis ont été rompus.

IPA [le puʁpaʁle ɑ̃tʁ la ʁysi e le z‿etazuni ɔ̃ ete ʁɔ̃py ‖]

2950

EN After college, Zahida was turned down from every job she applied for. Finding a job was difficult.

FR Après l'université, Zahida a été rejetée de chaque emploi pour lequel elle a postulé. Trouver un emploi fut difficile.

IPA [apʁɛ l‿ynivɛʁsite | (...) a ete ʁ°ʒte dø ʃak ɑ̃plwa puʁ l°kɛ l‿ɛ l‿a pɔstyle ‖ tʁuve ʁ‿œ̃ n‿ɑ̃plwa fy difisil ‖]

2951

EN When Ichirou had just arrived in London, a man came up to him in the street and asked for money, so he gave him a few Japanese yen.

FR Lorsque Ichirou venait d'arriver à Londres, un homme est venu vers lui dans la rue et lui a demandé de l'argent, alors il lui a donné un peu de yens japonais.

IPA [lɔʁsk° (...) v°nɛ d‿aʁive a lɔ̃dʁ° | œ̃ n‿ɔm e v°ny vɛʁ lɥi dɑ̃ la ʁy e lɥi a d°mɑ̃de dø l‿aʁʒɑ̃ | alɔ ʁ‿il lɥi a done œ̃ pø dø jɛn ʒaponɛ ‖]

2952

EN The police are going to ask us a lot of questions, so we need to back each other up.

FR La police va nous poser beaucoup de questions, donc nous avons besoin de nous soutenir les uns les autres.

IPA [la polis va nu poze boku də kɛstjɔ̃ | dɔ̃k nu z‿avɔ̃ bøzwɛ̃ də nu sut°niʁ le z‿œ̃ le z‿otʁ ‖]

2953

EN The police set up a special task force to investigate the murders.

FR La police a mis en place un groupe de travail spécial pour enquêter sur les meurtres.

IPA [la polis a mi z‿ɑ̃ plas œ̃ gʁup də tʁavaj spesjal pu ʁ‿ɑ̃kete syʁ le mœʁtʁ ‖]

2954

EN You should always back up your computer files just in case the hard drive dies.

FR Tu dois toujours sauvegarder tes fichiers informatiques au cas où le disque dur mourrait.

IPA [ty dwa tuʒuʁ sov°gaʁde te fiʃje ɛ̃fɔʁmatik o ka u lø disk dyʁ muʁɛ ‖]

2955

EN You should always save your files as you're working on them just in case your computer crashes.

FR Tu dois toujours sauvegarder les fichiers sur lesquels tu travailles au cas où ton ordinateur se bloquerait.

IPA [ty dwa tuʒuʁ sov°gaʁde le fiʃje syʁ lɛkɛl ty tʁavaj o ka u tɔ̃ n‿ɔʁdinatœʁ sø blɔk°ʁɛ ‖]

2956

EN The police accidentally shot and killed a man. They tried to cover up what really happened, but it became a big scandal.

FR La police a accidentellement tiré sur un homme et l'a tué. Ils ont essayé de cacher ce qui s'était réellement passé, mais c'est devenu un grand scandale.

IPA [la polis a aksidɑ̃tɛl°mɑ̃ tiʁe sy ʁ‿œ̃ n‿ɔm e l‿a tɥe ‖ i l‿ɔ̃ esɛje dø kaʃe sø ki s‿ete ʁeɛl°mɑ̃ pase | mɛ sɛ d°v°ny œ̃ gʁɑ̃ skɑ̃dal ‖]

2957

EN They couldn't just brush it under the carpet and expect everything to blow over and go away.

FR Ils ne pouvaient tout simplement pas le balayer sous le tapis et attendre que tout s'envole et disparaisse.

IPA [il nø puvɛ tu sɛ̃pl°mɑ̃ pa lø baleje su lø tapi e atɑ̃dʁ kø tu s‿ɑ̃vɔl e dispaʁɛs ‖]

2958

EN The murder suspect got bad press, but he wasn't the culprit; he was not the man who did it.

FR L'homme soupçonné de meurtre a eu mauvaise presse, mais il n'était pas coupable; ce n'est pas lui qui a fait le coup.

IPA [l‿ɔm supsone dø mœʁtʁ a y movɛz pʁɛs | mɛ il n‿etɛ pa kupabl;sø n‿e pa lɥi ki a fɛ lø ku ‖]

2959

EN Since he got so much bad press, it wouldn't just blow over. Everybody knew him now.

FR Comme il a tellement eu mauvaise presse, ça ne pouvait pas tout simplement pas s'estomper. Tout le monde le connaissait maintenant.

IPA [kɔm i l‿a tɛlᵊmã t‿y movɛz pʁɛs | sa nø puvɛ pa tu sɛplᵊmã pa s‿estɔpe ‖ tu lø mɔd lø konesɛ mɛtᵊnã ‖]

2960

EN So he sued and was awarded compensation for damage to his reputation.

FR Il s'est donc rendu en cour et on lui a accordé une indemnité pour atteinte à sa réputation.

IPA [il s‿e dɔk ʁãdy ã kuʁ e ɔ̃ lɥi a akɔʁde yn ɛdɛmnite pu ʁ‿atɛt a sa ʁepytasjɔ̃ ‖]

2961

EN We just won a new contract, but completing it will take up the next three (3) months.

FR Nous venons tout juste d'obtenir un nouveau contrat, mais le compléter prendra les trois prochains mois.

IPA [nu v°nɔ̃ tu ʒyst d‿ɔpt°niʁ œ̃ nuvo kɔ̃tʁa | mɛ lø kɔ̃plete pʁɑ̃dʁa le tʁwa pʁoʃɛ̃ mwa ||]

2962

EN My parents were away on business when I was a child, so my grandparents brought me up. > My grandparents raised me.

FR Mes parents étaient en voyage d'affaires quand j'étais un enfant, alors mes grands-parents m'ont élevé (♀ élevée). > Mes grands-parents m'ont élevé (♀ élevée).

IPA [me paʁɑ̃ ete t‿ɑ̃ vwajaʒ d‿afɛʁ kɑ̃ ʒ‿ete œ̃ n‿ɑ̃fɑ̃ | alɔʁ me gʁɑ̃paʁɑ̃ m‿ɔ̃ ɛl°ve (♀ ɛl°ve) || > me gʁɑ̃paʁɑ̃ m‿ɔ̃ ɛl°ve (♀ ɛl°ve) |||]

2963

EN If you can't find a hotel for the night, you'll end up sleeping on the street.

FR Si tu ne peux pas trouver un hôtel pour la nuit, tu finiras par dormir dans la rue.

IPA [si ty nø pø pa tʁuve ʁ‿œ̃ n‿otɛl puʁ la nɥi | ty finiʁa paʁ dɔʁmiʁ dɑ̃ la ʁy ||]

2964

EN There was a fight on the street and three (3) men ended up in the hospital.

FR Il y a eu une bagarre dans la rue et trois hommes se sont retrouvés à l'hôpital.

IPA [i l‿i a y yn bagaʁ dɑ̃ la ʁy e tʁwa ɔm sø sɔ̃ ʁ°tʁuve a l‿opital ‖]

2965

EN Don't argue with the police officer, or you'll just end up getting arrested.

FR Ne discute pas avec l'agent de police ou tu finiras par te faire arrêter.

IPA [nø diskyt pa z‿avɛk l‿aʒɑ̃ dø polis u ty finiʁa paʁ tø fɛʁ aʁete ‖]

2966

EN There are two (2) universities in the city, and students make up twenty percent (20%) of the population.

FR Il y a deux universités dans la ville, et les étudiants représentent vingt pour cent (20 %) de la population.

IPA [i l‿i a dø z‿ynivɛʁsite dɑ̃ la vil | e le z‿etydjɑ̃ ʁ°pʁezɑ̃t vɛ̃ puʁ sɑ̃ (20 %) dø la popylasjɔ̃ ‖]

2967

EN I'll be ready in a few minutes. You go on ahead and I'll catch up with you.

FR Je serai prêt (♀prête) dans quelques minutes. Partez et je vous rattraperai.

IPA [ʒø sᵊʁɛ pʁɛ (♀pʁɛt) dɑ̃ kɛlk minyt ‖ paʁte e ʒø vu ʁatʁapᵊʁɛ ‖]

2968

EN My parents dropped me off at the airport two (2) hours before my flight was scheduled to take off.

FR Mes parents m'ont déposé (♀déposée) à l'aéroport deux heures avant que mon vol ne décolle.

IPA [me paʁɑ̃ m‿ɔ̃ depoze (♀depoze) a l‿aeʁopɔʁ dø z‿œʁ avɑ̃ kø mɔ̃ vɔl nø dekɔl ‖]

2969

EN My parents were there again to pick me up when I flew back home.

FR Mes parents étaient encore là pour venir me chercher quand je suis rentré à la maison.

IPA [me paʁɑ̃ ete ɑ̃kɔʁ la puʁ vᵊniʁ mø ʃɛʁʃe kɑ̃ ʒø sɥi ʁɑ̃tʁe a la mɛzɔ̃ ‖]

2970

EN Simon is terribly creative, and is always coming up with great ideas.

FR Simon est terriblement créatif et songe toujours à de grandes idées.

IPA [(...) e tɛʁibl°mã kʁeatif e sɔ̃ʒ tuʒuʁ a dø gʁã d‿ide ‖]

2971

EN I'm saving my money up for a trip around the world.

FR J'économise mon argent pour un voyage autour du monde.

IPA [ʒ‿ekonomiz mɔ̃ n‿aʁʒã pu ʁ‿œ̃ vwajaʒ otuʁ dy mɔ̃d ‖]

2972

EN The F1 racer caught fire and blew up. Luckily the driver just narrowly escaped.

FR La voiture de F1 a pris feu et a explosé. Heureusement, le pilote s'est échappé de justesse.

IPA [lø vwatyʁ dø (...) a pʁi fø e a ɛksploze ‖ øʁøz°mã | lø pilɔt s‿e eʃape dø ʒystɛs ‖]

2973

EN A friend of mine was attacked and beaten up a few days ago. He's been in the hospital ever since.

FR Un de mes amis a été attaqué et battu il y a quelques jours. Il a été à l'hôpital depuis.

IPA [œ̃ də me z‿ami z‿a ete atake e baty i l ja kɛlk ʒuʁ ‖ i l‿a ete a l‿opital dᵊpɥi ‖‖]

2974

EN Ludwig and Rita broke up. > Ludwig and Rita split up.

FR Ludwig et Rita se sont séparés. > Ludwig et Rita se séparent.

IPA [(...) e (...) sø sɔ̃ sepaʁe ‖ > (...) e (...) sø sepaʁ ‖‖]

2975

EN Ludwig and Rita ended up breaking up. > Ludwig and Rita ended up splitting up.

FR Ludwig et Rita ont fini par rompre. > Ludwig et Rita ont fini par se quitter.

IPA [(...) e (...) ɔ̃ fini paʁ ʁɔ̃pʁ ‖ > (...) e (...) ɔ̃ fini paʁ sø kite ‖‖]

2976

EN They couldn't get along with each other, so the relationship didn't work out in the end.

FR Ils ne pouvaient pas s'entendre entre eux, alors la relation a fini par ne pas fonctionner.

IPA [il nø puvɛ pa s‿ɑ̃tɑ̃dʁ ɑ̃tʁ ø | alɔʁ la ʁᵊlasjɔ̃ a fini paʁ nø pa fɔ̃ksjone ||]

2977

EN Plans to build a new factory have been held up because of the company's financial problems.

FR Des plans pour construire une nouvelle usine ont été remisés à cause de problèmes financiers de la société.

IPA [de plɑ̃ puʁ kɔ̃stʁɥiʁ yn nuvɛ l‿yzin ɔ̃ ete ʁᵊmize a koz dø pʁoblɛm finɑ̃sje dø la sosjete ||]

2978

EN We live next to an international airport, so we have to put up with a lot of noise.

FR Nous vivons à côté d'un aéroport international, nous devons donc vivre avec beaucoup de bruit.

IPA [nu vivɔ̃ a kote d‿œ̃ aeʁopɔʁ ɛ̃tɛʁnasjonal | nu dᵊvɔ̃ dɔ̃k vivʁ avɛk boku dø bʁɥi ||]

2979

EN The two (2) brothers are identical twins, so everybody gets them mixed up.

FR Les deux frères sont de vrais jumeaux. Donc, tout le monde les mélange.

IPA [le dø fʁɛʁ sɔ̃ dø vʁɛ ʒymo ‖ dɔ̃k | tu lø mɔ̃d le melɑ̃ʒ ‖]

2980

EN Your house is an absolute mess. When are you going to get this place cleaned up?

FR Ta maison est dans un désordre absolu. Quand vas-tu faire nettoyer cet endroit?

IPA [ta mɛzɔ̃ e dɑ̃ z‿œ̃ dezɔʁdʁ apsoly ‖ kɑ̃ va ty fɛʁ netwaje sɛ t‿ɑ̃dʁwa ‖]

2981

EN When your language training starts getting tough, it means you're about to make a big breakthrough, so stick with it and don't give up.

FR Lorsque ta formation linguistique commence à devenir difficile, cela signifie que tu es sur le point de faire une percée importante, mieux vaut donc continuer et ne pas abandonner.

IPA [lɔʁskᵊ ta fɔʁmasjɔ̃ lɛ̃ɡɥistik komɑ̃s a dᵊvᵊniʁ difisil | sᵊla siɲifi kø ty ɛ syʁ lø pwɛ̃ dø fɛʁ yn pɛʁse ɛ̃pɔʁtɑ̃t | mjø vo dɔ̃k kɔ̃tinɥe e nø pa z‿abɑ̃done ‖]

2982

EN Whoever used up all the milk and eggs should go out and buy some more. And get some toilet paper while you're at it.

FR Celui qui a utilisé tout le lait et tous les œufs devrait sortir en acheter plus. Et achète du papier toilette pendant que tu y es!

IPA [sᵊlɥi ki a ytilize tu lø lɛ e tu le z‿ø dᵊvʁɛ sɔʁti ʁ‿ɑ̃ n‿aʃᵊte plys || e aʃɛt dy papje twalɛt pɑ̃dɑ̃ kø ty i ɛ ||]

2983

EN People used to carry pagers around, but they've completely fallen out of use.

FR Les gens avaient l'habitude de transporter des beepers, mais ces derniers sont complètement tombés en désuétude.

IPA [le ʒɑ̃ avɛ l‿abityd dø tʁɑ̃spɔʁte de (...) | mɛ se dɛʁnje sɔ̃ kɔ̃plɛtᵊmɑ̃ tɔ̃be z‿ɑ̃ desɥetyd ||]

2984

EN My manager pointed out a potential problem with our new marketing plan.

FR Mon manageur a un problème potentiel avec notre nouveau plan de marketing.

IPA [mɔ̃ manaʒœʁ a œ̃ pʁoblɛm potɑ̃sjɛl avɛk nɔtʁ nuvo plɑ̃ dø maʁketiŋ ||]

2985

EN A decision has to be made now. We can't put it off any longer.

FR Une décision doit être prise maintenant. Nous ne pouvons pas remettre ça à plus tard.

IPA [yn desizjɔ̃ dwa ɛtʁ pʁiz mɛ̃tᵊnã || nu nø puvɔ̃ pa ʁᵊmɛtʁ sa a plys taʁ ||]

2986

EN I was offered a job at the oil company, but I decided to turn it down.

FR On m'a offert un emploi dans la compagnie pétrolière, mais j'ai décidé de le refuser.

IPA [ɔ̃ m‿a ofɛ ʁ‿œ̃ n‿ãplwa dã la kɔ̃paɲi petʁoljɛʁ | mɛ ʒ‿ɛ deside dø lø ʁᵊfyze ||]

2987

EN Several men got angry with Jack in the bar and Jack told them he wasn't afraid to take them on.

FR Plusieurs hommes se sont fâchés avec Jack au bar et Jack leur a dit qu'il n'avait pas peur de les affronter.

IPA [plyzjœʁ ɔm sø sɔ̃ faʃe avɛk (...) o baʁ e (...) lœ ʁ‿a di k‿il n‿avɛ pa pøʁ dø le z‿afʁɔ̃te ||]

2988

EN They took it out into the street, and Jack let them have it. Jack put them down one by one, and the spectacle really drew a crowd.

FR Ils sont sortis dans la rue et Jack leur a donné ce qu'ils voulaient. Jack les a envoyés au sol un par un et le spectacle a vraiment attiré une foule.

IPA [il sɔ̃ sɔʁti dɑ̃ la ʁy e (...) lœ ʁ‿a done sø k‿il vulɛ ‖ (...) le z‿a ɑ̃vwaje o sɔl œ̃ pa ʁ‿œ̃ e lø spɛktakl a vʁɛmɑ̃ t‿atiʁe yn ful ‖‖]

2989

EN A man was knocked down by a car when crossing the street and had to be taken to the hospital.

FR Un homme a été renversé par une voiture en traversant la rue et a dû être transporté à l'hôpital.

IPA [œ̃ n‿ɔm a ete ʁɑ̃vɛʁse pa ʁ‿yn vwatyʁ ɑ̃ tʁavɛʁsɑ̃ la ʁy e a dy ɛtʁ tʁɑ̃spɔʁte a l‿opital ‖‖]

2990

EN In the aftermath of the tornado, they discovered a lot of uprooted trees and houses that had been blown down.

FR À la suite de la tornade, ils ont découvert un grand nombre d'arbres déracinés et de maisons démolies.

IPA [a la sɥit dø la tɔʁnad | i l‿ɔ̃ dekuvɛ ʁ‿œ̃ gʁɑ̃ nɔ̃bʁ d‿aʁbʁ deʁasine e dø mɛzɔ̃ demoli ‖‖]

2991

EN Please calm down. Everything will turn out all right.

FR S'il te plaît, calme-toi. Tout va s'arranger.

IPA [s͜il tø plɛ | kalm twa || tu va s͜aʁɑ̃ʒe |||]

2992

EN When the police questioned him, he decided to leave out an important detail.

FR Lorsque les policiers l'ont interrogé, il a décidé d'omettre un détail important.

IPA [lɔʁsk° le polisje l͜ɔ̃ ɛ̃teʁoʒe | i l͜a deside d͜omɛtʁ œ̃ detaj ɛ̃pɔʁtɑ̃ |||]

2993

EN When talking with the police, you shouldn't make up stories or lie.

FR Lorsque tu parles à la police, tu ne devrais pas raconter d'histoires ou de mensonges.

IPA [lɔʁsk° ty paʁl a la polis | ty nø d°vʁɛ pa ʁakɔ̃te d istwaʁ u dø mɑ̃sɔ̃ʒ |||]

2994

EN When Sara decided to move to India and start a new life, she gave away all of her belongings.

FR Quand Sara a décidé de déménager en Inde et commencer une nouvelle vie, elle a distribué tous ses biens.

IPA [kɑ̃ (...) a deside dø demenaʒe ʁ‿ɑ̃ n‿ɛ̃d e komɑ̃se ʁ‿yn nuvɛl vi | ɛ l‿a distʁibɥe tu se bjɛ̃ ‖]

2995

EN Put a smile on your face, and you'll certainly get lots of smiles back.

FR Affichez un sourire sur votre visage et vous obtiendrez certainement beaucoup de sourires en retour.

IPA [afiʃe z‿œ̃ suʁiʁ syʁ vɔtʁ vizaʒ e vu z‿ɔptjɛ̃dʁe sɛʁtɛnᵊmɑ̃ boku dø suʁiʁ ɑ̃ ʁᵊtuʁ ‖]

2996

EN I waved to the children on the bus, and they waved back.

FR J'ai salué de la main les enfants dans le bus et ils m'ont salué (♀saluée) en retour.

IPA [ʒ‿ɛ salɥe dø la mɛ̃ le z‿ɑ̃fɑ̃ dɑ̃ lø bys e il m‿ɔ̃ salɥe (♀salɥe) ɑ̃ ʁᵊtuʁ ‖]

2997

EN My first job was at a travel agency, and I didn't like it much. But now, looking back on the experience, I really learned a lot.

FR Mon premier emploi était dans une agence de voyages et je n'aimais pas vraiment ça. Mais maintenant, avec le recul, j'ai vraiment beaucoup appris lors de cette expérience.

IPA [mɔ̃ pʁømje ʁ‿ɑ̃plwa ete dɑ̃ z‿yn aʒɑ̃s dø vwajaʒ e ʒø n‿emɛ pa vʁɛmɑ̃ sa || mɛ mɛ̃t°nɑ̃ | avɛk lø ʁ°kyl | ʒ‿ɛ vʁɛmɑ̃ boku p‿apʁi lɔʁ dø sɛt ɛkspeʁjɑ̃s ||]

2998

EN When are you going to pay me back the money I lent you?

FR Quand vas-tu me rembourser l'argent que je t'ai prêté?

IPA [kɑ̃ va ty mø ʁɑ̃buʁse l‿aʁʒɑ̃ kø ʒø t‿ɛ pʁete ||]

2999

EN When you cause problems with the wrong people, those problems will come pay you back, or come back to haunt you.

FR Lorsque tu causes des ennuis aux mauvaises personnes, ces ennuis se retourneront contre toi ou te hanteront.

IPA [lɔʁsk° ty koz de z‿ɑ̃nɥi o movɛz pɛʁsɔn | se z‿ɑ̃nɥi sø ʁ°tuʁn°ʁɔ̃ kɔ̃tʁ twa u tø ɑ̃t°ʁɔ̃ ||]

3000

EN The lone ranger got on his horse and rode off into the sunset.

FR Le ranger solitaire est monté sur son cheval et il est parti vers le soleil couchant.

IPA [lø ʁɑ̃ʒe solitɛʁ e mɔ̃te syʁ sɔ̃ ʃ°val e i l‿e paʁti vɛʁ lø solɛj kuʃɑ̃ ‖]

French Index

à [a]: 2002, 2003, 2005, 2007, 2010, 2015, 2018, 2019, 2022, 2024, 2026, 2027, 2030, 2033, 2040, 2041, 2050, 2057... +289

a [a]: 2004, 2006, 2015, 2024, 2025, 2028, 2030, 2038, 2039, 2040, 2090, 2092, 2117, 2135, 2149, 2156, 2177, 2179, 2184, 2185... +100

a [l̩ a]: 2022, 2042, 2043, 2079, 2086, 2126, 2243, 2393, 2416, 2433, 2447, 2454, 2641, 2652, 2661, 2696, 2748, 2756... +10

a [n̩ a]: 2339, 2395, 2399, 2843

a [ʁ a]: 2750, 2987, 2988

a [t a]: 2467, 2713

a [z a]: 2014, 2112, 2183, 2257, 2505, 2943, 2973, 2988

abandonné [abãdone]: 2922

abandonner [z abãdone]: 2981

absent [apsã]: 2702

absolu [apsoly]: 2980

accepté [aksɛpte]: 2660, 2661

accident [ʁ aksidã]: 2760

accidentellement [aksidãtɛlˈmã]: 2956

accidents [ʁ aksidã]: 2076

accompagné [akɔ̃paɲe]: 2940

accord [akɔʁ]: 2928

accordé [akɔʁde]: 2960

accueillir [akœjiʁ]: 2485

accusé [akyze]: 2864

accusé [t akyze]: 2865

accusées [akyze]: 2108

accusés [akyze]: 2108

achalandé [aʃalãde]: 2616

achalandé [s aʃalãde]: 2605

achalandé [z aʃalãde]: 2584

achète [aʃɛt]: 2931, 2982

acheté [aʃˈte]: 2088, 2342, 2494, 2652

achète [l aʃɛt]: 2944

achetée [aʃˈte]: 2494

acheter [aʃˈte]: 2221, 2230, 2445

acheter [n aʃˈte]: 2982

acheter [ʁ aʃˈte]: 2137, 2253

achetons [aʃˈtɔ̃]: 2418

acteur [aktœʁ]: 2868

adjoint [adʒwɛ̃]: 2030

admirateurs [z admiʁatœʁ]: 2889

admission [n admisjɔ̃]: 2894

aéroport [aeʁopɔʁ]: 2978

affamé [afame]: 2446

affamée [afame]: 2446

affichaient [l afiʃɛ]: 2034

affichez [afiʃe]: 2995

affronter [z afʁɔ̃te]: 2987

afin [t afɛ̃]: 2854

afrique [afʁik]: 2311

âgé [aʒe]: 2628

âgées [aʒe]: 2797

agence [aʒãs]: 2997

agent [n aʒã]: 2242, 2534

âgés [aʒe]: 2851

agréable [s agʁeabl]: 2390

ai [ɛ]: 2499, 2651, 2754, 2806, 2844

ai [ʁ ɛ]: 2409, 2689, 2699

ai [z ɛ]: 2524

aidé [ɛde]: 2040, 2113

aide [n ɛd]: 2041

aider [ʁ ede]: 2293, 2452

aies [ɛ]: 2629, 2665

ai-je [ɛ ʒø]: 2858

aime [ɛm]: 2050

aimé [eme]: 2057, 2058, 2060, 2283, 2357

aimé [z eme]: 2059, 2451, 2806

aimerais-tu [ɛmˈʁɛ ty]: 2081

aimes-tu [ɛm ty]: 2045, 2282

aîné [ene]: 2628

allait [alɛ]: 2281, 2686
allé [ale]: 2129, 2209, 2273, 2313, 2382, 2516, 2527, 2639, 2922
allé [t̬ale]: 2521
allé [z̬ale]: 2441
allée [ale]: 2209, 2313, 2382, 2441, 2656, 2875
allée [t̬ale]: 2207
allées [ale]: 2288, 2439, 2459, 2630
aller [ale]: 2058, 2060, 2069, 2186, 2230, 2261, 2263, 2274, 2314, 2431, 2440, 2454, 2668
aller [ʁale]: 2704
aller [z̬ale]: 2262
allés [ale]: 2439, 2459, 2523, 2630
allés [z̬ale]: 2288
allions [z̬aljɔ̃]: 2503
allons [z̬alɔ̃]: 2654, 2721
allons-nous [alɔ̃ nu]: 2740
allumé [alyme]: 2664
alors [alɔ]: 2117, 2118, 2119, 2385, 2386, 2419, 2699, 2951
alors [alɔʁ]: 2040, 2116, 2156, 2172, 2281, 2288, 2366, 2673, 2674, 2675, 2714, 2757, 2763, 2861, 2868, 2880, 2898, 2899, 2962, 2976
alpes [z̬alp]: 2310
alphabet [n̬alfabɛ]: 2249
altercation [altɛʁkasjɔ̃]: 2369
altitude [altityd]: 2749
améliorer [ameljoʁe]: 2074
amende [amɑ̃d]: 2486
américain [n̬ameʁikɛ̃]: 2827
américaines [ameʁikɛn]: 2772
amérique [n̬ameʁik]: 2302, 2308
ami [l̬ami]: 2856
ami [n̬ami]: 2502, 2539, 2706
amie [ami]: 2370, 2501
amie [n̬ami]: 2504
amies [ami]: 2049, 2368, 2433, 2631, 2638, 2917
amies [n̬ami]: 2638, 2718
amis [s̬ami]: 2638

amis [z̬ami]: 2049, 2212, 2367, 2368, 2433, 2603, 2631, 2638, 2718, 2738, 2785, 2917, 2923, 2940, 2973
amour [amuʁ]: 2913
amour [n̬amuʁ]: 2496, 2745
amoureux [amuʁø]: 2496
amplement [ɑ̃plˀmɑ̃]: 2413
amples [s̬ɑ̃p]: 2233
amusant [z̬amyzɑ̃]: 2562
anesthésié [anɛstezje]: 2821
anesthésiée [anɛstezje]: 2821
anglais [ɑ̃glɛ]: 2419
anglais [n̬ɑ̃glɛ]: 2573, 2589, 2899
angleterre [ɑ̃gløtɛʁ]: 2315
angleterre [n̬ɑ̃gløtɛʁ]: 2093, 2877
anna [anna]: 2178
année [ane]: 2752, 2756, 2783, 2785
année [l̬ane]: 2781
années [k̬ane]: 2031, 2621
années [ʁane]: 2782
années [z̬ane]: 2786
annulé [anyle]: 2936
annulée [anyle]: 2339
ans [ɑ̃]: 2086, 2335, 2582, 2628, 2748, 2868, 2938
ans [t̬ɑ̃]: 2748
ans [v̬ɑ̃]: 2030
ans [z̬ɑ̃]: 2030, 2850
aperçu [apɛʁsy]: 2193
apparemment [apaʁamɑ̃]: 2948
appartement [apaʁtˀmɑ̃]: 2725
appartement [l̬apaʁtˀmɑ̃]: 2089
appel [n̬apɛl]: 2697
appelé [apˀle]: 2071, 2447
appeler [z̬apˀle]: 2181
appellerait [apɛlˀʁɛ]: 2664
appelons [z̬apˀlɔ̃]: 2922
application [aplikasjɔ̃]: 2780
apporté [z̬apɔʁte]: 2763
apprécié [apʁesje]: 2180
apprend [l̬apʁɑ̃]: 2143
apprendre [t̬apʁɑ̃dʁ]: 2575
apprennent [apʁɛn]: 2259, 2425
apprenties [apʁɑ̃ti]: 2378

apprentis [z_apʁɑ̃ti]: 2378
appris [apʁi]: 2002, 2251
appris [p_apʁi]: 2997
appropriées [apʁopʁije]: 2919
après [apʁɛ]: 2025, 2030, 2040, 2072, 2168, 2207, 2264, 2283, 2389, 2496, 2688, 2865, 2877, 2899, 2922, 2950
après-midi [apʁɛ midi]: 2280, 2709
araignées [z_aʁɛɲe]: 2284, 2810, 2811, 2812
architecture [n_aʁʃitektyʁ]: 2832
argent [aʁʒɑ̃]: 2900
argent [n_aʁʒɑ̃]: 2971
argent [t_aʁʒɑ̃]: 2156, 2404, 2432
argent [z_aʁʒɑ̃]: 2392
armes [ʁ_aʁm]: 2840
arnaquer [aʁnake]: 2943
arrangements [z_aʁɑ̃ʒ°mɑ̃]: 2852
arrêt [z_aʁɛ]: 2077, 2696
arrêté [aʁete]: 2556, 2727
arrêter [aʁete]: 2965
arrière [aʁjɛʁ]: 2723
arrivait [aʁivɛ]: 2826
arrive [aʁiv]: 2044, 2148
arrivé [aʁive]: 2163, 2503, 2768, 2915
arrivé [t_aʁive]: 2706
arrivée [z_aʁive]: 2641
arriver [aʁive]: 2162, 2740
arriverons [z_aʁiv°ʁɔ̃]: 2614
arrivés [aʁive]: 2503, 2603, 2831
arrivions [z_aʁivjɔ̃]: 2704, 2705
art [n_aʁ]: 2832
as [a]: 2017, 2097, 2225, 2233, 2289, 2297, 2396, 2466, 2493, 2505, 2515, 2582, 2613, 2667, 2776, 2830, 2896, 2919
asseoir [z_aswaʁ]: 2140
assez [ase]: 2080, 2594, 2609, 2690, 2763
assez [z_ase]: 2058, 2167, 2246, 2593, 2595, 2597, 2873, 2874, 2892
assis [asi]: 2497, 2552, 2676
assure-toi [asyʁ twa]: 2744

as-tu [a ty]: 2082, 2099, 2105, 2123, 2138, 2268, 2278, 2283, 2427, 2456, 2493, 2500, 2504, 2568, 2642, 2645, 2730, 2731, 2745... +6
a-t-elle [a t_ɛl]: 2915
athènes [atɛn]: 2319
a-t-il [a t_il]: 2261, 2383, 2594, 2875
atlantique [atlɑ̃tik]: 2300
attaqué [atake]: 2973
atteinte [ʁ_atɛt]: 2960
attend [atɑ̃]: 2646
attendant [atɑ̃dɑ̃]: 2187
attendions [z_atɑ̃djɔ̃]: 2324, 2610
attendre [atɑ̃dʁ]: 2014, 2048, 2084, 2824, 2957
attendu [atɑ̃dy]: 2609
attention [atɑ̃sjɔ̃]: 2205
attentivement [s_atɑ̃tiv°mɑ̃]: 2384
attentivement [z_atɑ̃tiv°mɑ̃]: 2172
atterri [atɛʁi]: 2647
atterrir [atɛʁiʁ]: 2647
attiré [t_atiʁe]: 2988
attitude [n_atityd]: 2788
au [o]: 2020, 2049, 2063, 2069, 2082, 2083, 2088, 2089, 2092, 2094, 2119, 2134, 2166, 2199, 2200, 2209, 2210, 2260... +54
aucun [okœ̃]: 2214, 2405, 2433, 2437, 2439, 2450
aucune [okyn]: 2401, 2433, 2442, 2469, 2540
augmentation [ogmɑ̃tasjɔ̃]: 2380, 2781
augmente [ogmɑ̃t]: 2788
augmenté [ogmɑ̃te]: 2770, 2884
aujourd'hui [oʒuʁdɥi]: 2065, 2221, 2237, 2251, 2261, 2276, 2455, 2699, 2704, 2755
auparavant [opaʁavɑ̃]: 2366
auprès [opʁɛ]: 2860
aura [oʁa]: 2169, 2260, 2389, 2705
auraient [l_oʁɛ]: 2600
aurais [oʁɛ]: 2680
aurais-tu [oʁɛ ty]: 2056
aurait [l_oʁɛ]: 2578, 2663
aurait [oʁɛ]: 2384, 2391, 2948

auras [oʁa]: 2231
aurions [z‿oʁjɔ̃]: 2058
aussi [osi]: 2052, 2618, 2624, 2923
aussi [z‿osi]: 2324, 2616, 2633
australie [ostʁali]: 2104, 2143
autant [otã]: 2619
autant [z‿otã]: 2617
autorisées [otoʁize]: 2183, 2378
autorisés [z‿otoʁize]: 2183, 2378
autorités [z‿otoʁite]: 2778, 2865
autour [otuʁ]: 2267, 2781, 2940, 2971
autre [n‿otʁ]: 2629, 2640
autre [ʁ‿otʁ]: 2416
autrefois [t‿otʁ°fwa]: 2532
autres [z‿otʁ]: 2741, 2952
aux [o]: 2008, 2152, 2298, 2729, 2772, 2817, 2828, 2941, 2999
avaient [avɛ]: 2040, 2533, 2983
avais [avɛ]: 2504
avait [avɛ]: 2121, 2140, 2171, 2379, 2391, 2400, 2402, 2410, 2423, 2490, 2504, 2584, 2605, 2733, 2734, 2865
avant [avã]: 2019, 2071, 2256, 2418, 2653, 2701, 2931, 2934, 2940, 2947, 2968
avant [ʁ‿avã]: 2920
avantages [z‿avãtaʒ]: 2777
avec [avɛk]: 2146, 2153, 2212, 2359, 2368, 2369, 2372, 2419, 2426, 2434, 2447, 2496, 2506, 2510, 2516, 2520, 2544, 2645, 2649, 2665... +12
avec [z‿avɛk]: 2965
aventure [n‿avãtyʁ]: 2940
avérée [aveʁe]: 2929
avertir [z‿aveʁtiʁ]: 2863
avez-vous [ave vu]: 2189, 2193, 2222
avion [avjɔ̃]: 2939
avion [n‿avjɔ̃]: 2162, 2766
avions [z‿avjɔ̃]: 2172, 2238, 2538
avis [n‿avi]: 2006, 2525
avocat [n‿avoka]: 2015, 2837, 2904
avoir [avwa]: 2017, 2375

avoir [avwaʁ]: 2019, 2248, 2385, 2386, 2444, 2769
avoir [ʁ‿avwaʁ]: 2895
avoir [z‿avwaʁ]: 2025, 2072, 2080, 2084, 2098, 2114, 2145, 2207, 2211, 2865, 2877
avons [avɔ̃]: 2434, 2861
avons [n‿avɔ̃]: 2623
avons [z‿avɔ̃]: 2023, 2034, 2077, 2096, 2104, 2140, 2147, 2172, 2206, 2226, 2236, 2254, 2258, 2269, 2283, 2368, 2400, 2413, 2418, 2430... +14
ayant [ɛjã]: 2206, 2212
bagages [bagaʒ]: 2238, 2613
bagarre [bagaʁ]: 2964
baisse [bɛs]: 2532, 2783
balayer [baleje]: 2957
banque [bãk]: 2261, 2263, 2639, 2704
bar [baʁ]: 2987
barrière [baʁjɛʁ]: 2906
bas [ba]: 2661, 2892
basé [baze]: 2791
bateau [bato]: 2733
bâtiment [batimã]: 2183, 2216, 2334, 2387, 2467, 2482
battu [baty]: 2973
beau [bo]: 2216, 2231, 2236, 2237, 2258
beaucoup [boku]: 2042, 2090, 2127, 2138, 2169, 2210, 2229, 2235, 2238, 2250, 2254, 2281, 2340, 2379, 2386, 2412, 2414, 2415, 2476... +18
beaux [bo]: 2579
bébé [bebe]: 2920
belle [bɛl]: 2237, 2934
besoin [bøzwɛ̃]: 2036, 2038, 2039, 2040, 2041, 2079, 2136, 2139, 2156, 2220, 2233, 2247, 2253, 2289, 2327, 2396, 2413, 2422, 2560... +9
beurre [bœʁ]: 2872
bicyclette [bisiklɛt]: 2322
bien [bjɛ̃]: 2056, 2075, 2445, 2494, 2579, 2580, 2589, 2655, 2656, 2658, 2659, 2718, 2743, 2826

biens [bjɛ̃]: 2994
billet [bijɛ]: 2132
billets [bijɛ]: 2403, 2875
bizarre [bizaʁ]: 2086
blague [blag]: 2838
blâme [blam]: 2881, 2885
blâmée [blame]: 2886
blâmer [blame]: 2347, 2348, 2883
blâmes-tu [blam ty]: 2513, 2883
blessé [blese]: 2410, 2548
blessée [blese]: 2200
blessées [blese]: 2217, 2571, 2576
bloquerait [blɔkᵊʁɛ]: 2955
boire [bwaʁ]: 2151, 2418
bois [bwa]: 2298
boisson [bwasɔ̃]: 2849
boîte [bwat]: 2729
bombe [bɔ̃b]: 2198
bon [bɔ̃]: 2240, 2357, 2382, 2460,
    2562, 2565, 2588
bondé [bɔ̃de]: 2616, 2735
bonjour [bɔ̃ʒuʁ]: 2649
bonne [bɔn]: 2164, 2240, 2789, 2858
bonnes [bɔ]: 2638, 2718
bons [bɔ̃]: 2438, 2638, 2718
bonté [bɔ̃te]: 2857
bord [bɔʁ]: 2390, 2716, 2735
bordés [bɔʁde]: 2542
bouillir [bujiʁ]: 2912
bouleversé [bulᵊvɛʁse]: 2946
bout [bu]: 2751
bouteille [butɛj]: 2136
bouton [butɔ̃]: 2035
branché [bʁɑ̃ʃe]: 2921
bruit [bʁ4i]: 2089, 2111, 2222, 2223,
    2386, 2978
brûle [bʁyl]: 2947
brûler [bʁyle]: 2196
bu [by]: 2283
bureau [byʁo]: 2051, 2263
bus [bys]: 2142, 2187, 2400, 2460,
    2604, 2605, 2673, 2735, 2741,
    2765, 2911, 2996
but [byt]: 2543

ça [sa]: 2026, 2053, 2064, 2090, 2091,
    2383, 2440, 2567, 2601, 2680,
    2835, 2879, 2890, 2943, 2959,
    2985, 2997
cacher [kaʃe]: 2956
cadre [kadʁ]: 2790
café [kafe]: 2201, 2282, 2283
caire [kaiʁ]: 2299
calmer [kalme]: 2948
calme-toi [kalm twa]: 2991
cambriolage [kɑ̃bʁijolaʒ]: 2323, 2549
cambrioleurs [kɑ̃bʁijolœʁ]: 2073, 2121
camion [kamjɔ̃]: 2911
campagne [kɑ̃paɲ]: 2062, 2476
canada [kanada]: 2307
capable [kapabl]: 2361, 2822
capitale [kapital]: 2299, 2309
capitales [kapital]: 2744
car [kaʁ]: 2088, 2450, 2572, 2686,
    2783, 2862, 2890, 2926
carambolage [kaʁɑ̃bolaʒ]: 2911
cardiaque [kaʁdjak]: 2868, 2869, 2884
carte [kaʁt]: 2538, 2662, 2762, 2763,
    2780, 2876
cartes [kaʁt]: 2933
cas [ka]: 2662, 2663, 2664, 2665, 2666,
    2915, 2954, 2955
cassée [kase]: 2769
causant [kozɑ̃]: 2911
cause [koz]: 2218, 2660, 2778, 2977
causé [koze]: 2340, 2486
causer [koze]: 2397
causes [koz]: 2999
causés [koze]: 2076, 2784
ce [sø]: 2010, 2016, 2021, 2052, 2063,
    2064, 2067, 2070, 2086, 2089,
    2091, 2097, 2105, 2160, 2165,
    2169, 2171, 2178... + 63
ceci [sᵊsi]: 2539
ceintures [sɛ̃tyʁ]: 2473
cela [sᵊla]: 2404, 2764, 2801, 2830,
    2981
célèbre [selɛbʁ]: 2832, 2868
célibataire [selibatɛʁ]: 2377
celui [sᵊl4i]: 2982

cent [sã]: 2751, 2966
centrale [sãtʀal]: 2310
centre [sãtʀ]: 2616
centre-ville [sãtʀ°vil]: 2134
cents [sã]: 2486, 2749, 2750, 2770, 2773
certainement [seʀten°mã]: 2995
certaines [seʀtɛ]: 2772
certaines [seʀten]: 2284, 2363, 2425, 2426, 2897, 2945
certains [seʀtɛ̃]: 2211, 2259, 2260, 2435, 2679, 2752, 2814, 2866
ces [se]: 2094, 2239, 2427, 2438, 2439, 2440, 2441, 2449, 2468, 2470, 2597, 2833, 2983, 2999
cesse [sɛs]: 2672
c'est [se]: 2057, 2089, 2134, 2154, 2237, 2240, 2252, 2326, 2330, 2348, 2373, 2455, 2563, 2567, 2589, 2596, 2613, 2762, 2776... +6
cet [sɛ]: 2007, 2156, 2404, 2432, 2507, 2510, 2533, 2611, 2980
c'était [se etɛ]: 2060, 2078, 2155, 2387, 2423, 2467, 2559, 2584, 2586, 2592, 2605, 2629, 2793
cette [sɛt]: 2041, 2136, 2151, 2167, 2170, 2370, 2550, 2585, 2684, 2756, 2785, 2816, 2912, 2946, 2997
chacun [ʃakœ̃]: 2468, 2471
chacune [ʃakyn]: 2469, 2470
chaise [ʃɛz]: 2167
chaises [ʃɛz]: 2140, 2239
chaleur [ʃalœʀ]: 2011, 2326, 2536
chambre [ʃãbʀ]: 2197, 2226, 2372, 2547, 2584, 2671
chambres [ʃãbʀ]: 2469
chandails [ʃãdaj]: 2902
change [ʃãʒ]: 2487
changé [ʃãʒe]: 2582
changer [ʃãʒe]: 2026
chanteurs [ʃãtœʀ]: 2752
chaque [ʃak]: 2094, 2466, 2473, 2474, 2752, 2788, 2918, 2950
charité [ʃaʀite]: 2794
chat [ʃa]: 2948
chaud [ʃo]: 2326, 2648, 2742

chaude [ʃod]: 2849
chauds [ʃo]: 2145, 2901
chaussure [ʃosyʀ]: 2843
chaussures [ʃosy]: 2920
chaussures [ʃosyʀ]: 2088, 2574
chemin [ʃ°mɛ̃]: 2442, 2592, 2662, 2706, 2755
chemises [ʃ°miz]: 2445
chèque [ʃɛk]: 2772, 2773
cher [ʃɛʀ]: 2439, 2611, 2621, 2944
cherché [ʃɛʀʃe]: 2206, 2464
chercher [ʃɛʀʃe]: 2969
cherches [ʃɛʀʃ]: 2932
chères [ʃɛʀ]: 2380
cheval [ʃ°val]: 3000
cheveu [ʃ°vø]: 2224
cheveux [ʃ°vø]: 2225
chez [ʃe]: 2226, 2262
chien [ʃjɛ̃]: 2174
chiens [ʃjɛ̃]: 2173
chine [ʃin]: 2316, 2738
chinois [ʃinwa]: 2295
chocolat [ʃokola]: 2330
chocolats [ʃokola]: 2551
chômage [ʃomaʒ]: 2210
chômeurs [ʃomœʀ]: 2297
choqué [ʃoke]: 2804
chose [ʃoz]: 2078, 2136, 2181, 2196, 2203, 2416, 2418, 2484, 2825, 2846
choses [ʃoz]: 2297, 2342, 2380, 2500, 2690, 2690, 2927, 2944
ciel [sjɛl]: 2269
cimetière [sim°tjɛʀ]: 2526
cinéma [sinema]: 2063, 2387, 2705, 2723, 2875
cinq [sɛ̃]: 2276, 2334, 2700
cinq [sɛ̃k]: 2162, 2770, 2772, 2911
cinquante [sɛ̃kãt]: 2770, 2868
circulation [siʀkylasjɔ̃]: 2169, 2379, 2386, 2633
clairement [klɛʀ°mã]: 2018
claquer [klake]: 2199
classe [klas]: 2276, 2277, 2681, 2823, 2942

clé [kle]: 2208, 2450, 2769
clés [kle]: 2493, 2844
client [klijã]: 2166
climatique [klimatik]: 2863
cloche [klɔʃ]: 2535
club [klœb]: 2175, 2668
coco [koko]: 2910
cœur [kœʁ]: 2884
coin [kwɛ̃]: 2728, 2729
colère [kolɛʁ]: 2796, 2797, 2800
collision [kolizjɔ̃]: 2911
combien [kɔ̃bjɛ̃]: 2353, 2879, 2918
comme [kɔm]: 2026, 2169, 2377, 2529, 2676, 2679, 2680, 2681, 2682, 2683, 2688, 2689, 2690, 2742, 2784, 2900, 2959
commençait [komãsɛ]: 2675
commence [komãs]: 2169, 2940, 2981
commencé [komãse]: 2022, 2705, 2713, 2841, 2842
commencer [komãse]: 2148, 2724, 2994
comment [komã]: 2120, 2325, 2575
commercial [komɛʁsjal]: 2616
communiquer [komynike]: 2146, 2213, 2419, 2544, 2665, 2678
communiquerait [komynikᵊʁɛ]: 2447
compagnie [kɔ̃paɲi]: 2333, 2773, 2986
compétences [kɔ̃petãs]: 2074
compétitif [kɔ̃petitif]: 2914
complet [kɔ̃plɛ]: 2034, 2467
complète [kɔ̃plɛt]: 2381
complètement [kɔ̃plɛtᵊmã]: 2029, 2829, 2983
compléter [kɔ̃plete]: 2961
complique [kɔ̃plik]: 2544
compliquée [kɔ̃plike]: 2598
compliquées [kɔ̃plike]: 2600
comportement [kɔ̃pɔʁtᵊmã]: 2881
comporter [kɔ̃pɔʁte]: 2775
compose [kɔ̃poz]: 2872
composé [kɔ̃poze]: 2870
comprenant [kɔ̃pʁᵊnã]: 2334
comprends [kɔ̃pʁã]: 2835
comprise [kɔ̃pʁiz]: 2558

compter [kɔ̃te]: 2509, 2896
concentrer [kɔ̃sãtʁe]: 2350, 2360
concernant [kɔ̃sɛʁnã]: 2329
concert [kɔ̃sɛʁ]: 2936
condamné [kɔ̃dane]: 2486
condition [kɔ̃disjɔ̃]: 2671
conditions [kɔ̃disjɔ̃]: 2890
conducteur [kɔ̃dyktœ]: 2750
conducteur [kɔ̃dyktœʁ]: 2473, 2486
conducteurs [kɔ̃dyktœʁ]: 2378
conductrices [kɔ̃dyktʁis]: 2378
conduire [kɔ̃dɥiʁ]: 2002, 2061, 2092, 2093, 2378, 2652, 2670
conduisaient [kɔ̃dɥizɛ]: 2384
conduisent [kɔ̃dɥiz]: 2076
conduises [kɔ̃dɥiz]: 2670
conduit [kɔ̃dɥi]: 2019, 2241
conférence [kɔ̃feʁãs]: 2389, 2577, 2800
confiant [kɔ̃fjã]: 2822
connais [konɛ]: 2411, 2617
connaissait [konɛsɛ]: 2442, 2959
connaissent-ils [konɛ s_il]: 2218
connaissez-vous [konɛse vu]: 2353
connaissons [konɛsɔ̃]: 2476
connais-tu [konɛ ty]: 2286, 2415, 2528
connaît [konɛ]: 2517, 2518
connaître [konɛtʁ]: 2502
conscient [kɔ̃sjã]: 2820, 2821
consciente [kɔ̃sjãt]: 2821
conseil [kɔ̃sɛj]: 2240
conseillé [kɔ̃seje]: 2861
conseils [kɔ̃sɛj]: 2247, 2256
considérable [kɔ̃sideʁabl]: 2782
consiste [kɔ̃sist]: 2331
constituée [kɔ̃stitɥe]: 2871
construire [kɔ̃stʁɥiʁ]: 2977
consulter [kɔ̃sylte]: 2861
contact [kɔ̃takt]: 2762
contents [kɔ̃tã]: 2160
continent [kɔ̃tinã]: 2303
continua [kɔ̃tinɥa]: 2688
continué [kɔ̃tinɥe]: 2024
continue [kɔ̃tiny]: 2935
continuent [kɔ̃tiny]: 2863

continuer [kɔ̃tinɥe]: 2026, 2941, 2981
contrat [kɔ̃tʁa]: 2961
contre [kɔ̃tʁ]: 2182, 2291, 2797, 2808, 2839, 2862, 2888, 2906, 2999
contrepartie [kɔ̃tʁ°paʁti]: 2177
contrôle [kɔ̃tʁol]: 2750, 2906
convenait [kɔ̃v°nɛ]: 2540
convenu [kɔ̃v°ny]: 2928
conversation [kɔ̃vɛʁsasjɔ̃]: 2147
conviction [kɔ̃viksjɔ̃]: 2916
coopération [koopeʁasjɔ̃]: 2928
copain [kopɛ̃]: 2875
corps [kɔʁ]: 2889
correctement [kɔʁɛkt°mɑ̃]: 2569, 2921
corriger [kɔʁiʒe]: 2764
corsé [kɔʁse]: 2282
côté [kote]: 2286, 2475, 2481, 2488, 2489, 2497, 2552, 2687, 2736, 2900, 2978
côtés [kote]: 2542
couchant [kuʃɑ̃]: 3000
couloir [kulwaʁ]: 2736
coup [ku]: 2958
coupable [kupabl]: 2958
coupé [kupe]: 2204
couramment [kuʁamɑ̃]: 2630
coureur [kuʁœʁ]: 2972
courir [kuʁiʁ]: 2624
courriel [kuʁjɛl]: 2762, 2834
courriels [kuʁjɛl]: 2197
cours [kuʁ]: 2336, 2695, 2926, 2960
course [kuʁs]: 2679, 2757, 2771
courses [kuʁs]: 2342
court [kuʁ]: 2578, 2930, 2933
couru [kuʁy]: 2077
coût [ku]: 2380
coûté [kute]: 2943
coutumes [kutym]: 2828
couvertures [kuvɛʁtyʁ]: 2902
crains-tu [kʁɛ̃ ty]: 2811
créatif [kʁeatif]: 2970
crédit [kʁedi]: 2763, 2876
criait [kʁijɛ]: 2839
criant [kʁijɑ̃]: 2202

crié [kʁije]: 2182, 2808
crime [kʁim]: 2545, 2667, 2820
crimes [kʁim]: 2878, 2885
criminalité [kʁiminalite]: 2782
crise [kʁiz]: 2868, 2883
critiqué [kʁitike]: 2818
critiquer [kʁitike]: 2157
croirais [kʁwaʁɛ]: 2589
croire [kʁwaʁ]: 2016
crois [kʁwa]: 2903
croisière [kʁwazjɛʁ]: 2733
croit [kʁwa]: 2791
croyait [kʁwajɛ]: 2929
cuisine [kɥizin]: 2052, 2053, 2201, 2294, 2559, 2832
cuisinière [kɥizinjɛʁ]: 2912
culture [kyltyʁ]: 2832
d'à [d a]: 2489, 2687
d'accidents [d aksidɑ̃]: 2384, 2781
d'accord [d akɔʁ]: 2081, 2434
d'affaires [d afɛʁ]: 2519, 2543, 2678, 2962
d'afrique [afrique]: 2306
d'aide [d ɛd]: 2040, 2896
d'air [d ɛʁ]: 2255
d'aller [d ale]: 2063, 2119, 2174, 2799
d'amis [d ami]: 2226, 2417
dangereuse [dɑ̃ʒ°ʁøz]: 2170
dangereux [dɑ̃ʒ°ʁø]: 2004, 2679
d'anglais [d ɑ̃glɛ]: 2918
dans [dɑ̃]: 2007, 2059, 2073, 2084, 2085, 2095, 2121, 2186, 2197, 2201, 2211, 2217, 2224, 2260, 2271, 2313, 2321, 2364, 2449... +56
d'appeler [d ap°le]: 2001, 2029
d'apprendre [d apʁɑ̃dʁ]: 2158, 2179
d'appuyer [d apɥije]: 2035
d'arbres [d aʁbʁ]: 2542, 2990
d'argent [d aʁʒɑ̃]: 2058, 2085, 2210, 2235, 2253, 2293, 2412, 2623, 2651, 2763, 2873, 2874
d'arriver [d aʁive]: 2951
d'assurance [d asyʁɑ̃s]: 2773
d'attendre [d atɑ̃dʁ]: 2116

d'autre [d_otʁ]: 2847
d'autres [dot]: 2814
d'autres [dotʁ]: 2425, 2815, 2897
davantage [davãtaʒ]: 2270
d'avoir [d_avwaʁ]: 2021, 2042, 2115,
     2182, 2808, 2866
de [dø]: 2003, 2004, 2005, 2007, 2008,
     2009, 2010, 2015, 2016, 2017,
     2018, 2019, 2020, 2022, 2023,
     2025, 2027... +497
d'eau [d_o]: 2912
début [deby]: 2088, 2608, 2718, 2719,
     2929
décédé [desede]: 2514
décembre [desãbʁ]: 2707, 2720
déchets [deʃɛ]: 2919
décidé [deside]: 2104, 2986, 2992,
     2994
décider [deside]: 2445
décision [desizjɔ̃]: 2422, 2629, 2985
décisions [desizjɔ̃]: 2683, 2848
décolle [dekɔl]: 2968
décollé [dekole]: 2646, 2749
décoller [dekole]: 2939
déconcertées [dekɔ̃sɛʁte]: 2778
d'économie [d_ekonomi]: 2025
d'économiser [d_ekonomize]: 2543
découvert [dekuvɛ]: 2990
découvert [dekuvɛʁ]: 2865
décrire [dekʁiʁ]: 2836
décrocheur [dekroʃœʁ]: 2922
défendre [defãdʁ]: 2361
dégoûtant [degutã]: 2559
degrés [d_gʁe]: 2326, 2751
déjà [deʒa]: 2212, 2268, 2275, 2278,
     2313, 2514, 2573, 2629, 2643,
     2644, 2645, 2690, 2705, 2730,
     2731, 2745, 2850, 2855
déjeuner [deʒœne]: 2081, 2185, 2185,
     2278, 2644
déjeunons [deʒœnɔ̃]: 2081
déjoué [deʒwe]: 2925
d'elles [d_ɛl]: 2442, 2540, 2933

demain [d_mɛ̃]: 2001, 2029, 2065,
     2081, 2260, 2280, 2339, 2653,
     2654, 2669, 2937
demande [d_mãd]: 2178, 2690, 2774
demandé [d_mãde]: 2003, 2409, 2437,
     2442, 2806, 2844, 2951
demander [d_mãde]: 2102, 2181, 2245,
     2525
demandes [d_mãd]: 2006
déménager [demenaʒe]: 2104, 2629,
     2994
déménagés [demenaʒe]: 2144
demeurait [d_mœʁɛ]: 2817
demi-heures [d_miœʁ]: 2483
démissionner [demisjone]: 2806
démolies [demoli]: 2945, 2990
d'enfants [d_ãfã]: 2444, 2815
d'entendre [d_ãtãdʁ]: 2177, 2801
dentiste [dãtist]: 2262
d'entre [d_ãtʁ]: 2435, 2437, 2450, 2741
d'entrer [d_ãtʁe]: 2920
département [depaʁt_mã]: 2724
dépassé [depase]: 2737
dépassée [depase]: 2737
dépasser [depase]: 2150
dépêché [depeʃe]: 2141
dépêchée [depeʃe]: 2141
dépêcher [depeʃe]: 2413
dépend [depã]: 2890, 2900
dépendant [depãdã]: 2830
dépendante [depãdãt]: 2830
dépensé [depãse]: 2412, 2458
dépensent [depãs]: 2235
dépit [depi]: 2655, 2656, 2657, 2658,
     2661
déplacé [deplase]: 2003
déplacer [deplase]: 2017, 2041, 2211
déposé [depoze]: 2968
déposée [depoze]: 2968
déprimantes [depʁimãt]: 2234
depuis [d_pɥi]: 2353, 2524, 2531, 2559,
     2591, 2692, 2786, 2973
déracinés [deʁasine]: 2990
dérange [deʁãʒ]: 2053, 2064, 2091
dérangent [deʁãʒ]: 2079

déranger [deʁɑ̃ʒe]: 2149

dernier [dɛʁnje]: 2258, 2637, 2806

dernière [dɛʁnjɛʁ]: 2129, 2195, 2323, 2340, 2342, 2733, 2856

dernières [dɛʁnjɛ]: 2782

derniers [dɛʁnje]: 2983

d'erreurs [d_ɛʁœʁ]: 2823

derrière [dɛʁjɛʁ]: 2150

des [de]: 2024, 2037, 2047, 2076, 2080, 2121, 2126, 2130, 2145, 2216, 2271, 2284, 2298, 2308, 2310, 2322, 2329, 2389... +58

dès [dɛ]: 2620, 2861

désastre [dezastʁ]: 2454

descendait [desɑ̃dɛ]: 2673

désert [dezɛʁ]: 2311

désires [deziʁ]: 2905

désolé [dezole]: 2044, 2158, 2179, 2181, 2182, 2379, 2397, 2618, 2801, 2807, 2808, 2809, 2932

désolée [dezole]: 2179

désordre [dezɔʁdʁ]: 2807, 2980

d'essence [d_esɑ̃s]: 2930

dessus [d°sy]: 2167

destiné [destine]: 2168

destinée [destine]: 2164, 2168

désuétude [desyetyd]: 2983

détail [detaj]: 2992

d'été [d_ete]: 2454

détendre [detɑ̃dʁ]: 2349, 2362

déterminer [detɛʁmine]: 2833

déteste [detɛst]: 2046, 2585

détesté [deteste]: 2051

d'étoiles [d_etwal]: 2271, 2536

d'être [d_ɛtʁ]: 2033, 2038, 2039, 2043, 2109, 2120, 2121, 2289, 2618, 2655, 2657, 2658, 2668, 2864, 2924

détruit [detʁɥi]: 2467, 2482

d'étudier [d_etydje]: 2360

d'europe [d_øʁop]: 2305, 2310

d'eux [d_ø]: 2814, 2830

deux [dø]: 2014, 2030, 2162, 2212, 2264, 2323, 2328, 2337, 2338, 2355, 2438, 2442, 2443, 2445, 2449, 2541... +17

deuxième [døzjɛm]: 2166, 2725

devait [d°vɛ]: 2385

devant [d°vɑ̃]: 2008, 2009, 2771

développée [dev°lope]: 2774

devenait [d°v°nɛ]: 2564

devenir [d°v°niʁ]: 2855, 2981

devenu [d°v°ny]: 2030, 2031, 2956

devenus [d°v°ny]: 2718

déverrouilla [dev°ʁuija]: 2208

devoirs [d°vwaʁ]: 2918

devons [d°vɔ̃]: 2026, 2270, 2780, 2978

devraient [d°vʁɛ]: 2292, 2699

devrais [d°vʁɛ]: 2015, 2097, 2098, 2350, 2666, 2667, 2854, 2993

devrais-je [d°vʁɛ ʒø]: 2066, 2643

devrait [d°vʁɛ]: 2647, 2982

devrions [d°vʁijɔ̃]: 2348, 2845

devrions-nous [d°vʁijɔ̃ nu]: 2351, 2612

d'examen [d_ɛgzamɛ̃]: 2332

d'exercice [d_ɛgzɛʁsis]: 2036

d'expérience [d_ɛkspeʁjɑ̃s]: 2229, 2246, 2594

d'habitude [d_abityd]: 2605, 2616, 2681

d'histoires [d istwaʁ]: 2993

d'hydrogène [d_idʁoʒɛn]: 2871

d'ici [d_isi]: 2118, 2261, 2398, 2477, 2596, 2699, 2703, 2704, 2705

différences [difeʁɑ̃s]: 2792

différent [difeʁɑ̃]: 2466, 2825, 2829

différente [difeʁɑ̃t]: 2469

différentes [difeʁɑ̃t]: 2434

difficile [difisil]: 2090, 2154, 2211, 2252, 2419, 2677, 2878, 2950, 2981

difficulté [difikylte]: 2123, 2124, 2125, 2131, 2401

d'îles [d_il]: 2312

diminution [diminysjɔ̃]: 2782

d'impôts [d_ɛ̃po]: 2292

d'imprimer [d_ɛ̃pʁime]: 2744

dîner [dine]: 2055, 2100, 2206, 2283, 2565, 2715

d'intéressant [d_ɛ̃teʁesɑ̃]: 2563

d'invitations [d_ɛ̃vitasjɔ̃]: 2785

diplôme [diplom]: 2243, 2923

diplômés [diplome]: 2772
dirait [diʁɛ]: 2685, 2687
dire [diʁ]: 2015, 2021, 2066, 2070, 2078, 2398, 2643, 2714, 2903
directement [diʁɛkt°mã]: 2207
directeur [diʁɛktœʁ]: 2860
dis [di]: 2714
discours [disku]: 2899
discours [diskuʁ]: 2802, 2803, 2805
discussion [diskysjɔ̃]: 2845
discute [diskyt]: 2965
discuté [diskyte]: 2025
discuter [diskyte]: 2941
dise [diz]: 2070
dises [diz]: 2067
dis-moi [di mwa]: 2512
disparaisse [dispaʁɛs]: 2957
disparus [dispaʁy]: 2195
dispose [dispoz]: 2373, 2543
disque [disk]: 2954
distribué [distʁibɥe]: 2933, 2994
district [distʁikt]: 2321
dit [di]: 2004, 2015, 2016, 2021, 2067, 2097, 2098, 2298, 2391, 2433, 2447, 2463, 2498, 2500, 2527, 2563... +9
d'italie [italie]: 2539
dite [dit]: 2078
divisé [divize]: 2909
dix [di]: 2714
dix [dis]: 2077, 2460, 2540, 2749
dix-huit [dizɥit]: 2938
dix-sept [disɛ]: 2748
dix-sept [disɛt]: 2748
d'obtenir [d_ɔpt°niʁ]: 2961
d'occasions [d_okazjɔ̃]: 2138
dois [dwa]: 2181, 2245, 2261, 2263, 2361, 2700, 2703, 2709, 2881, 2954, 2955
doit [dwa]: 2026, 2037, 2090, 2386, 2398, 2473, 2477, 2683, 2769, 2886, 2985
doive [dwav]: 2669
dollar [dolaʁ]: 2296
dollars [dolaʁ]: 2772

d'omettre [d_omɛtʁ]: 2992
dommage [domaʒ]: 2057
dommages [domaʒ]: 2340, 2784
don [dɔ̃]: 2794
donc [dɔ̃k]: 2850, 2952, 2960, 2978, 2979, 2981
donna [dona]: 2186
donnant [donã]: 2547
donné [done]: 2137, 2257, 2298, 2458, 2499, 2951, 2988
donnent [dɔn]: 2511, 2772
donner [done]: 2256, 2422, 2802
donnerai [dɔn°ʁɛ]: 2665
donnez [done]: 2474
dont [dɔ̃]: 2331, 2496, 2507, 2514, 2516, 2518, 2542, 2543
dormi [dɔʁmi]: 2701
dormir [dɔʁmi]: 2658
dormir [dɔʁmiʁ]: 2034, 2658, 2963
dormira [dɔʁmiʁa]: 2033
doucement [dus°mã]: 2581
douleur [dulœʁ]: 2861
doute [dut]: 2653
douze [duz]: 2336, 2336
droit [dʁwa]: 2732, 2894, 2904
drôle [dʁol]: 2838
drôles [dʁol]: 2562
dû [dy]: 2021, 2092, 2140, 2400, 2675, 2680, 2784, 2898, 2936, 2989
du [dy]: 2034, 2096, 2125, 2129, 2130, 2166, 2174, 2201, 2213, 2231, 2242, 2258, 2260, 2267, 2269, 2287, 2301, 2302, 2303, 2308... +45
d'un [d_œ̃]: 2543, 2721, 2856, 2889, 2923, 2928, 2978
d'une [d_yn]: 2342, 2501, 2774, 2861, 2868, 2869, 2884
duquel [dykɛl]: 2497
dur [dyʁ]: 2134, 2954
durant [dyʁã]: 2276, 2464, 2866
dure [dyʁ]: 2336, 2337
duré [dyʁe]: 2290
durer [dyʁe]: 2342
d'usines [d_yzin]: 2331

d'y   [d_i]: 2395, 2854
eau   [o]: 2151, 2151
échappé   [eʃape]: 2972
économique   [ekonomik]: 2883, 2883, 2942
écrasé   [ekʁaze]: 2906
écrire   [ekʁiʁ]: 2764
écrit   [ekʁi]: 2447, 2642, 2773, 2823
écriture   [n_ekʁityʁ]: 2124
éducation   [edykasjõ]: 2913
effets   [z_efɛ]: 2863, 2888
effrayantes   [efʁejãt]: 2810
effrayé   [efʁeje]: 2813
égoïste   [egoist]: 2864
égoïste   [t_egoist]: 2847
égoïstes   [z_egoist]: 2363
égout   [n_egu]: 2844
eiffel   [eiffel]: 2831
élève   [elɛv]: 2164, 2277
élevé   [ɛl°ve]: 2962, 2962
élève   [l_elɛv]: 2377
élevé   [z_ɛl°ve]: 2660
élevée   [ɛl°ve]: 2962
élèves   [z_elɛv]: 2471, 2866
elle   [d_ɛl]: 2433, 2798
elle   [ɛ]: 2043, 2079, 2086, 2087, 2091, 2143, 2164, 2207, 2377, 2392, 2416, 2433, 2447, 2488, 2491, 2504, 2641, 2652, 2656... +11
elle   [ɛl]: 2043, 2075, 2131, 2359, 2371, 2401, 2433, 2447, 2544, 2580, 2589, 2610, 2641, 2652, 2660, 2690, 2704, 2756, 2769, 2826... +9
elle   [l_ɛ]: 2950
elle   [ʁ_ɛl]: 2086, 2690
elle   [t_ɛ]: 2827
elle-même   [ɛlmɛm]: 2358
elles   [d_ɛ]: 2844
elles   [ɛ]: 2088, 2152, 2600
elles   [ɛl]: 2040, 2066, 2088, 2100, 2137, 2354, 2363, 2381, 2465, 2844
elles-mêmes   [ɛl mɛm]: 2378
elles-mêmes   [ɛlmɛm]: 2363
éloquent   [elokã]: 2805
emmenant   [z_ãm°nã]: 2553

emmenées   [ãm°ne]: 2264
empêché   [ãpeʃe]: 2110, 2183
empêchées   [ãpeʃe]: 2112
empêchés   [z_ãpeʃe]: 2112
emploi   [ãplwa]: 2640, 2950
emploi   [l_ãplwa]: 2090, 2107, 2252, 2358
emploi   [n_ãplwa]: 2099, 2131, 2156, 2177, 2179, 2297, 2401, 2416, 2640, 2950, 2986
emploi   [ʁ_ãplwa]: 2806, 2997
emploi   [t_ãplwa]: 2533
emploi   [z_ãplwa]: 2281
empruntant   [n_ãpʁœ̃tã]: 2085
emprunté   [ãpʁœ̃te]: 2515
emprunter   [ãpʁœ̃te]: 2374, 2670
en   [ã]: 2020, 2028, 2073, 2074, 2075, 2084, 2085, 2093, 2094, 2141, 2177, 2195, 2196, 2197, 2200, 2201, 2202, 2204, 2205... +56
en   [ʁ_ã]: 2058, 2061, 2061, 2104, 2143, 2658, 2709, 2738, 2765, 2766, 2899, 2942, 2982, 2994
en   [s_ã]: 2564
en   [t_ã]: 2119, 2163, 2272, 2316, 2491, 2492, 2519, 2532, 2678, 2738, 2755, 2767, 2796, 2797, 2916, 2945, 2962
en   [z_ã]: 2379, 2459, 2560, 2623, 2636, 2685, 2800, 2862, 2903, 2932, 2953, 2983
encore   [ãkɔʁ]: 2418, 2573, 2637, 2650, 2651, 2798, 2824, 2830, 2969
encore   [z_ãkɔʁ]: 2422, 2639, 2640, 2646, 2647
endommagée   [ãdomaʒe]: 2554
endormi   [ãdɔʁmi]: 2693
endormie   [ãdɔʁmi]: 2693
endroit   [n_ãdʁwa]: 2122, 2125, 2134, 2206, 2423, 2522, 2526
endroit   [t_ãdʁwa]: 2980
endroits   [z_ãdʁwa]: 2211, 2260
enfant   [n_ãfã]: 2962
enfants   [n_ãfã]: 2289
enfants   [ʁ_ãfã]: 2511

enfants [zᵊɑ̃fɑ̃]: 2144, 2195, 2259, 2377, 2814, 2827, 2996
enfermées [ɑ̃fɛʀme]: 2364
enfermés [ɑ̃fɛʀme]: 2364
enfilé [ɑ̃file]: 2145
enfin [ɑ̃fɛ̃]: 2206
enlève [ɑ̃lɛv]: 2920
ennuis [zᵊɑ̃nɥi]: 2999
ennuyant [sᵊɑ̃nɥijɑ̃]: 2564
ennuyantes [ennuyantes]: 2563
ennuyeux [sᵊɑ̃nɥijø]: 2625
ennuyeux [zᵊɑ̃nɥijø]: 2089, 2423
énorme [enɔʀm]: 2783
enquête [ɑ̃kɛt]: 2545
enquêter [ʀᵊɑ̃kete]: 2953
enregistrer [ɑ̃ʀᵊʒistʀe]: 2666
enseignante [ɑ̃sɛɲɑ̃t]: 2558
enseignantes [zᵊɑ̃sɛɲɑ̃t]: 2541
enseigner [ʀᵊɑ̃sɛɲe]: 2289
ensemble [lᵊɑ̃sɑ̃bl]: 2945
ensuite [ɑ̃sɥit]: 2025
entendez-vous [ɑ̃tɑ̃de vu]: 2687
entendions [zᵊɑ̃tɑ̃djɔ̃]: 2718
entendre [ɑ̃tɑ̃dʀ]: 2147, 2194
entendu [ɑ̃tɑ̃dy]: 2198, 2199, 2222, 2385, 2500, 2798
entendu [zᵊɑ̃tɑ̃dy]: 2191, 2753
entendue [ɑ̃tɑ̃dy]: 2191
enterrés [ɑ̃teʀe]: 2526
entier [nᵊɑ̃tje]: 2456
entre [ɑ̃tʀ]: 2300, 2307, 2791, 2792, 2949, 2976
entré [ɑ̃tʀe]: 2911
entreprise [ɑ̃tʀᵊpʀiz]: 2530
entreprise [nᵊɑ̃tʀᵊpʀiz]: 2682
entreprises [nᵊɑ̃tʀᵊpʀiz]: 2772
entreprises [zᵊɑ̃tʀᵊpʀiz]: 2904, 2928
entrer [ɑ̃tʀe]: 2186, 2191, 2255
entrés [ɑ̃tʀe]: 2084
envahie [ɑ̃vai]: 2831
envers [ɑ̃vɛʀ]: 2788, 2795
envers [zᵊɑ̃vɛʀ]: 2819
envie [ɑ̃vi]: 2105
envieuse [ɑ̃vjøz]: 2816

environ [ɑ̃viʀɔ̃]: 2461
envoyé [ɑ̃vwaje]: 2699
envoyés [ɑ̃vwaje]: 2988
épreuve [epʀœv]: 2946
épuisé [epɥize]: 2561
épuisée [epɥize]: 2561
erreur [ʀᵊɛʀœʀ]: 2761
erreurs [zᵊɛʀœʀ]: 2573
es [ɛ]: 2168, 2362, 2503, 2593, 2599, 2619, 2681, 2830, 2838, 2846, 2848, 2875, 2981, 2982
espace [ɛspas]: 2373
espagne [espagne]: 2938
espagnols [ɛspaɲɔl]: 2435
espérons [zᵊespeʀɔ̃]: 2927
espion [nᵊespjɔ̃]: 2109
espionne [ɛspjɔn]: 2109
essaie [ɛsɛ]: 2033, 2035
essayé [eseje]: 2032, 2034, 2043, 2176, 2360, 2945, 2956
essayées [eseje]: 2574
essayer [eseje]: 2126, 2350, 2512
essayons [esejɔ̃]: 2825
est [e]: 2030, 2087, 2089, 2091, 2092, 2151, 2158, 2164, 2170, 2201, 2202, 2262, 2272, 2273, 2275, 2277, 2287, 2291... +88
est [lᵊe]: 2009, 2031, 2087, 2091, 2115, 2117, 2118, 2153, 2156, 2164, 2178, 2207, 2266, 2272, 2298, 2392, 2488, 2496... +24
est [nᵊe]: 2242, 2285
est [ʀᵊe]: 2239
est [tᵊe]: 2404, 2432, 2882, 2932
est [zᵊe]: 2370, 2573, 2885
est-ce [ɛsᵊ]: 2355, 2431, 2594, 2811
est-il [e tᵊil]: 2490, 2594, 2647
es-tu [ɛ ty]: 2028, 2129, 2313, 2568, 2639, 2802, 2820, 2826
et [e]: 2004, 2022, 2030, 2073, 2186, 2238, 2252, 2263, 2267, 2290, 2298, 2300, 2307, 2315, 2322, 2352, 2353, 2354, 2355, 2359... +98
et [gᵊe]: 2160
et [zᵊe]: 2609

étage [etaʒ]: 2725
étages [k‿etaʒ]: 2334
étaient [ete]: 2234, 2281, 2435, 2541, 2542, 2600, 2962, 2969
étaient [l‿etɛ]: 2088, 2152
étaient [z‿etɛ]: 2435
étais [ete]: 2697
étais-tu [ete ty]: 2464, 2692
était [ete]: 2004, 2051, 2119, 2157, 2163, 2172, 2469, 2490, 2491, 2492, 2498, 2503, 2510, 2519, 2532, 2556, 2558, 2577, 2586, 2590... +21
était [l‿ete]: 2116, 2119, 2152, 2244, 2419, 2491, 2503, 2831
était [t‿ete]: 2120
était-il [ete t‿il]: 2159
étant [etã]: 2214
états-unis [z‿etazuni]: 2307, 2949
été [ete]: 2005, 2016, 2158, 2177, 2179, 2195, 2217, 2264, 2339, 2403, 2410, 2421, 2454, 2467, 2486, 2548, 2571, 2576, 2730, 2731... +18
été [t‿ete]: 2482, 2554
été [z‿ete]: 2343, 2559
éteindre [etɛ̃dʁ]: 2947
étions [z‿etjɔ̃]: 2057, 2160, 2364, 2366, 2443, 2459, 2638
étoiles [z‿etwal]: 2269
étrange [etʁãʒ]: 2566, 2862
étrangère [etʁãʒɛʁ]: 2025, 2138, 2802
étrangers [z‿etʁãʒe]: 2795, 2819
étranges [etʁãʒ]: 2088
être [ɛtʁ]: 2059, 2163, 2168, 2361, 2562, 2578, 2600, 2679, 2700, 2715, 2758, 2795, 2854, 2886, 2919, 2929, 2936, 2985, 2989
être [ʁ‿etʁ]: 2597, 2914
être [z‿etʁ]: 2141, 2213, 2484, 2800
étroite [z‿etʁwat]: 2546
études [z‿etyd]: 2923
étudiant [n‿etydjã]: 2244, 2275
étudiants [z‿etydjã]: 2558, 2966
étudier [etydje]: 2143
eu [t‿y]: 2959

eu [y]: 2123, 2125, 2213, 2228, 2258, 2369, 2380, 2629, 2697, 2736, 2806, 2845, 2856, 2948, 2958, 2964
eu [z‿y]: 2122, 2131, 2343, 2508, 2655, 2657, 2659
europe [øʁop]: 2301, 2799
européennes [øʁopeɛn]: 2792
euros [øʁo]: 2770
euros [z‿øʁo]: 2327, 2486, 2770, 2773
eux [ø]: 2435, 2437, 2976
eux-mêmes [ʁ‿ømɛm]: 2378
évidentes [evidãt]: 2823
examens [z‿ɛgzamɛ̃]: 2332
examiné [ɛgzamine]: 2535
excusé [ɛkskyze]: 2880
excusée [ɛkskyze]: 2880
excuses [z‿ɛkskyz]: 2881
existe [l‿ɛgzist]: 2792
expérience [ɛkspeʁjãs]: 2997
expériences [k‿ɛkspeʁjãs]: 2228
expérimenté [z‿ɛkspeʁimãte]: 2594
expliqué [ɛksplike]: 2484
expliquer [ɛksplike]: 2598
explosé [ɛksploze]: 2972
exploser [ɛksploze]: 2198
exportés [ɛkspɔʁte]: 2550
exprès [t‿ɛkspʁɛ]: 2759
extrêmement [ɛkstʁɛmˀmã]: 2657
fabrique [fabʁik]: 2530
fabriqués [fabʁike]: 2550
face [fas]: 2783
fâchés [faʃe]: 2987
facile [fasil]: 2762
facilement [fasilˀmã]: 2017, 2425
faciles [fasil]: 2297
facture [faktyʁ]: 2876
faim [fɛ̃]: 2644, 2897
faire [fɛʁ]: 2022, 2036, 2037, 2117, 2129, 2149, 2173, 2174, 2201, 2203, 2255, 2270, 2356, 2375, 2409, 2423, 2477, 2504... +19
fais [fɛ]: 2203, 2205, 2569, 2846, 2848
faisait [fˀzɛ]: 2742
fais-moi [fɛ mwa]: 2175, 2233, 2396

fait [fɛ]: 2010, 2014, 2072, 2211, 2237,
    2330, 2368, 2409, 2544, 2573,
    2602, 2732, 2733, 2759, 2777,
    2783, 2794, 2798, 2800, 2822... +8
faites [fɛt]: 2555
famille [famij]: 2054, 2779
farine [faʁin]: 2872
fasse [fas]: 2048
fasses [fas]: 2065
fatigant [fatigã]: 2160
fatigue [fatig]: 2011
fatigué [fatige]: 2064, 2168, 2209,
    2446, 2658, 2825
fatiguée [fatige]: 2064, 2168, 2209,
    2446, 2658, 2825
fatiguées [fatige]: 2443
fatigués [fatige]: 2443
faute [fot]: 2347, 2348, 2480, 2784,
    2880, 2882, 2885, 2898
fédéral [fedeʁal]: 2321
félicité [felisite]: 2107, 2895
félicitée [felisite]: 2899
féliciter [felisite]: 2894
femme [fam]: 2370, 2475, 2481, 2488,
    2489, 2491, 2492, 2496, 2514,
    2519, 2754, 2893, 2948
fendu [fãdy]: 2910
fenêtre [fᵊnetʁ]: 2073, 2255, 2844
fenêtres [fᵊnetʁ]: 2018
fer [fɛʁ]: 2755
ferai [fᵊʁe]: 2452
ferait [fᵊʁe]: 2666
fermé [fɛʁme]: 2503
fermée [fɛʁme]: 2704
fermer [fɛʁme]: 2018, 2056
fesses [fes]: 2943
fête [fɛt]: 2040, 2060, 2169, 2254,
    2431, 2451, 2687, 2894
feu [fø]: 2757, 2947, 2972
feuille [fœj]: 2474
fiche [fiʃ]: 2671, 2848
fichiers [fiʃje]: 2954, 2955
fie [fi]: 2891
fiers [fjɛʁ]: 2814, 2815
fille [fij]: 2816

film [film]: 2120, 2212, 2357, 2436,
    2502, 2564, 2578, 2625, 2693,
    2705, 2746, 2829
fils [fis]: 2534, 2628
fin [fɛ̃]: 2718, 2720
finalement [final°mã]: 2910
financier [finãsje]: 2085
financièrement [finãsjɛʁ°mã]: 2830
financiers [finãsje]: 2977
fini [fini]: 2072, 2207, 2504, 2703,
    2915, 2975, 2976
finirai [finiʁe]: 2274
finiras [finiʁa]: 2963, 2965
finis-tu [fini ty]: 2279
finit [fini]: 2636
fleurs [flœʁ]: 2429
fleuve [flœv]: 2266, 2302, 2305
fluide [flɥid]: 2573
fois [fwa]: 2129, 2195, 2212, 2446,
    2466, 2621, 2879
fonctionne [fɔ̃ksjɔn]: 2479, 2678, 2921
fonctionner [fɔ̃ksjone]: 2035, 2976
font [fɔ̃]: 2687, 2752, 2811
forcément [fɔʁsemã]: 2388
formation [fɔʁmasjɔ̃]: 2981
formulaires [fɔʁmylɛʁ]: 2744
fort [fɔʁ]: 2037, 2561, 2590, 2593,
    2839
forte [fɔʁt]: 2380, 2774
fortune [fɔʁtyn]: 2794
fou [fu]: 2689
foule [ful]: 2988
fournir [fuʁniʁ]: 2293
fournissent [fuʁnis]: 2913
fournit [fuʁni]: 2536
fous [fu]: 2889
fracassant [fʁakasã]: 2073
frais [fʁɛ]: 2255
français [fʁãsɛ]: 2294, 2435, 2528,
    2529
france [fʁãs]: 2313
freiné [fʁene]: 2717
fréquence [fʁekãs]: 2128
frère [fʁɛʁ]: 2272, 2273, 2516, 2732,
    2796, 2895

frères [fʁɛʁ]: 2979
frimer [fʁime]: 2944
froid [fʁwa]: 2022, 2145, 2901
fromage [fʁomaʒ]: 2490, 2490
fur [fyʁ]: 2564
furieuse [fyʁjøz]: 2798
fut [fy]: 2160, 2381, 2783, 2945, 2950
gagne [gaɲ]: 2421
gagné [gaɲe]: 2771
gagner [gaɲe]: 2421
galles [gal]: 2315
garçon [gaʁsɔ̃]: 2548
garde [gaʁd]: 2862, 2889
gardé [gaʁde]: 2433
garder [gaʁde]: 2032
gare [gaʁ]: 2008, 2442
garer [gaʁe]: 2008, 2009, 2134
gâteau [gato]: 2872
gauche [goʃ]: 2092, 2093, 2726
gaz [gaz]: 2621
géante [ʒeɑ̃t]: 2813
généralement [ʒeneʁalˀmɑ̃]: 2279, 2633
généreuse [ʒeneʁøz]: 2877
généreux [ʒeneʁø]: 2794
genou [ʒˀnu]: 2200
genre [ʒɑ̃ʁ]: 2855
gens [ʒɑ̃]: 2008, 2047, 2076, 2079,
   2124, 2130, 2170, 2216, 2254,
   2281, 2286, 2384, 2415, 2421,
   2437, 2476, 2506, 2520, 2526,
   2587... +7
gentil [ʒɑ̃ti]: 2155, 2793, 2795
gentille [ʒɑ̃tij]: 2795
gentils [ʒɑ̃ti]: 2520, 2587
gérant [ʒeʁɑ̃]: 2166
glacé [glase]: 2172
glissé [glise]: 2673
goûte [gut]: 2566
gouvernement [guvɛʁnˀmɑ̃]: 2293,
   2883
grand [gʁɑ̃]: 2303, 2304, 2956, 2990
grande [gʁɑ̃d]: 2260, 2316, 2386, 2428,
   2436, 2532, 2547, 2610, 2767
grande-bretagne [gʁɑ̃d bʁˀtaɲ]: 2315,
   2726

grandes [gʁɑ̃]: 2970
grandi [gʁɑ̃di]: 2093, 2521
grand-père [gʁɑ̃pɛʁ]: 2850
grands-parents [gʁɑ̃paʁɑ̃]: 2962
grave [gʁav]: 2410, 2608
gravité [gʁavite]: 2820
grève [gʁɛv]: 2755
grièvement [gʁijɛvˀmɑ̃]: 2571, 2576
grimpant [gʁɛ̃pɑ̃]: 2073
groupe [gʁup]: 2312, 2435, 2953
guerre [gɛʁ]: 2291
guide [gid]: 2257, 2529, 2630
gym [ʒim]: 2926
habillé [abije]: 2352, 2579
habite [abit]: 2475, 2481, 2488
habitez [abite]: 2355
habitions [z_abitjɔ̃]: 2095
habitué [abitɥe]: 2093, 2094
habitué [z_abitɥe]: 2088, 2090
habituée [abitɥe]: 2088, 2093, 2094
habituée [t_abitɥe]: 2087, 2091
hanteront [ɑ̃tˀʁɔ̃]: 2999
hasard [azaʁ]: 2907
hâte [at]: 2082, 2106, 2799
hélicoptère [n_elikoptɛʁ]: 2766
heure [l_œʁ]: 2279, 2351, 2612
heure [œʁ]: 2641, 2749, 2939
heures [k_œʁ]: 2276, 2700
heures [t_œʁ]: 2265, 2768
heures [z_œʁ]: 2014, 2024, 2126, 2337,
   2472, 2703, 2714, 2767, 2968
heureusement [øʁøzˀmɑ̃]: 2324, 2410,
   2538, 2972
heureux [øʁø]: 2395, 2859
heureux [z_øʁø]: 2803
heurta [œʁta]: 2760, 2761
hier [jɛʁ]: 2182, 2283, 2342, 2382,
   2428, 2737, 2757, 2808
histoire [istwaʁ]: 2586
histoire [n_istwaʁ]: 2832, 2935
histoires [istwaʁ]: 2478, 2562
hobbit [hobbit]: 2813
homme [n_ɔm]: 2202, 2335, 2517,
   2518, 2946, 2951, 2956, 2989

homme [t‿ɔm]: 2510
hommes [ɔm]: 2323, 2545, 2964, 2987
honte [ɔ̃t]: 2373, 2814
honteux [ɔ̃tø]: 2815
horrible [ɔʁibl]: 2051
horrible [t‿ɔʁibl]: 2567
hospitalité [ɔspitalite]: 2877
hôtel [l‿otɛl]: 2216, 2671
hôtel [n‿otɛl]: 2206, 2963
hôtel [t‿otɛl]: 2007, 2507, 2611
hôtels [otɛl]: 2034, 2248, 2449
hôtes [z‿ot]: 2877
huit [ɥi]: 2265
hygiénique [iʒjenik]: 2931
ici [isi]: 2170, 2180, 2223, 2227, 2414, 2637
ici [s‿isi]: 2637
idée [ide]: 2858
idées [d‿ide]: 2970
idées [z‿ide]: 2434
identifier [idɑ̃tifje]: 2677
idiote [idjɔt]: 2078
il [d‿i]: 2706
il [i]: 2009, 2022, 2028, 2030, 2031, 2042, 2115, 2116, 2126, 2152, 2153, 2156, 2169, 2208, 2223, 2224, 2243, 2244... +51
il [il]: 2019, 2037, 2090, 2103, 2117, 2121, 2227, 2237, 2352, 2384, 2391, 2402, 2403, 2406, 2414, 2419, 2420, 2453... +35
il [l‿il]: 2154
il [ʁ‿i]: 2117, 2118, 2119, 2419
il [ʁ‿il]: 2385, 2386, 2951
il [t‿i]: 2496
île [il]: 2721
ils [i]: 2008, 2034, 2623, 2956, 2990
ils [il]: 2040, 2100, 2108, 2137, 2229, 2235, 2365, 2386, 2465, 2511, 2524, 2570, 2587, 2595, 2649, 2689... +15
ils [ʁ‿il]: 2699
impeccable [ɛ̃pekabl]: 2899
impliquant [ɛ̃plikɑ̃]: 2333
impoliment [ɛ̃pɔlimɑ̃]: 2775

important [ɛ̃pɔʁtɑ̃]: 2992
importante [ɛ̃pɔʁtɑ̃t]: 2981
importante [s‿ɛ̃pɔʁtɑ̃t]: 2629, 2800
importante [z‿ɛ̃pɔʁtɑ̃t]: 2916
importantes [ɛ̃pɔʁtɑ̃t]: 2683
importe [ɛ̃pɔʁt]: 2879
impossible [ɛ̃pɔsibl]: 2060, 2152
impossibles [ɛ̃pɔsibl]: 2152
impressionné [z‿ɛ̃pʁesjone]: 2805
incendie [ɛ̃sɑ̃di]: 2467
incroyablement [ɛ̃kʁwajablᵊmɑ̃]: 2575
inculquent [z‿ɛ̃kylk]: 2914
inde [n‿ɛ̃d]: 2457, 2994
indemnité [ɛ̃dɛmnite]: 2960
indépendant [t‿ɛ̃depɑ̃dɑ̃]: 2830
indépendante [ɛ̃depɑ̃dɑ̃t]: 2830, 2848
indications [z‿ɛ̃dikasjɔ̃]: 2437
industrie [ɛ̃dystʁi]: 2341, 2341
informations [l‿ɛ̃fɔʁmasjɔ̃]: 2233
informations [z‿ɛ̃fɔʁmasjɔ̃]: 2762
informatique [ɛ̃fɔʁmatik]: 2764
informatiques [ɛ̃fɔʁmatik]: 2954
informer [z‿ɛ̃fɔʁme]: 2023
injuste [t‿ɛ̃ʒyst]: 2157
injustement [ɛ̃ʒystᵊmɑ̃]: 2865
inquiet [ɛ̃kjɛ]: 2846
inquiète [ɛ̃kjɛt]: 2846
insensé [t‿ɛ̃sɑ̃se]: 2156
insisté [ɛ̃siste]: 2100, 2185, 2917
inspecter [ɛ̃spɛkte]: 2331
inspecteur [n‿ɛ̃spɛktœʁ]: 2331
instructions [z‿ɛ̃stʁyksjɔ̃]: 2600
interdisent [l‿ɛ̃tɛʁdiz]: 2008
interdit [t‿ɛ̃tɛʁdi]: 2009
intéressant [ɛ̃teʁesɑ̃]: 2177
intéressant [t‿ɛ̃teʁesɑ̃]: 2153
intéressantes [ɛ̃teʁesɑ̃t]: 2228
intéressants [ɛ̃teʁesɑ̃]: 2254
intéressé [ɛ̃teʁese]: 2178
intéressé [z‿ɛ̃teʁese]: 2537
intéressée [ɛ̃teʁese]: 2178
international [ɛ̃tɛʁnasjonal]: 2978
internet [ʁ‿ɛ̃tɛʁnɛt]: 2753

interrogé [ɛ̃teʁoʒe]: 2992
interroger [ɛ̃teʁoʒe]: 2323, 2790
introduits [ɛ̃tʁodɥi]: 2073, 2121
inutile [inytil]: 2116, 2119
inutile [t‿inytil]: 2115, 2117, 2118
inutilement [inytil°mã]: 2578
inventé [ɛ̃vãte]: 2295
invité [ɛ̃vite]: 2800
invitée [ɛ̃vite]: 2800
italie [italie]: 2738
italien [italjɛ̃]: 2528, 2529
j'adore [ʒ‿adɔʁ]: 2047
j'adorerais [ʒ‿adɔʁ°ʁɛ]: 2054
j'ai [ʒ‿ɛ]: 2003, 2005, 2016, 2018,
    2021, 2029, 2032, 2036, 2041,
    2051, 2067, 2071, 2080, 2082,
    2088, 2093... +86
j'aie [ʒ‿ɛ]: 2397, 2625, 2627, 2659
j'aimais [ʒ‿ɛmɛ]: 2445
j'aime [ʒ‿ɛm]: 2052, 2053, 2390, 2501,
    2506, 2723, 2758
j'aimerais [ʒ‿ɛm°ʁɛ]: 2248, 2375, 2522,
    2860
jalouse [ʒaluz]: 2816
jamais [ʒamɛ]: 2115, 2366, 2448, 2465,
    2481, 2549, 2563, 2563, 2625,
    2627, 2754
janvier [ʒãvje]: 2719
japon [ʒapõ]: 2092, 2376, 2678, 2726
japonais [ʒaponɛ]: 2951
j'apprécie [ʒ‿apʁesi]: 2758
jardin [ʒaʁdɛ̃]: 2375, 2429, 2547
j'attends [ʒ‿atã]: 2692
j'aurai [ʒ‿oʁe]: 2703
j'aurais [ʒ‿oʁɛ]: 2057, 2060
j'avais [ʒ‿avɛ]: 2174, 2229, 2499, 2859,
    2924
je [ʒø]: 2003, 2006, 2007, 2010, 2015,
    2018, 2021, 2027, 2028, 2029,
    2032, 2042, 2044... +249
jeans [dʒins]: 2221
j'économise [ʒ‿ekonomiz]: 2971
j'en [ʒ‿ã]: 2651, 2806
j'espère [ʒ‿ɛspɛʁ]: 2231, 2314, 2698,
    2905

j'étais [ʒ‿etɛ]: 2163, 2166, 2276, 2428,
    2446, 2497, 2655, 2658, 2689, 2962
jeté [ʒ°te]: 2843, 2910
jette-les [ʒɛt le]: 2919
jeune [ʒœn]: 2277
jeunes [ʒœ]: 2289
jeunes [ʒœn]: 2595
j'habite [ʒ‿abit]: 2118
jogging [dʒɔgiŋ]: 2926
john [john]: 2698
joindre [ʒwɛ̃dʁ]: 2175
joint [ʒwɛ̃]: 2030
jouant [ʒwã]: 2200
jouer [ʒwe]: 2069, 2195
jour [ʒuʁ]: 2094, 2265, 2523, 2918
journaux [ʒuʁno]: 2632
journée [ʒuʁne]: 2237, 2343, 2428,
    2462, 2561, 2933
jours [ʒuʁ]: 2139, 2265, 2328, 2459,
    2527, 2696, 2825, 2926, 2973
jours-ci [ʒuʁ si]: 2094
jules [ʒyl]: 2509
jumeaux [ʒymo]: 2979
jurons [ʒyʁõ]: 2103
jusqu'à [ʒyska]: 2400, 2701, 2702, 2703
juste [ʒyst]: 2019, 2560, 2567, 2716,
    2717, 2724, 2929, 2961
justesse [ʒystɛs]: 2972
j'utilise [ʒ‿ytiliz]: 2094
j'y [ʒ‿i]: 2382, 2698
kilomètres [kilomɛtʁ]: 2077, 2590,
    2749
kilomètres-heure [kilomɛtʁœʁ]: 2750
kremlin [kʁɛmlɛ̃]: 2320
l'a [l‿a]: 2298, 2433, 2496, 2505, 2798,
    2956
la [la]: 2011, 2012, 2015, 2018, 2019,
    2020, 2027, 2033, 2040, 2052,
    2053, 2056, 2060, 2062, 2063,
    2073... +289
là [la]: 2203, 2634, 2641, 2846, 2969
là-bas [laba]: 2051, 2370, 2678, 2739
lac [lak]: 2721

l'accident [l_aksidã]: 2019, 2189, 2215, 2217, 2264, 2325, 2410, 2486, 2548, 2571, 2576, 2784, 2898
l'acheter [l_aʃ°te]: 2176, 2934
l'acropole [l_akʁopɔl]: 2319
l'aérobie [l_aeʁobi]: 2926
l'aéroport [l_aeʁopɔʁ]: 2155, 2391, 2483, 2553, 2740, 2767, 2940, 2968
l'afrique [l afrique]: 2300
l'âge [l_aʒ]: 2748, 2938
l'agent [l_aʒã]: 2965
l'ai [l_ɛ]: 2010, 2078, 2188, 2190, 2591, 2753, 2759, 2899
l'aimais [l_ɛmɛ]: 2615
l'aime [l_ɛm]: 2042, 2583
l'aiment [l_ɛm]: 2216
l'aimes [l_ɛm]: 2501
l'air [l_ɛʁ]: 2288, 2410, 2466, 2568, 2582, 2684, 2926
laissaient [lɛsɛ]: 2012
laissé [lese]: 2146
laisse-moi [lɛs mwa]: 2013
laisser [lese]: 2664
laissez-moi [lese mwa]: 2383
lait [lɛ]: 2330, 2566, 2982
l'amazone [l_amazon]: 2302
l'amérique [l_ameʁik]: 2300
lancer [lãse]: 2844
l'anglais [l_ãglɛ]: 2143, 2249, 2250, 2630, 2908
langue [lãg]: 2138, 2213, 2589, 2802
langues [lãg]: 2425, 2575, 2792, 2908
l'année [l_ane]: 2314, 2524, 2719, 2720
l'appareil [l_apaʁɛj]: 2599
l'appartement [l_apaʁt°mã]: 2373
l'appellerai [l_apɛl°ʁɛ]: 2029
l'apprécie [l_apʁesi]: 2793
l'après-midi [l apʁɛ midi]: 2695
laquelle [lakɛ]: 2154
laquelle [lakɛl]: 2525, 2538
l'araignée [l_aʁɛɲe]: 2813
l'argent [l_aʁʒã]: 2028, 2028, 2102, 2137, 2298, 2458, 2499, 2543, 2549, 2620, 2830, 2951, 2998
l'arrêter [l_aʁete]: 2867

l'article [l_aʁtikl]: 2823
l'as [l_a]: 2921
l'asie [l asie]: 2303
l'assassinat [l_asasina]: 2790
l'audience [l_odjãs]: 2803
l'augmentation [l_ogmãtasjɔ̃]: 2885, 2886
l'autoroute [l_otoʁut]: 2906, 2911
l'autre [l_otʁ]: 2353, 2354, 2355, 2366, 2432, 2440, 2441, 2444, 2607, 2611, 2784
l'avantage [l_avãtaʒ]: 2776
lavé [lave]: 2039, 2352
l'avion [l_avjɔ̃]: 2046, 2497, 2552, 2646, 2736, 2740
l'avoir [l_avwaʁ]: 2018
le [lø]: 2003, 2019, 2021, 2023, 2024, 2025, 2031, 2033, 2035, 2040, 2051, 2057, 2065, 2066, 2085, 2089, 2091, 2100, 2111... +218
l'eau [l_o]: 2288, 2751, 2871
l'école [l_ekɔl]: 2072, 2274, 2516, 2732, 2748, 2816, 2856, 2894
l'économie [l_ekonomi]: 2281, 2411, 2886
l'écosse [l_ekɔs]: 2315
l'écran [l_ekʁã]: 2888
l'édifice [l_edifis]: 2008, 2009
l'éducation [l_edykasjɔ̃]: 2914
légèrement [leʒɛʁ°mã]: 2607
légumes [legym]: 2375
l'égypte [l_eʒypt]: 2299
l'empêcher [l_ãpeʃe]: 2902
l'emploi [l_ãplwa]: 2023, 2246, 2477, 2508, 2540, 2657, 2905
l'employé [l_ãplwaje]: 2109
l'employée [l_ãplwaje]: 2109
l'endroit [l_ãdʁwa]: 2390
l'enfant [l_ãfã]: 2717
l'enseignant [l_ãsɛɲã]: 2558
l'ensemble [l_ãsãbl]: 2758
lentement [lãt°mã]: 2606
l'entendre [l_ãtãdʁ]: 2177, 2590
l'entreprise [l_ãtʁ°pʁiz]: 2030, 2031, 2783

l'environnement [l_ãviʁɔn°mã]: 2270
l'épaule [l_epol]: 2192
l'équateur [l_ekwatœʁ]: 2268
lequel [l°kɛ]: 2950
lequel [l°kɛl]: 2508
l'équivalent [l_ekivalã]: 2342
les [le]: 2018, 2034, 2073, 2103, 2113,
    2124, 2169, 2170, 2173, 2195,
    2217, 2218, 2219, 2220, 2225,
    2234, 2248, 2269, 2286, 2292...
    + 106
l'espace [l_ɛspas]: 2271
lesquels [lekɛl]: 2955
l'essayer [l_eseje]: 2567, 2934
l'essence [l_esãs]: 2727
l'est [l_e]: 2306
l'était [l_etɛ]: 2633
l'étoile [l_etwal]: 2889
l'être [l_etʁ]: 2636
lettre [letʁ]: 2020
lettres [letʁ]: 2249, 2729, 2744
l'étude [l_etyd]: 2287
leur [lœ]: 2409, 2689, 2699, 2987,
    2988
leur [lœʁ]: 2066, 2102, 2290, 2294,
    2610, 2828, 2877
leurs [lœ]: 2511, 2840
leurs [lœʁ]: 2235, 2797, 2814, 2815,
    2851
levé [l°ve]: 2352, 2650, 2701
levée [l°ve]: 2650
lever [l°ve]: 2045, 2090
l'examen [l_ɛgzamɛ̃]: 2152, 2164, 2394,
    2398, 2602, 2822, 2866
l'explication [l_ɛksplikasjɔ̃]: 2558
l'expliquer [l_ɛksplike]: 2835
l'explosion [l_ɛksplozjɔ̃]: 2218, 2778
l'exposition [l_ɛkspozisjɔ̃]: 2084
l'extérieur [l_ɛksteʁjœʁ]: 2364
l'habitude [l_abityd]: 2983
l'heure [l_œʁ]: 2148, 2163, 2222, 2714,
    2749
l'histoire [l_istwaʁ]: 2287, 2586
l'homme [l_ɔm]: 2497, 2515, 2552,
    2556, 2841, 2958

l'hôpital [l_opital]: 2264, 2548, 2730,
    2964, 2973, 2989
l'horloge [l_ɔʁlɔʒ]: 2126
l'hôtel [l_otɛl]: 2505, 2671, 2674, 2721
liberté [libɛʁte]: 2776
libre [libʁ]: 2619
l'idée [l_ide]: 2802, 2903
lien [ljɛ̃]: 2791
lieu [ljø]: 2083
ligne [liɲ]: 2084
l'immeuble [l_imœbl]: 2725
l'imprimante [l_ɛ̃pʁimãt]: 2479
l'imprimerie [l_ɛ̃pʁim°ʁi]: 2295
l'incendie [l_ɛ̃sãdi]: 2482, 2948
l'information [l_ɛ̃fɔʁmasjɔ̃]: 2248, 2257,
    2667
linguistique [lɛ̃gɥistik]: 2981
linguistiques [lɛ̃gɥistik]: 2074
l'interrupteur [l_ɛ̃teʁyptœʁ]: 2004, 2005
l'interruption [l_ɛ̃teʁypsjɔ̃]: 2688
lire [liʁ]: 2124, 2197
lis [lis]: 2470
lisant [lizã]: 2074
lisible [lizibl]: 2744
lit [li]: 2119, 2209, 2278, 2428, 2632
l'italie [l italie]: 2832
livre [livʁ]: 2456, 2471, 2909, 2932
livres [livʁ]: 2427, 2468, 2495
l'obligeance [l_obliʒãs]: 2056
l'obtenir [l_ɔpt°niʁ]: 2512
l'obtention [l_ɔptãsjɔ̃]: 2107
locale [lokal]: 2213
l'océan [l_oseã]: 2300, 2390
logements [lɔʒ°mã]: 2945
loin [lwɛ̃]: 2596
l'ombre [l_ɔ̃bʁ]: 2742
londres [lɔ̃dʁ°]: 2050, 2417, 2532,
    2698, 2951
long [lɔ̃]: 2019, 2160, 2168, 2190,
    2266, 2542, 2578, 2592
longs [lɔ̃]: 2225
longtemps [lɔ̃tã]: 2116, 2290, 2531,
    2591, 2609
l'ont [l_ɔ̃]: 2558, 2992

l'opération [l_opeʁasjɔ̃]: 2821
l'orateur [l_oʁatœʁ]: 2688
lors [lɔʁ]: 2537, 2549, 2554, 2602, 2744, 2997
lorsque [lɔʁskə]: 2033, 2057, 2459, 2613, 2735, 2750, 2951, 2981, 2992, 2993, 2999
lorsqu'elle [lɔʁsk ɛl]: 2092
lourd [luʁ]: 2607
loyer [lwaje]: 2874
lu [ly]: 2427, 2456, 2468
lui [lɥi]: 2042, 2070, 2153, 2192, 2419, 2494, 2499, 2624, 2642, 2643, 2663, 2754, 2797, 2824, 2840, 2841, 2844, 2850... +10
lui-même [lɥimɛm]: 2019
lumière [lymjɛʁ]: 2536
l'un [lœ̃]: 2353, 2355, 2366, 2427, 2440, 2441, 2444
lundi [lœ̃di]: 2699, 2907
lune [lyn]: 2267
l'une [lyn]: 2354, 2366, 2536
lunes [lyn]: 2559
lunettes [lynɛt]: 2220
l'univers [l_ynivɛʁ]: 2536
l'université [l_ynivɛʁsite]: 2256, 2274, 2275, 2371, 2732, 2853, 2922, 2950
l'utiliser [l_ytilize]: 2931
l'utilises [l_ytiliz]: 2115
lycée [lise]: 2732
m'a [m_a]: 2004, 2015, 2016, 2391, 2527, 2534, 2535, 2737, 2813, 2826, 2864, 2986
ma [ma]: 2052, 2176, 2197, 2224, 2262, 2370, 2371, 2372, 2374, 2480, 2664, 2670, 2739, 2747, 2762, 2779, 2784, 2787... +8
m'accueillerait [m_akœj°ʁɛ]: 2391
m'acheter [m_aʃ°te]: 2101
magasin [magazɛ̃]: 2934
magasins [magazɛ̃]: 2402, 2405
magnat [magna]: 2766
magnifique [maɲifik]: 2926
magnifiques [maɲifik]: 2429
mai [mɛ]: 2708

m'aider [m_ede]: 2003, 2041, 2437, 2793
m'aies [m_ɛ]: 2028, 2859
main [mɛ̃]: 2764, 2841, 2996
maintenant [mɛ̃t°nã]: 2021, 2055, 2090, 2095, 2380, 2387, 2479, 2482, 2532, 2554, 2561, 2582, 2749, 2827, 2916, 2924, 2933, 2959, 2985, 2997
mais [mɛ]: 2018, 2019, 2032, 2034, 2043, 2052, 2058, 2060, 2089, 2094, 2095, 2121, 2176, 2181, 2220, 2260, 2290, 2297, 2357, 2360... +37
maison [mɛzɔ̃]: 2033, 2063, 2073, 2083, 2095, 2101, 2121, 2160, 2202, 2207, 2280, 2364, 2385, 2400, 2406, 2424, 2465, 2588, 2596... +18
maisons [mɛzɔ̃]: 2945, 2990
majorité [maʒɔʁite]: 2428
mal [ma]: 2454, 2577
mal [mal]: 2122, 2125, 2130, 2132, 2213, 2281, 2297, 2454, 2478, 2513, 2656, 2948
malade [malad]: 2075, 2158, 2428, 2902
maladie [maladi]: 2608, 2869, 2884
maladies [maladi]: 2884
malentendu [malãtãdy]: 2880
manager [manadʒe]: 2030, 2031
manageur [manaʒœʁ]: 2682, 2683, 2984
mange [mãʒ]: 2214, 2285
mangé [mãʒe]: 2455, 2645
mangeant [mãʒã]: 2075
mangées [mãʒe]: 2597
mangent [mãʒ]: 2897
manger [mãʒe]: 2346, 2393, 2407, 2567, 2619, 2645, 2825
manquer [mãke]: 2142
manteau [mãto]: 2022, 2648
manuellement [manɥɛl°mã]: 2764
m'appellent [m_apɛl]: 2049
marché [maʁʃe]: 2172
marcher [maʁʃe]: 2170, 2190, 2400

mari [maʁi]: 2091, 2514
mariage [maʁjaʒ]: 2290, 2785, 2924
marie [maʁi]: 2367
mariée [maʁje]: 2433, 2827
marient [maʁi]: 2785
marier [maʁje]: 2595, 2712
mariés [maʁje]: 2290, 2524
marketing [maʁketiŋ]: 2754, 2941, 2984
marre [maʁ]: 2806
m'as [m a]: 2458, 2507
masque [mask]: 2677
m'asseoir [m aswaʁ]: 2723
maternelle [matɛʁnɛl]: 2589
matin [matɛ̃]: 2531, 2633, 2701, 2708, 2911
matinale [matinal]: 2845
matinée [matine]: 2119, 2464
m'attendais [m atɑ̃dɛ]: 2381, 2829
m'attends [m atɑ̃]: 2089
mauvaise [movɛz]: 2633, 2783, 2943, 2958, 2959
mauvaises [movɛz]: 2324, 2999
maux [mo]: 2887
m'avait [m avɛ]: 2862
m'avoir [m avwaʁ]: 2113
me [mø]: 2001, 2011, 2018, 2028, 2048, 2053, 2080, 2094, 2130, 2135, 2141, 2150, 2157, 2166, 2173, 2174, 2209, 2245, 2343, 2349... +29
médecin [medsɛ̃]: 2475, 2488, 2489, 2527, 2535, 2861
médecine [medsin]: 2732
médecins [medsɛ̃]: 2821
méfiante [mefjɑ̃t]: 2817
meilleure [mɛjœʁ]: 2747
mélange [melɑ̃ʒ]: 2979
mélangeante [melɑ̃ʒɑ̃t]: 2558
membre [mɑ̃bʁ]: 2668
membres [mɑ̃bʁ]: 2668
même [mɛm]: 2343, 2358, 2469, 2573, 2582, 2622, 2648, 2649, 2652, 2653, 2654, 2655, 2656, 2825
m'emmener [m ɑ̃mᵊne]: 2155

m'empêche [m ɑ̃pɛʃ]: 2111
m'empêcher [m ɑ̃pɛʃe]: 2042
m'en [m ɑ̃]: 2924
m'endormir [m ɑ̃dɔʁmiʁ]: 2111
m'ennuie [m ɑ̃nɥi]: 2557
mensonges [mɑ̃sɔ̃ʒ]: 2993
mentir [mɑ̃tiʁ]: 2108
m'entraîner [m ɑ̃tʁene]: 2036
m'envoyer [m ɑ̃vwaje]: 2620
merci [mɛʁsi]: 2808
mercredi [mɛʁkʁᵊdi]: 2707
mère [mɛʁ]: 2029, 2377, 2664, 2747, 2857, 2887
méritait [meʁitɛ]: 2121
mes [me]: 2032, 2049, 2080, 2197, 2212, 2220, 2367, 2375, 2376, 2603, 2631, 2738, 2739, 2762, 2785, 2877, 2917, 2940, 2962... +5
m'est [m e]: 2154
mesure [mᵊzyʁ]: 2213, 2343, 2430, 2437, 2564
mètres [mɛtʁ]: 2749, 2771
métro [metʁo]: 2907
mets-la [me la]: 2912
mettent [mɛt]: 2927
mettre [mɛtʁ]: 2232, 2797
meubles [mœbl]: 2232, 2530
meurent [mœʁ]: 2897
meurtre [mœʁtʁ]: 2865, 2915, 2925, 2958
meurtres [mœʁtʁ]: 2791, 2833, 2953
meurtrier [mœʁtʁije]: 2878, 2879, 2925
m'excuser [m ɛkskyze]: 2114
mexique [meksik]: 2307
miche [miʃ]: 2230
midi [midi]: 2081, 2701, 2707
mien [mjɛ̃]: 2622
mieux [mjø]: 2611, 2612, 2613, 2930, 2981
milieu [miljø]: 2199, 2721
mille [mil]: 2708, 2749, 2770, 2772, 2804
millions [miljɔ̃]: 2271, 2536
m'importe [m ɛ̃pɔʁt]: 2440
mineures [minœʁ]: 2792

minimum [minimɔm]: 2876
minute [minyt]: 2343
minutes [miny]: 2767
minutes [minyt]: 2460, 2560, 2647, 2710, 2967
m'inviter [m‿ɛ̃vite]: 2185
mis [mi]: 2085, 2841, 2862, 2953
mobilier [mobilje]: 2239
m'occuper [m‿okype]: 2852
mode [mɔd]: 2832
moi [mwa]: 2146, 2150, 2163, 2177, 2239, 2326, 2344, 2404, 2432, 2434, 2447, 2552, 2602, 2622, 2665, 2746, 2760, 2761, 2896... +1
moi-même [mwamɛm]: 2003, 2344
moins [mwɛ̃]: 2613, 2615, 2616, 2617, 2651, 2668, 2669, 2672
mois [mwa]: 2028, 2258, 2461, 2496, 2637, 2640, 2712, 2770, 2788, 2961
moitié [mwatje]: 2432, 2794
moment [momɑ̃]: 2089, 2626, 2841
mon [mɔ̃]: 2015, 2038, 2039, 2094, 2124, 2146, 2180, 2185, 2241, 2242, 2452, 2539, 2650, 2664, 2665, 2689, 2703, 2732, 2758... +14
monde [mɔ̃d]: 2033, 2040, 2163, 2198, 2266, 2303, 2421, 2487, 2532, 2706, 2804, 2824, 2862, 2883, 2891, 2914, 2940, 2959, 2971, 2979
mondiale [mɔ̃djal]: 2752
monnaie [monɛ]: 2296
monsieur [m°sjø]: 2537, 2740
m'ont [m‿ɔ̃]: 2229, 2689, 2821, 2940, 2962, 2968, 2996
montagnes [mɔ̃taɲ]: 2308, 2310
montant [mɔ̃tɑ̃]: 2876
monté [mɔ̃te]: 2741, 3000
montées [mɔ̃te]: 2734, 2735, 2741
monter [mɔ̃te]: 2167
montés [mɔ̃te]: 2716, 2734, 2735, 2741
montré [mɔ̃tʁe]: 2534, 2680
mordre [mɔʁdʁ]: 2173, 2174
mort [mɔʁ]: 2813, 2868, 2869
moscou [mɔsku]: 2320
mot [mo]: 2463

motifs [motif]: 2817
moto [moto]: 2679
mots [mo]: 2251
mouillé [muje]: 2568, 2743
mouillée [muje]: 2568, 2743
mourrait [muʁɛ]: 2954
moyens [mwajɛ̃]: 2322, 2371, 2376, 2377
muraille [myʁaj]: 2316
mûres [myʁ]: 2597
murmuré [myʁmyʁe]: 2147
musée [myze]: 2318, 2503
musicale [myzikal]: 2818
musique [myzik]: 2357, 2385, 2590, 2687
mystère [mistɛʁ]: 2484
n'est [n'est]: 2404
n'a [n‿a]: 2034, 2131, 2184, 2210, 2246, 2290, 2394, 2408, 2409, 2410, 2447, 2463, 2544, 2549, 2640, 2642, 2646, 2660, 2892, 2900
nager [naʒe]: 2069, 2128, 2288
n'ai [n‿ɛ]: 2003, 2032, 2122, 2343, 2481, 2508, 2552, 2557, 2655, 2657, 2659, 2717, 2753, 2754, 2763, 2806
n'aies [n‿ɛ]: 2852
n'aimais [n‿ɛmɛ]: 2997
n'aime [n‿ɛm]: 2048, 2049, 2103, 2173, 2262, 2326, 2478
n'approuvent [n‿apʁuv]: 2867
n'arrête [n‿aʁɛt]: 2563, 2935
n'arrivait [n‿aʁivɛ]: 2019
n'arrive [n‿aʁiv]: 2418
n'as [n‿a]: 2560, 2764
n'attendrai [n‿atɑ̃dʁɛ]: 2609
n'aura [n‿oʁa]: 2401
n'aurais [n‿oʁɛ]: 2021, 2059
n'auras [n‿oʁa]: 2132
n'avais [n‿avɛ]: 2531, 2651, 2690, 2873, 2874
n'avait [n‿avɛ]: 2288, 2450, 2559, 2868, 2987
navette [navɛt]: 2483
n'avions [n‿avjɔ̃]: 2058, 2407

n'avons [n̩avɔ̃]: 2412, 2939
n'ayons [n̩ɛjɔ̃]: 2057
ne [nø]: 2004, 2005, 2007, 2009, 2010,
2012, 2015, 2016, 2022, 2023,
2026, 2027, 2028, 2035, 2042...
+151
nécessaire [neseseʁ]: 2914
nécessaires [neseseʁ]: 2533, 2659
n'en [n̩ɑ̃]: 2403
nerveuse [nɛʁvøz]: 2044, 2802
nerveux [nɛʁvø]: 2044, 2349, 2802
n'est [n̩e]: 2052, 2086, 2090, 2167,
2216, 2297, 2347, 2439, 2580,
2583, 2610, 2611, 2616, 2633,
2641, 2769, 2932, 2958
n'est-ce [n̩e sø]: 2409, 2685
n'étaient [n̩etɛ]: 2324, 2555, 2649
n'étais [n̩etɛ]: 2088, 2821
n'était [n̩etɛ]: 2357, 2405, 2437, 2439,
2469, 2746, 2958
n'étions [n̩etjɔ̃]: 2183
nettoyée [netwaje]: 2559
nettoyer [netwaje]: 2040, 2052, 2053,
2807, 2980
neuf [nœ]: 2030
neuf [nœf]: 2749, 2770
new [nuw]: 2318, 2328
ni [ni]: 2441, 2444, 2447, 2753
nocifs [nosif]: 2888
noir [nwaʁ]: 2282
noix [nwa]: 2910
nom [nɔ̃]: 2502, 2507, 2515, 2556,
2744
nombre [nɔ̃bʁ]: 2781, 2884, 2990
nombreuses [nɔ̃bʁø]: 2786
nombreuses [nɔ̃bʁøz]: 2792
nombreux [nɔ̃bʁø]: 2296, 2777, 2923
noms [nɔ̃]: 2130
non [nɔ̃]: 2029, 2066, 2070, 2715
n'ont [n̩ɔ̃]: 2649, 2902
nord [nɔʁ]: 2301, 2311
nos [no]: 2112, 2144, 2368, 2454,
2694, 2913, 2914
n'oserais [n̩ozᵒʁɛ]: 2102

notre [nɔtʁ]: 2089, 2119, 2147, 2347,
2348, 2537, 2583, 2630, 2662,
2725, 2870, 2939, 2984
nôtre [notʁ]: 2610
nôtres [notʁ]: 2828
n'oublie [n̩ubli]: 2020
nourriture [nuʁityʁ]: 2137, 2253, 2619,
2747, 2825, 2913, 2943
nous [nu]: 2014, 2023, 2026, 2034,
2057, 2058, 2077, 2084, 2095,
2096, 2104, 2108, 2110, 2112,
2116... +137
nous-mêmes [numɛm]: 2348
nouveau [nuvo]: 2382, 2479, 2543,
2583, 2910, 2961, 2984
nouveaux [nuvo]: 2221, 2251
nouvel [nuvɛ]: 2089, 2090, 2107, 2216,
2252, 2358, 2945
nouvelle [nuvɛ]: 2781, 2977
nouvelle [nuvɛl]: 2994
nouvelles [nuvɛl]: 2088, 2161, 2234,
2324, 2753, 2804, 2856
nuit [nɥi]: 2170, 2199, 2342, 2463,
2856, 2963
nul [nyl]: 2413, 2943
nulle [nyl]: 2034, 2584, 2585
numéro [nymeʁo]: 2146, 2162, 2665
n'utilises-tu [n̩ytiliz ty]: 2374
n'y [n̩i]: 2044, 2117, 2121, 2135, 2140,
2227, 2384, 2391, 2400, 2402,
2406, 2414, 2551, 2584, 2585,
2672, 2733, 2734, 2755, 2775... +2
obtenir [ɔptᵊni]: 2123, 2132, 2780
obtenir [ɔptᵊniʁ]: 2246
obtenu [ɔptᵊny]: 2243
obtiendra [ɔptjɛ̃dʁa]: 2358
obtiendrez [z̩ɔptjɛ̃dʁe]: 2995
occupée [z̩okype]: 2416
océan [d̩oseɑ̃]: 2304
œufs [z̩ø]: 2893, 2982
offert [ofɛ]: 2986
offert [ofɛʁ]: 2229
offrir [z̩ofʁiʁ]: 2023
oh [o]: 2029

on [ɔ̃]: 2014, 2016, 2026, 2034, 2183, 2391, 2671, 2685, 2687, 2866, 2926, 2960, 2986

ont [ɔ̃]: 2100, 2124, 2170, 2195, 2217, 2264, 2284, 2295, 2403, 2454, 2471, 2498, 2500, 2533, 2540, 2571, 2576, 2635, 2782... +15

ont [l‿ɔ̃]: 2623, 2844, 2956, 2990

ont [ʁ‿ɔ̃]: 2814

ont [z‿ɔ̃]: 2108, 2137

onze [ɔ̃z]: 2804

opinion [n‿opinjɔ̃]: 2178

opinions [z‿opinjɔ̃]: 2434

orateur [n‿oʁatœʁ]: 2805

ordinateur [n‿ɔʁdinatœʁ]: 2955

organisé [ɔʁganize]: 2894

organisée [l‿ɔʁganize]: 2577

ou [n‿u]: 2440

où [ʁ‿u]: 2034, 2584, 2585

ou [t‿u]: 2055

où [u]: 2051, 2122, 2125, 2134, 2140, 2232, 2275, 2390, 2423, 2439, 2464, 2490, 2521, 2522, 2523, 2524, 2526, 2662... +9

ou [u]: 2066, 2070, 2643, 2645, 2743, 2762, 2816, 2849, 2965, 2993, 2999

oublié [t‿ublije]: 2029, 2859

oublié [ublije]: 2018, 2113, 2399, 2663

oui [wi]: 2056, 2082, 2642

ouvert [uveʁ]: 2405

ouverte [uveʁt]: 2769

ouverts [uveʁ]: 2032, 2402

ouvrir [ʁ‿uvʁiʁ]: 2136

ouvrir [uvʁi]: 2255

ouvrir [z‿uvʁiʁ]: 2450

ouvrit [l‿uvʁi]: 2208

oxyde [ɔksid]: 2871

pacifique [pasifik]: 2304

pacifiste [pasifist]: 2291

paies [pɛ]: 2344

pain [pɛ̃]: 2230, 2893

panne [pan]: 2479, 2553, 2706

pantalon [pɑ̃talɔ̃]: 2039

papier [papje]: 2474, 2931, 2982

paquet [pakɛ]: 2699

par [pa]: 2378, 2760, 2761, 2988, 2989

par [paʁ]: 2003, 2076, 2140, 2265, 2371, 2376, 2377, 2416, 2537, 2556, 2636, 2648, 2762, 2763, 2769, 2770, 2778... +14

parapluie [paʁaplɥi]: 2399, 2686

parce [paʁs]: 2090, 2093, 2174, 2229, 2246, 2364, 2400, 2560, 2677, 2678, 2755, 2797, 2859, 2891, 2921

pardonner [paʁdone]: 2878

parents [paʁɑ̃]: 2012, 2171, 2739, 2789, 2797, 2814, 2815, 2830, 2851, 2867, 2900, 2913, 2940, 2962, 2968, 2969

paresseuse [paʁɛsøz]: 2593

paresseux [paʁɛsø]: 2593

parfaitement [paʁfɛtᵊmɑ̃]: 2574

parfois [paʁfwa]: 2345, 2758, 2765

parlais [paʁlɛ]: 2539

parlait [paʁlɛ]: 2419, 2630

parle [paʁl]: 2528, 2529, 2589

parlé [paʁle]: 2025, 2096, 2408, 2481, 2497, 2507, 2537, 2552, 2754, 2859

parlent [paʁl]: 2365

parler [paʁle]: 2024, 2135, 2153, 2213, 2215, 2247, 2563, 2606, 2667, 2688

parles [paʁl]: 2581, 2993

parles-tu [paʁl ty]: 2345

pars [paʁ]: 2142, 2719, 2937

part [pa]: 2034, 2584, 2585

part [paʁ]: 2155, 2156, 2157, 2691, 2793, 2794

partager [paʁtaʒe]: 2372

partes [paʁt]: 2256

partez [paʁte]: 2967

parti [paʁti]: 2091, 2637, 2706, 2938, 3000

partie [paʁti]: 2132, 2170, 2260, 2436

parties [paʁti]: 2338, 2909

partions [paʁtjɔ̃]: 2674

partir [paʁtiʁ]: 2180, 2245, 2330, 2612, 2675, 2710, 2854

partis [paʁti]: 2116, 2570

partons [paʁtɔ̃]: 2614

pas [pa]: 2003, 2004, 2005, 2007, 2009, 2012, 2016, 2019, 2020, 2021,

2022, 2023, 2026, 2027, 2028, 2032, 2034... +229

passante [pasãt]: 2089

passe [pas]: 2483

passé [pase]: 2010, 2070, 2126, 2171, 2236, 2287, 2428, 2462, 2480, 2588, 2643, 2688, 2836, 2956

passent [pas]: 2604

passer [pase]: 2164, 2398, 2822

passes-tu [pas ty]: 2918

passons [pasɔ̃]: 2941

patient [pasjã]: 2289

patiente [pasjãt]: 2627

patron [patʁɔ̃]: 2583, 2795, 2834

pauvre [povʁ]: 2059

pauvres [povʁ]: 2298

payé [peje]: 2875

payée [peje]: 2580

payer [peje]: 2100, 2185, 2292, 2344, 2763, 2784, 2873, 2874, 2876, 2898

pays [pei]: 2260, 2296, 2301, 2306, 2315, 2629, 2819, 2828

peau [po]: 2888, 2943

peine [pɛn]: 2581, 2582, 2632

pékin [pekɛ̃]: 2162

pendant [pãdã]: 2024, 2086, 2228, 2527, 2693, 2694, 2696, 2697, 2698, 2821, 2939, 2982

pensais [pãsɛ]: 2615, 2651

pense [pãs]: 2133, 2157, 2178, 2246, 2358, 2453, 2780, 2883, 2885, 2886, 2903

pensé [pãse]: 2018, 2858

pensent [pãs]: 2363, 2838

penser [pãse]: 2139, 2422

penses-tu [pãs ty]: 2039, 2041, 2151, 2292, 2328

pensions [pãsjɔ̃]: 2608

pentagone [pɛ̃tagon]: 2321

percée [pɛʁse]: 2981

perdant [pɛʁdã]: 2809

perds [pɛʁ]: 2127, 2133

perdu [pɛʁdy]: 2179, 2640, 2750, 2906

perdues [pɛʁdy]: 2493

perdus [pɛʁdy]: 2538, 2780

père [pɛʁ]: 2158, 2765, 2766, 2856

performance [pɛʁfɔʁmãs]: 2818

péri [peʁi]: 2948

permet [pɛʁmɛ]: 2017

permets-moi [pɛʁmɛ mwa]: 2836

permis [pɛʁmi]: 2865

permission [pɛʁmisjɔ̃]: 2245

personne [pɛʁsɔn]: 2007, 2010, 2067, 2109, 2135, 2147, 2161, 2176, 2291, 2391, 2394, 2406, 2408, 2409, 2410, 2583, 2627, 2847, 2848, 2855... +1

personnes [pɛʁsɔn]: 2217, 2264, 2284, 2363, 2425, 2426, 2442, 2533, 2540, 2563, 2571, 2576, 2797, 2884, 2897, 2999

petit [pᵊti]: 2278

petite [pᵊtit]: 2095, 2721

pétrin [petʁɛ̃]: 2085

pétrole [petʁɔl]: 2766

pétrolière [petʁoljɛʁ]: 2333, 2986

peu [pø]: 2255, 2416, 2417, 2418, 2419, 2420, 2421, 2423, 2533, 2566, 2599, 2606, 2879, 2951

peur [pøʁ]: 2170, 2171, 2172, 2173, 2174, 2284, 2810, 2810, 2811, 2987

peut [pø]: 2026, 2211, 2484, 2562, 2624, 2652, 2758, 2926

peuvent [pœv]: 2679, 2867, 2919

peux [pø]: 2009, 2017, 2042, 2074, 2220, 2223, 2226, 2227, 2347, 2349, 2356, 2422, 2452, 2509, 2567, 2581, 2624, 2668, 2670... +5

peux-tu [pø ty]: 2001, 2599, 2835

philippines [filipin]: 2312

photo [foto]: 2534

photocopieur [fotokopjœʁ]: 2035

photos [foto]: 2779

phrases [fʁaz]: 2470

piano [pjano]: 2003

pièce [pjɛs]: 2728, 2916

pied [pje]: 2068, 2596

pilote [pilɔt]: 2972

pire [piʁ]: 2602, 2626

piscine [pisin]: 2288, 2359

piste [pist]: 2646, 2939

pitié [pitje]: 2042, 2809
place [plas]: 2227, 2945, 2953
plage [plaʒ]: 2459, 2462, 2654
plaignait [plɛɲɛ]: 2861
plaindre [plɛ̃dʁ]: 2166
plainte [plɛ̃t]: 2860
plaît [plɛ]: 2020, 2033, 2056, 2148,
    2722, 2912, 2920, 2931, 2935, 2991
plan [plɑ̃]: 2537, 2543, 2615, 2689,
    2984
planète [planɛt]: 2485
plans [plɑ̃]: 2408, 2977
plante [plɑ̃t]: 2728
plein [plɛ̃]: 2823
pleinement [plɛnəmɑ̃]: 2822
pleut [pløt]: 2654
pleuvait [pløvɛ]: 2572
pleuvoir [pløvwaʁ]: 2686
plu [ply]: 2696
pluie [plɥi]: 2112, 2194, 2260, 2568,
    2672, 2743
plupart [plypaʁ]: 2216, 2424, 2430,
    2550, 2555, 2558
plus [ply]: 2233, 2384, 2390, 2563,
    2564, 2605, 2625, 2629, 2637,
    2638, 2800
plus [plys]: 2017, 2031, 2036, 2037,
    2055, 2074, 2090, 2116, 2144,
    2145, 2161, 2245, 2260, 2266,
    2277, 2292, 2293... +45
plusieurs [plyzjœ]: 2076
plusieurs [plyzjœʁ]: 2434, 2987
plutôt [plyto]: 2061, 2062, 2063, 2068,
    2069, 2661, 2853
poche [pɔʃ]: 2208
poches [pɔʃ]: 2841
poids [pwa]: 2756, 2926
point [pwɛ̃]: 2927, 2981
pointé [pwɛ̃te]: 2840
poli [poli]: 2795
police [polis]: 2015, 2215, 2323, 2534,
    2545, 2549, 2556, 2667, 2790,
    2791, 2817, 2833, 2839, 2841,
    2915, 2925, 2952, 2953, 2956... +2
policier [polisje]: 2837

policiers [polisje]: 2218, 2219, 2325,
    2840, 2992
polie [poli]: 2795
politicien [politisjɛ̃]: 2843
politique [politik]: 2025
pommes [pɔm]: 2597
pompiers [pɔ̃pje]: 2947, 2948
populaire [popylɛʁ]: 2583, 2816
population [popylasjɔ̃]: 2532, 2966
portable [pɔʁtabl]: 2038, 2664, 2678,
    2762, 2779
portaient [pɔʁtɛ]: 2901
portait [pɔʁtɛ]: 2677
porte [pɔʁt]: 2018, 2027, 2056, 2149,
    2162, 2199, 2208, 2450, 2579,
    2648, 2722, 2769
porter [pɔʁte]: 2013, 2022, 2473, 2860
portes [pɔʁt]: 2501
poser [poze]: 2389, 2952
positive [pozitiv]: 2788
possibilité [posibilite]: 2389
possible [posibl]: 2052, 2452, 2620,
    2626, 2861
poste [pɔst]: 2229, 2263, 2594, 2635,
    2655, 2659, 2660, 2661, 2853
poster [pɔste]: 2020
postulé [pɔstyle]: 2508, 2533, 2540,
    2635, 2950
postuler [pɔstyle]: 2477, 2594, 2853
postules-tu [pɔstyl ty]: 2853
potentiel [potɑ̃sjɛl]: 2984
poubelles [pubɛl]: 2919
pour [pu]: 2086, 2136, 2137, 2253,
    2289, 2293, 2343, 2416, 2422,
    2452, 2530, 2597, 2690, 2691,
    2704, 2895, 2914, 2953, 2960... +1
pour [puʁ]: 2040, 2041, 2081, 2089,
    2097, 2100, 2107, 2129, 2132,
    2138, 2139, 2141, 2142, 2143,
    2144, 2145, 2146, 2147, 2148,
    2149... +90
pourparlers [puʁpaʁle]: 2949
pourquoi [puʁkwa]: 2083, 2362, 2374,
    2513, 2568, 2626, 2853, 2858
pourraient [puʁɛ]: 2795
pourrais [puʁɛ]: 2041

pourrais-je [puʁɛ ʒø]: 2763
pourrais-tu [puʁɛ ty]: 2606, 2620, 2722
pourrait [puʁɛ]: 2383
pourvu [puʁvy]: 2670, 2671
pousser [puse]: 2375
pouvaient [puvɛ]: 2957, 2976
pouvais [puvɛ]: 2194, 2360, 2445, 2658, 2678, 2876
pouvait [puvɛ]: 2043, 2454, 2535, 2590, 2925, 2959
pouvez [puve]: 2449
pouvions [puvjõ]: 2364, 2450
pouvoir [puvwaʁ]: 2143, 2144, 2375, 2485
pouvons [puvõ]: 2023, 2026, 2440, 2985
pratiquement [pʁatik°mã]: 2584, 2585, 2585
pratiquer [pʁatike]: 2138
préfère [pʁefɛʁ]: 2061, 2062, 2063, 2064
préférée [pʁefeʁe]: 2052
préférerais [pʁefeʁ°ʁɛ]: 2055, 2063, 2065, 2067, 2068, 2069, 2853
préférerais-tu [pʁefeʁ°ʁɛ ty]: 2055, 2066
préfères-tu [pʁefeʁ ty]: 2070
premier [pʁømje]: 2997
première [pʁømjɛʁ]: 2161
prend [pʁã]: 2601, 2926
prendra [pʁãdʁa]: 2961
prendre [pʁãdʁ]: 2046, 2068, 2118, 2629, 2683, 2727, 2740, 2757, 2848, 2850
prennent [pʁɛn]: 2851
près [pʁɛ]: 2174, 2195, 2261, 2355, 2599
présent [pʁezã]: 2924
présente [pʁezãt]: 2924
présentées [pʁezãte]: 2366
présentés [pʁezãte]: 2366
président [pʁezidã]: 2024, 2025
presque [pʁɛsk]: 2394, 2583
presse [pʁɛs]: 2958, 2959
pressé [pʁese]: 2362, 2740

prêt [pʁɛ]: 2967
prête [pʁɛt]: 2967
prêté [pʁete]: 2028, 2998
preuves [pʁœv]: 2791
prévenu [pʁɛv°ny]: 2004, 2005, 2016
prévenue [pʁɛv°ny]: 2016
prévu [pʁevy]: 2603
prime [pʁim]: 2772
principale [pʁɛ̃sipal]: 2341
principalement [pʁɛ̃sipal°mã]: 2872
pris [pʁi]: 2278, 2298, 2686, 2756, 2972
prise [pʁiz]: 2985
prison [pʁizõ]: 2272, 2273, 2731, 2865, 2916
probablement [pʁobabl°mã]: 2169, 2634
problème [pʁoblɛm]: 2096, 2184, 2397, 2764, 2786, 2984
problèmes [pʁoblɛm]: 2042, 2080, 2329, 2430, 2927, 2977
prochain [pʁoʃɛ̃]: 2162, 2795
prochaine [pʁoʃɛn]: 2314, 2634, 2698, 2738, 2799
prochaines [pʁoʃɛn]: 2570
prochains [pʁoʃɛ̃]: 2961
proches [pʁoʃ]: 2312
production [pʁodyksjõ]: 2941
produire [pʁodɥiʁ]: 2189
produit [pʁodɥi]: 2325
produits [pʁodɥi]: 2550, 2774
professeur [pʁofɛsœʁ]: 2650
professeurs [pʁofɛsœʁ]: 2914
professionnel [pʁofɛsjonɛl]: 2923
profite [pʁofit]: 2231
profiter [pʁofite]: 2112
programme [pʁogʁam]: 2764
progrès [pʁogʁɛ]: 2037
progressait [pʁogʁɛse]: 2564
promesses [pʁomɛs]: 2891
promettes [pʁomɛt]: 2670
promettre [pʁomɛtʁ]: 2010
promis [pʁomi]: 2185, 2293, 2924
propos [pʁopo]: 2117, 2323, 2667, 2796

proposition [pʁopozisjɔ̃]: 2139
propre [pʁɔpʁ]: 2288, 2372, 2671
propres [pʁɔpʁ]: 2080, 2371, 2375,
    2376, 2377, 2848
propriétaires [pʁopʁijetɛʁ]: 2945
protège [pʁotɛʒ]: 2888
protéger [pʁoteʒe]: 2270, 2889, 2901
protester [pʁotɛste]: 2945
provenant [pʁovˀnɑ̃]: 2386
pu [py]: 2032, 2034, 2397, 2578, 2600,
    2618, 2939
public [pyblik]: 2818
puis [pɥi]: 2263, 2842, 2943
puis-je [pɥi ʒø]: 2247
puisqu'il [pɥisk il]: 2140
puisse [pɥis]: 2146, 2147, 2150, 2924
puisses [pɥis]: 2117, 2662
puissions [pɥisjɔ̃]: 2148
qu'à [k a]: 2363, 2660
qualifications [kalifikasjɔ̃]: 2533, 2659
qualifié [kalifje]: 2655, 2657
qualifiée [kalifje]: 2655, 2657
quand [kɑ̃]: 2129, 2274, 2433, 2446,
    2503, 2630, 2689, 2706, 2734,
    2740, 2798, 2806, 2831, 2844,
    2875, 2890, 2962, 2969, 2980... +2
quant [kɑ̃]: 2817
quarante [kaʁɑ̃t]: 2767
qu'arturo [k (...)]: 2177
qu'as-tu [k a ty]: 2072, 2923
quatorze [katɔʁz]: 2708
quatre [katʁ]: 2162, 2486, 2741, 2773
quatre-vingt-dix [katʁˀvɛ̃di]: 2850
qu'avant [k avɑ̃]: 2090
que [kø]: 2004, 2006, 2015, 2018,
    2021, 2023, 2028, 2039, 2041,
    2049, 2052, 2057, 2061, 2063,
    2065, 2067, 2068, 2069... +154
quel [kɛ]: 2266, 2502, 2507, 2515,
    2671
quel [kɛl]: 2556, 2855
qu'elle [k ɛl]: 2156, 2178, 2358, 2447,
    2494, 2633, 2641, 2656, 2685,
    2826, 2891

quelle [kɛ]: 2178, 2279, 2351, 2612,
    2629
quelle [kɛl]: 2128, 2445
quelque [kɛlk]: 2136, 2181, 2196,
    2203, 2418, 2484, 2825, 2846
quelques [kɛl]: 2031, 2228, 2621
quelques [kɛlk]: 2028, 2118, 2139,
    2247, 2256, 2527, 2551, 2560,
    2710, 2754, 2922, 2967, 2973
quelques-uns [kɛlkˀzœ̃]: 2368
quelqu'un [kɛlkœ̃]: 2003, 2192, 2193,
    2199, 2285, 2331, 2361, 2372,
    2385, 2391, 2395, 2399, 2509,
    2516, 2528, 2531, 2722, 2745,
    2769, 2843... +1
qu'en [k ɑ̃]: 2062, 2601
qu'est-ce [kɛsˀ]: 2110
qu'est-il [k e t il]: 2915
question [kɛstjɔ̃]: 2154, 2338, 2474,
    2837
questions [kɛstjɔ̃]: 2152, 2389, 2395,
    2941, 2952
qui [ki]: 2002, 2010, 2070, 2076, 2079,
    2110, 2121, 2135, 2171, 2277,
    2285, 2286, 2291, 2335, 2336,
    2337, 2338, 2391, 2406, 2426...
    +48
quiconque [kikɔ̃k]: 2215, 2398, 2477
qu'il [k il]: 2016, 2090, 2091, 2146,
    2151, 2157, 2210, 2246, 2391,
    2400, 2421, 2453, 2582, 2621,
    2624, 2636, 2673... +15
qu'ils [k il]: 2066, 2381, 2498, 2500,
    2511, 2687, 2927, 2988
quinze [kɛ̃z]: 2086, 2582
quitté [kite]: 2177, 2496, 2748, 2938
quitter [kite]: 2156, 2183, 2975
quoi [kwa]: 2324, 2393, 2396, 2535,
    2829
qu'on [k ɔ̃]: 2008, 2048, 2081, 2089,
    2590
raconter [ʁakɔ̃te]: 2010, 2171, 2562,
    2935, 2993
radio [ʁadjo]: 2753
raison [ʁɛzɔ̃]: 2525, 2774, 2936
raisonnables [ʁɛzonabl]: 2555
ralenti [ʁalɑ̃ti]: 2150

ramène [ʁamɛn]: 2879
rangée [ʁɑ̃ʒe]: 2723
ranger [ʁɑ̃ʒe]: 3000
rapidement [ʁapidᵊmɑ̃]: 2575, 2670, 2774
rappelé [ʁapᵊle]: 2114
rappeler [ʁapᵊle]: 2001
rappelles [ʁapɛl]: 2857
rarement [ʁaʁᵊmɑ̃]: 2632
rasant [ʁazɑ̃]: 2204
rasé [ʁaze]: 2352
rattraperai [ʁatʁapᵊʁɛ]: 2967
rayons [ʁɛjɔ̃]: 2888
réaction [ʁeaksjɔ̃]: 2787
récemment [ʁesamɑ̃]: 2521
récente [ʁesɑ̃t]: 2886
réception [ʁesɛpsjɔ̃]: 2803
réceptions [ʁesɛpsjɔ̃]: 2785
recevoir [ʁᵊsᵊvwaʁ]: 2699
rechargé [ʁᵊʃaʁʒe]: 2038
réchauffement [ʁeʃofmɑ̃]: 2863
recherche [ʁᵊʃɛʁʃ]: 2219, 2545
recherché [ʁᵊʃɛʁʃe]: 2269
rechercher [ʁᵊʃɛʁʃe]: 2780
recherchiez [ʁᵊʃɛʁʃje]: 2495
reçois [ʁᵊswa]: 2785
reçoit [ʁᵊswa]: 2622
recommandé [ʁᵊkomɑ̃de]: 2015, 2505
recommanderais [ʁᵊkomɑ̃dᵊʁɛ]: 2007
reconnus [ʁᵊkony]: 2294
reconstruit [ʁᵊkɔ̃stʁɥi]: 2482
reçu [ʁᵊsy]: 2471
recul [ʁᵊkyl]: 2997
recyclés [ʁᵊsikle]: 2919
redéménagée [ʁᵊdemenaʒe]: 2092
réel [ʁeɛl]: 2914
réellement [ʁeɛlᵊmɑ̃]: 2956
réfléchir [ʁefleʃiʁ]: 2078
réfrigérateur [ʁefʁiʒeʁatœʁ]: 2490, 2921
refusé [ʁᵊfyze]: 2393, 2837
refuser [ʁᵊfyze]: 2986
regardais [ʁᵊgaʁdɛ]: 2693, 2757
regarde [ʁᵊgaʁd]: 2632

regardé [ʁᵊgaʁde]: 2436, 2689
regarder [ʁᵊgaʁde]: 2133
régime [ʁeʒim]: 2756
région [ʁeʒjɔ̃]: 2341
regret [ʁᵊgʁɛ]: 2023
regrette [ʁᵊgʁɛt]: 2021
regretté [ʁᵊgʁete]: 2022
rejetée [ʁᵊʒte]: 2950
rejoindre [ʁᵊʒwɛ̃dʁ]: 2762
relation [ʁᵊlasjɔ̃]: 2789, 2927, 2976
relayons [ʁᵊlejɔ̃]: 2850
reliant [ʁᵊljɑ̃]: 2546
rembourser [ʁɑ̃buʁse]: 2998
remercié [ʁᵊmɛʁsje]: 2877
remercier [ʁᵊmɛʁsje]: 2113
remettre [ʁᵊmetʁ]: 2985
remisés [ʁᵊmize]: 2977
remplis [ʁɑ̃pli]: 2912
remplissage [ʁɑ̃plisaʒ]: 2744
remporté [ʁɑ̃pɔʁte]: 2895
rencontre [ʁɑ̃kɔ̃tʁ]: 2081
rencontré [ʁɑ̃kɔ̃tʁe]: 2254, 2516, 2517, 2518, 2531, 2631, 2674, 2694, 2754
rencontrée [ʁɑ̃kɔ̃tʁe]: 2627
rencontrées [ʁɑ̃kɔ̃tʁe]: 2366, 2563, 2907
rencontrer [ʁɑ̃kɔ̃tʁe]: 2047, 2054, 2106, 2351, 2739
rencontrés [ʁɑ̃kɔ̃tʁe]: 2366, 2907
rendant [ʁɑ̃dɑ̃]: 2020
rendent [ʁɑ̃d]: 2815
rendre [ʁɑ̃dʁ]: 2094, 2211, 2273
rendu [ʁɑ̃dy]: 2960
rendue [ʁɑ̃dy]: 2075
rentrant [ʁɑ̃tʁɑ̃]: 2631, 2727
rentré [ʁɑ̃tʁe]: 2446, 2969
rentrée [ʁɑ̃tʁe]: 2446
rentrer [ʁɑ̃tʁe]: 2068, 2160, 2165, 2588, 2596, 2890
rentreras [ʁɑ̃tʁᵊʁa]: 2033
renversé [ʁɑ̃vɛʁse]: 2989
réparations [ʁepaʁasjɔ̃]: 2898
réparée [ʁepaʁe]: 2554
réparer [ʁepaʁe]: 2065, 2126

reparlerai [ʁəpaʁlˠʁɛ]: 2448, 2663

repas [ʁəpa]: 2870, 2873

répondre [ʁepɔ̃dʁ]: 2152, 2154, 2395, 2722, 2837

répondu [ʁepɔ̃dy]: 2642, 2834

réponse [ʁepɔ̃s]: 2474

repos [ʁəpo]: 2343

reposer [ʁəpoze]: 2343, 2527

représentent [ʁəpʁezɑ̃t]: 2966

reprises [ʁəpʁiz]: 2754

reproche [ʁəpʁɔʃ]: 2882

réputation [ʁepytasjɔ̃]: 2960

résoudre [ʁezudʁ]: 2184, 2430, 2764

responsabilités [ʁɛspɔ̃sabilite]: 2580

responsable [ʁɛspɔ̃sabl]: 2754, 2833

restants [ʁɛstɑ̃]: 2551

restaurant [ʁɛstoʁɑ̃]: 2166, 2382, 2510, 2747

restaurants [ʁɛstoʁɑ̃]: 2438, 2439, 2440, 2441

reste [ʁɛst]: 2203, 2403, 2420, 2424

rester [ʁɛste]: 2063, 2083, 2917

restes [ʁɛst]: 2846

résultats [ʁezylta]: 2332

retard [ʁətaʁ]: 2141, 2163, 2379, 2560, 2618, 2636, 2681, 2685, 2715, 2824

retardé [ʁətaʁde]: 2939

retour [ʁətuʁ]: 2702, 2995, 2996

retourner [ʁətuʁne]: 2212, 2738

retourneront [ʁətuʁnˠʁɔ̃]: 2999

retrouvés [ʁətʁuve]: 2964

réunion [ʁeynjɔ̃]: 2148, 2339, 2537, 2555, 2663, 2675, 2845, 2859

réussi [ʁeysi]: 2099, 2184, 2394, 2947

réussiras [ʁeysiʁa]: 2905

rêvasser [ʁɛvase]: 2127

rêvé [ʁeve]: 2855

réveille [ʁevɛj]: 2920

revenir [ʁəvˠniʁ]: 2364, 2720

reverrons [ʁəvɛʁɔ̃]: 2653

reviens [ʁəvjɛ̃]: 2027, 2711, 2720

revoir [ʁəvwaʁ]: 2057, 2653

rhin [ʁin]: 2305

riaient [ʁjɛ]: 2838

riche [ʁiʃ]: 2832

riches [ʁiʃ]: 2292, 2298

rien [ʁjɛ̃]: 2015, 2117, 2121, 2203, 2404, 2407, 2411, 2557, 2563, 2569, 2585, 2688, 2852, 2924

rire [ʁiʁ]: 2043

risque [ʁisk]: 2165

rivière [ʁivjɛʁ]: 2195

robe [ʁɔb]: 2494, 2501, 2934

robin [ʁɔbɛ̃]: 2298

roche [ʁɔʃ]: 2910

rock [ʁɔk]: 2889

rôle [ʁol]: 2851

romans [ʁomɑ̃]: 2908

rompre [ʁɔ̃pʁ]: 2975

rompus [ʁɔ̃py]: 2949

roulait [ʁulɛ]: 2750

roulé [ʁule]: 2542

roulent [ʁul]: 2726

route [ʁut]: 2019, 2542, 2546, 2554, 2767, 2781, 2890

routes [ʁut]: 2169

royaume-uni [ʁwajom yni]: 2314, 2315

rue [ʁy]: 2089, 2190, 2205, 2386, 2729, 2951, 2963, 2964, 2988, 2989

russie [ʁysi]: 2949

s'il [s'il]: 2654

sa [sa]: 2059, 2157, 2186, 2208, 2450, 2457, 2589, 2608, 2787, 2794, 2798, 2832, 2906, 2960

sac [sak]: 2013, 2607

sachent [saʃ]: 2066

sacs [sak]: 2238

s'agit-il [s‿aʒi t‿il]: 2495

s'aiment [s‿ɛm]: 2354

sais [sɛ]: 2018, 2890, 2896

sait [sɛ]: 2453

sait-il [sɛ t‿il]: 2643

salaire [salɛʁ]: 2622, 2660, 2661, 2770, 2892

salle [sal]: 2387

s'allonger [s‿alɔ̃ʒe]: 2840

salué [salɥe]: 2996

saluée [salɥe]: 2996

samedi [samˠdi]: 2367, 2702

samia [samia]: 2861
s'amuser [s̬amyze]: 2585
sandwich [sãdwitʃ]: 2455
sans [sã]: 2077, 2078, 2079, 2080,
  2084, 2281, 2392, 2538, 2653, 2696
sans-abri [sã z̬abʁi]: 2293
santé [sãte]: 2329, 2329, 2913
s'arranger [s̬aʁãʒe]: 2991
s'asseoir [s̬aswaʁ]: 2584, 2742
s'attendaient [s̬atãdɛ]: 2421
sauf [sof]: 2163
sauvegarder [sov°gaʁde]: 2954, 2955
sauvent [sov]: 2473
savais [savɛ]: 2592, 2651, 2862
savent-ils [sa v̬il]: 2325
savoir [savwaʁ]: 2161, 2175, 2178,
  2233, 2396, 2504
savons [savɔ̃]: 2575
scandale [skãdal]: 2333, 2956
scientifiques [sjãtifik]: 2786, 2863
se [søʔ]: 2008, 2009, 2019, 2073, 2081,
  2090, 2121, 2131, 2134, 2149,
  2189, 2211, 2290, 2359, 2365,
  2367, 2383... +27
sec [sɛk]: 2260
sécha [seʃa]: 2359
secondaire [s°gɔ̃dɛʁ]: 2274, 2856
secret [s°kʁɛ]: 2433
sécuritaire [sekyʁitɛʁ]: 2151, 2167
sécurité [sekyʁite]: 2473
sein [sɛ̃]: 2682
seize [sɛz]: 2628
séjour [seʒuʁ]: 2180, 2877
séjourne [seʒuʁn]: 2671
séjourné [seʒuʁne]: 2505
séjourner [seʒuʁne]: 2007, 2226, 2449
selon [s°lɔ̃]: 2746, 2747
semaine [s°mɛn]: 2265, 2323, 2340,
  2342, 2634, 2691, 2698, 2711,
  2733, 2738, 2799
semaines [s°mɛn]: 2336, 2570
semblables [sãblabl]: 2828
semblait [sãblɛ]: 2686
semble [sãbl]: 2035, 2485, 2684, 2685,
  2927

semestres [s°mɛstʁ]: 2922
s'empêcher [s̬ãpeʃe]: 2043
s'en [s̬ã]: 2186, 2925
s'engueuler [s̬ãgøle]: 2842
sens [sãs]: 2135, 2349, 2809
sens-tu [sãs ty]: 2196
sent [sã]: 2565
sentait [sãte]: 2656
sentant [sãtã]: 2209
s'entendre [s̬ãtãdʁ]: 2976
sentent [sãt]: 2814
senti [sãti]: 2192
sentir [sãtiʁ]: 2656
s'envole [s̬ãvɔl]: 2957
séparée [sepaʁe]: 2474
séparent [sepaʁ]: 2974
séparés [sepaʁe]: 2974
sept [sɛ]: 2768
sept [sɛt]: 2870
septembre [sɛptãbʁ]: 2691, 2804
sera [s°ʁa]: 2162, 2260, 2636, 2702,
  2704
serai [s°ʁɛ]: 2180, 2395, 2634, 2698,
  2967
serais [s°ʁɛ]: 2178
serait [s°ʁɛ]: 2390, 2612, 2641
seras [s°ʁa]: 2161, 2743
seras-tu [s°ʁa ty]: 2280, 2715
sérieuse [seʁjøz]: 2043
serions [s°ʁjɔ̃]: 2538
seront [s°ʁɔ̃]: 2570
sers-toi [se twa]: 2346
sert [sɛʁ]: 2569
service [sɛʁvis]: 2460, 2755, 2860,
  2943
services [sɛʁvis]: 2870
serviette [sɛʁvjɛt]: 2359
ses [se]: 2012, 2171, 2369, 2371, 2377,
  2408, 2433, 2434, 2774, 2788,
  2841, 2867, 2878, 2891, 2900,
  2908, 2994
s'est [s̬e]: 2030, 2070, 2075, 2085,
  2171, 2200, 2325, 2352, 2433,
  2480, 2643, 2650, 2713, 2774,
  2827, 2836, 2906... +4

s'estomper [s_ɛstɔ̃pe]: 2959
s'était [s_etɛ]: 2010, 2688, 2956
seul [sœl]: 2135, 2163, 2776, 2777
seule [sœl]: 2012, 2086, 2087, 2135, 2485
seulement [sœlᵊmã]: 2118, 2420, 2551, 2668, 2767, 2893
s'excuse [s_ɛkskyz]: 2879
s'habitue [s abity]: 2089
s'habituer [s abitɥe]: 2092
shopping [ʃɔpiŋ]: 2129
si [si]: 2017, 2064, 2090, 2115, 2161, 2168, 2175, 2181, 2233, 2245, 2297, 2346, 2361, 2384, 2395, 2396, 2504, 2569... +21
siècles [sjɛkl]: 2692
siège [sjɛʒ]: 2736
sièges [sjɛʒ]: 2734
signature [siɲatyʁ]: 2772
signifie [siɲifi]: 2210, 2213, 2830, 2981
s'il [s_il]: 2020, 2033, 2037, 2056, 2135, 2148, 2722, 2912, 2920, 2931, 2935, 2991
silencieuse [silãsjøz]: 2033
silencieux [silãsjø]: 2033
simple [sɛ̃pl]: 2787, 2893
simplement [sɛ̃plᵊmã]: 2925, 2957, 2959
simples [sɛ̃pl]: 2600
singapour [singapuʁ]: 2726
sinon [sinɔ̃]: 2830
situation [sitɥasjɔ̃]: 2059, 2117, 2598
situé [sitɥe]: 2725
six [si]: 2327
six [sis]: 2265, 2461, 2640, 2712
s'occuper [s_okype]: 2850
société [sosjete]: 2543, 2774, 2977
sœur [sœʁ]: 2262, 2370, 2371, 2518, 2798, 2881, 2894
sœurs [sœʁ]: 2541
soigneusement [swaɲøzᵊmã]: 2470
soin [swɛ̃]: 2850, 2851
soir [swaʁ]: 2063, 2064, 2105, 2165, 2283, 2342, 2382, 2383, 2388, 2431, 2826

sois [swa]: 2714, 2795, 2816, 2822
soit [swa]: 2091, 2210, 2393, 2396, 2448, 2485, 2535, 2610, 2671, 2744
sol [sɔl]: 2840, 2844, 2988
solaire [sɔlɛʁ]: 2888
soleil [sɔlɛj]: 2267, 2522, 2536, 2742, 2888, 3000
solitaire [sɔlitɛʁ]: 3000
solution [sɔlysjɔ̃]: 2786
sommes [sɔm]: 2084, 2116, 2144, 2288, 2366, 2430, 2439, 2459, 2503, 2523, 2572, 2630, 2638, 2716, 2718, 2734, 2735, 2780, 2831... +3
somnole [sɔmnɔl]: 2942
son [sɔ̃]: 2022, 2107, 2156, 2177, 2178, 2179, 2188, 2273, 2373, 2399, 2416, 2534, 2573, 2580, 2628, 2640, 2647, 2678, 2682, 2706... +15
songe [sɔ̃ʒ]: 2101, 2970
sonné [sone]: 2676
sont [sɔ̃]: 2073, 2076, 2121, 2219, 2239, 2290, 2294, 2297, 2307, 2308, 2310, 2312, 2315, 2322, 2329, 2332, 2363, 2378, 2380, 2426... +31
sont-elles [sɔ̃ t_ɛl]: 2810
sors [sɔʁ]: 2424, 2743
sors-tu [sɔʁ ty]: 2083
sortant [sɔʁtã]: 2208
sortent [sɔʁt]: 2465
sorti [sɔʁti]: 2202, 2568, 2697
sortie [sɔʁti]: 2392, 2568, 2697
sorties [sɔʁti]: 2572
sortir [sɔʁti]: 2982
sortir [sɔʁtiʁ]: 2012, 2064, 2071, 2105, 2193, 2865, 2924
sortis [sɔʁti]: 2572, 2988
sortit [sɔʁti]: 2359
soucie [susi]: 2847
soucier [susje]: 2080, 2852
soudainement [sudɛnᵊmã]: 2192
souffrant [sufʁã]: 2884
souffre [sufʁ]: 2887, 2927
souhaitait [swɛtɛ]: 2176

souhaitant [swɛtɑ̃]: 2477
souhaite [swɛt]: 2398
souhaites [swɛt]: 2175, 2245
soulève [sulev]: 2926
soupçonnait [supsonɛ]: 2109
soupçonne [supsɔn]: 2866
soupçonné [supsone]: 2958
soupe [sup]: 2224, 2849
sourire [suʁiʁ]: 2995
sourires [suʁiʁ]: 2995
sous [su]: 2568, 2743, 2957
soutenir [sut°niʁ]: 2952
souvenait [suv°nɛ]: 2019
souvenir [suv°niʁ]: 2019, 2130
souvent [suvɑ̃]: 2052, 2091, 2124,
    2144, 2424, 2461, 2604
souvenu [suv°ny]: 2029
souviens [suvjɛ̃]: 2018, 2028
souviens-tu [suvjɛ̃ ty]: 2523
spécial [spesjal]: 2953
spécialisé [spesjalize]: 2904
spectacle [spɛktakl]: 2988
spectateurs [spɛktatœʁ]: 2842
sports [spɔʁ]: 2679
stan [stan]: 2006
station [stasjɔ̃]: 2930
stationnement [stasjɔn°mɑ̃]: 2373
stock [stɔk]: 2932
stressant [stʁɛsɑ̃]: 2758
stupide [stypid]: 2586, 2586
sucre [sykʁ]: 2872
sud [syd]: 2302, 2308, 2313
suède [sɥed]: 2301
suffi [syfi]: 2902
suffisamment [syfizamɑ̃]: 2342
suffisent [syfiz]: 2327, 2328
suggéré [sygʒeʁe]: 2006
suggestion [sygʒɛstjɔ̃]: 2240, 2787
suggestions [sygʒɛstjɔ̃]: 2555
suicidé [sɥiside]: 2946
suicides [sɥisid]: 2886
suis [sɥi]: 2044, 2064, 2093, 2094,
    2141, 2181, 2182, 2209, 2379,
    2382, 2397, 2434, 2441, 2446,
    2516, 2521, 2527, 2560, 2561...
    +27
suite [sɥit]: 2027, 2990
suivre [sɥivʁ]: 2662
sujet [syʒɛ]: 2846
supermarché [sypɛʁmaʁʃe]: 2342, 2387
sur [sy]: 2089, 2386, 2474, 2753, 2786,
    2916, 2956
sûr [syʁ]: 2028, 2056, 2653, 2826
sur [syʁ]: 2035, 2169, 2235, 2248,
    2257, 2509, 2545, 2547, 2646,
    2706, 2721, 2733, 2736, 2737,
    2762, 2791, 2840, 2841, 2845...
    +11
sûre [syʁ]: 2028
surpris [syʁpʁi]: 2159, 2177, 2421,
    2787
surprise [syʁpʁiz]: 2177, 2381, 2787
suspect [syspɛ]: 2790, 2817, 2839,
    2840
sympa [sɛ̃pa]: 2649, 2694
sympathiques [sɛ̃patik]: 2426
t'a [t a]: 2002, 2110
ta [ta]: 2029, 2054, 2065, 2138, 2139,
    2155, 2793, 2838, 2881, 2980, 2981
table [tabl]: 2041, 2742
tâche [taʃ]: 2052
t'ai [t ɛ]: 2028, 2191, 2464, 2510, 2680,
    2998
t'aider [t ede]: 2764
taïwan [taiwan]: 2312
tandis [tandis]: 2184, 2814, 2815, 2897
tant [tɑ̃]: 2384
tante [tɑ̃t]: 2739
tapis [tapi]: 2957
t'appelle [t apɛl]: 2525
t'appellerai [t apɛl°ʁe]: 2695
tard [taʁ]: 2031, 2055, 2165, 2181,
    2669, 2699, 2700, 2704, 2807, 2985
t'asseoir [t aswaʁ]: 2227, 2362
t'attaque [t atak]: 2361
taxi [taksi]: 2068, 2118, 2553, 2765
te [tø]: 2006, 2007, 2009, 2017, 2020,
    2033, 2045, 2056, 2064, 2099,

2148, 2159, 2204, 2247, 2256,
2345, 2350... +30

t'effraient-elles [tˬefʁɛ tˬɛl]: 2810, 2811

tel [tɛl]: 2454

télé [tele]: 2133

téléphone [telefɔn]: 2146, 2544, 2665,
2676, 2678, 2754, 2762, 2779

téléphonique [telefonik]: 2697

télévision [televizjɔ̃]: 2632, 2753, 2885

tellement [tɛlˬmɑ̃]: 2044, 2587, 2588,
2788, 2847, 2946, 2959

t'éloigner [tˬelwaɲe]: 2599

t'embête [tˬɑ̃bɛt]: 2027

température [tɑ̃peʁatyʁ]: 2751

tempête [tɑ̃pɛt]: 2340, 2554

temps [tɑ̃]: 2127, 2133, 2231, 2258,
2353, 2413, 2416, 2418, 2420,
2422, 2424, 2465, 2487, 2497,
2588, 2601, 2648, 2713, 2715... +5

t'en [tˬɑ̃]: 2117

t'énerver [tˬenɛʁve]: 2560

tennis [tenis]: 2895

tente [tɑ̃t]: 2833

t'entendre [tˬɑ̃tɑ̃dʁ]: 2581

t'enverrai [tˬɑ̃vɛʁɛ]: 2662

terminé [tɛʁmine]: 2371, 2504, 2713,
2771

terminent [tɛʁmin]: 2478

terre [tɛʁ]: 2140, 2267, 2485

terrible [tɛʁibl]: 2467, 2746, 2897

terriblement [tɛʁiblˬmɑ̃]: 2970

terribles [tɛʁibl]: 2887

terrifié [tɛʁifje]: 2812

terrifiée [tɛʁifje]: 2812

terrifient [tɛʁifi]: 2812

tes [te]: 2074, 2231, 2232, 2332, 2789,
2830, 2848, 2918, 2920, 2923, 2954

t'es-tu [tˬɛ ty]: 2029, 2204

tête [tɛt]: 2887

t'excuser [tˬekskyze]: 2097, 2098, 2808

t'excuses [tˬekskyz]: 2448

thaïlande [tailɑ̃d]: 2309

théière [tejɛʁ]: 2912

tienne [tjɛn]: 2374

tiens [tjɛ̃]: 2080

tient [tjɛ̃]: 2891

t'importuner [tˬɛ̃pɔʁtyne]: 2759

t'inquiète [tˬɛ̃kjɛt]: 2838

tiré [tiʁe]: 2923, 2956

tirer [tiʁe]: 2841, 2925

titre [titʁ]: 2772

toi [twa]: 2182, 2353, 2355, 2356,
2404, 2432, 2512, 2617, 2617,
2697, 2771, 2808, 2838, 2999

toilette [twalɛt]: 2982

toi-même [twamɛm]: 2345, 2356

tolérants [toleʁɑ̃]: 2819

tombé [tɔ̃be]: 2496, 2553

tombée [tɔ̃be]: 2479, 2706

tombées [tɔ̃be]: 2844

tomber [tɔ̃be]: 2172, 2188, 2684, 2902

tombés [tɔ̃be]: 2916, 2983

ton [tɔ̃]: 2006, 2013, 2041, 2158, 2356,
2504, 2525, 2666, 2744, 2795,
2834, 2860, 2875, 2881, 2935, 2955

tornade [tɔʁnad]: 2990

tôt [to]: 2045, 2090, 2119, 2142, 2148,
2209, 2245, 2603, 2612, 2614,
2650, 2854

totalement [totalˬmɑ̃]: 2859, 2943

totalité [totalite]: 2436

touché [tuʃe]: 2717, 2844

toucher [tuʃe]: 2004, 2005, 2192

toujours [tuʒu]: 2648, 2781, 2942

toujours [tuʒuʁ]: 2083, 2173, 2362,
2579, 2626, 2636, 2641, 2642,
2646, 2681, 2690, 2732, 2778,
2795, 2833, 2882, 2891... +4

tour [tuʁ]: 2831, 2851

tourisme [tuʁizm]: 2341

touristes [tuʁist]: 2414, 2435, 2831

touristique [tuʁistik]: 2529

tourne [tuʁn]: 2267

tourné [tuʁne]: 2454

tournée [tuʁne]: 2752

tournoi [tuʁnwa]: 2895

tous [tu]: 2034, 2232, 2315, 2403,
2435, 2443, 2451, 2459, 2461,
2635, 2755, 2825, 2851, 2852,
2902, 2926, 2982, 2994

tout [tu]: 2016, 2027, 2033, 2040, 2163, 2198, 2222, 2397, 2404, 2421, 2452, 2453, 2454, 2455, 2458, 2465, 2480, 2487... +33

toute [tut]: 2343, 2457, 2462, 2463, 2464, 2561, 2568, 2743, 2933, 2946

toutefois [tut°fwa]: 2948

toutes [tut]: 2269, 2429, 2443, 2460, 2472, 2483, 2541, 2659, 2762, 2779

traduits [tʁadɥi]: 2908

train [tʁɛ̃]: 2061, 2195, 2196, 2197, 2201, 2418, 2472, 2601, 2710, 2716, 2734, 2750, 2755, 2767, 2768

trains [tʁɛ̃]: 2604

trajet [tʁaʒɛ]: 2337

transport [tʁɑ̃spɔʁ]: 2322

transporté [tʁɑ̃spɔʁte]: 2548, 2989

transporter [tʁɑ̃spɔʁte]: 2983

travail [tʁavaj]: 2020, 2049, 2094, 2252, 2331, 2356, 2504, 2569, 2580, 2656, 2703, 2727, 2758, 2788, 2795, 2854, 2900... +1

travaille [tʁavaj]: 2265, 2426, 2506, 2520, 2529, 2530, 2637, 2682, 2926

travaillé [tʁavaje]: 2051, 2275, 2561

travaillent [tʁavaj]: 2786

travailler [tʁavaje]: 2037, 2051, 2079, 2207, 2223, 2279, 2669, 2703, 2709, 2724, 2765, 2766

travailles [tʁavaj]: 2593, 2955

travailleurs [tʁavajœʁ]: 2755

travers [tʁavɛʁ]: 2376

traversant [tʁavɛʁsɑ̃]: 2205, 2989

traversé [tʁavɛʁse]: 2268

trentaine [tʁɑ̃ten]: 2647

trente [tʁɑ̃t]: 2335, 2708, 2908

trente-deux [tʁɑ̃tdø]: 2326

très [tʁɛ]: 2089, 2119, 2164, 2172, 2216, 2225, 2234, 2236, 2258, 2259, 2290, 2357, 2363, 2382, 2416, 2417, 2423, 2424, 2426... +39

triché [tʁiʃe]: 2866

triste [tʁist]: 2180

trois [tʁwa]: 2545, 2696, 2770, 2771, 2909, 2961, 2964

trop [tʁo]: 2076, 2085, 2133, 2223, 2326, 2581, 2595, 2596, 2598, 2599, 2670, 2704, 2742, 2897

trottoir [tʁotwaʁ]: 2172

trouve [tʁuv]: 2090

trouvé [tʁuve]: 2177, 2197, 2206, 2493, 2549, 2640, 2742, 2934

trouver [tʁuve]: 2034, 2099, 2122, 2125, 2131, 2134, 2220, 2401, 2535, 2662, 2905, 2915, 2930, 2950, 2963

tu [ty]: 2009, 2017, 2028, 2033, 2041, 2065, 2067, 2074, 2097, 2098, 2115, 2117, 2132, 2133, 2161, 2168, 2175, 2225... +102

tué [tɥe]: 2956

tueur [tɥœʁ]: 2915

type [tip]: 2214

typhon [tifɔ̃]: 2936

typique [tipik]: 2824

ultraviolets [yl°tʁavjolɛ]: 2888

un [d‿œ̃]: 2926

un [œ̃]: 2068, 2090, 2109, 2118, 2162, 2202, 2206, 2222, 2224, 2236, 2243, 2249, 2252, 2285, 2291, 2333, 2334, 2335, 2336... +51

un [ʁ‿œ̃]: 2099, 2122, 2123, 2125, 2131, 2132, 2134, 2255, 2375, 2401, 2502, 2503, 2606, 2648, 2790, 2802, 2861, 2950, 2956... +5

un [t‿œ̃]: 2160, 2187, 2240, 2241, 2242, 2244, 2252, 2275, 2301, 2302, 2305, 2306, 2311, 2312, 2331, 2333, 2334, 2335, 2336, 2337... +15

un [z‿œ̃]: 2168, 2216, 2297, 2449, 2487, 2496, 2522, 2629, 2686, 2741, 2844, 2922, 2926, 2980, 2995

une [ʁ‿yn]: 2017, 2089, 2230, 2255, 2342, 2343, 2386, 2473, 2474, 2491, 2530, 2691, 2780, 2781, 2786, 2916, 2930, 2948, 2989... +1

une [t‿yn]: 2073, 2154, 2164, 2208, 2237, 2240, 2291, 2333, 2338, 2370, 2373, 2381, 2514, 2563, 2687, 2733, 2752, 2783, 2858, 2893... +1 une [yn]: 2078, 2101, 2109, 2115, 2261, 2338, 2343, 2359, 2369, 2377, 2380, 2387, 2431, 2486, 2488, 2501, 2514, 2534, 2547... +29

une [z‿yn]: 2017, 2095, 2226, 2538, 2647, 2711, 2741, 2797, 2802, 2997

unes [yn]: 2368

universitaire [yniveʁsiteʁ]: 2243

universitaires [yniveʁsiteʁ]: 2923

universitaires [z‿yniveʁsiteʁ]: 2772

universités [z‿yniveʁsite]: 2966

uns [z‿œ̃]: 2952

usine [l‿yzin]: 2977

usine [yzin]: 2550

usines [z‿yzin]: 2331

utilisé [ytilize]: 2982

va [va]: 2246, 2472, 2483, 2494, 2502, 2513, 2594, 2710, 2739, 2765, 2766, 2952, 2991

vacances [vakɑ̃s]: 2058, 2112, 2231, 2454, 2459, 2491, 2492, 2588, 2694

vain [vɛ̃]: 2945

vais [vɛ]: 2065, 2066, 2070, 2221, 2230, 2255, 2263, 2344, 2356, 2512, 2634, 2653, 2664, 2672, 2715, 2720, 2765, 2780, 2807, 2852... +1

valait-il [valɛ t‿il]: 2120

valises [valiz]: 2238

vas [va]: 2502

vas-tu [va ty]: 2070, 2128, 2232, 2980, 2998

vaut [vo]: 2930, 2981

vécu [veky]: 2086, 2457

végétarien [veʒetaʁjɛ̃]: 2214, 2285

vélo [velo]: 2094, 2188, 2666, 2737

venait [v°nɛ]: 2951

venant [v°nɑ̃]: 2687

vendre [vɑ̃dʁ]: 2176

vendredi [vɑ̃dʁ°di]: 2169, 2398, 2477

vendu [vɑ̃dy]: 2932

vendus [vɑ̃dy]: 2403

venir [v°niʁ]: 2110, 2969

venons [v°nɔ̃]: 2625, 2961

ventes [vɑ̃t]: 2724, 2783, 2788

ventre [vɑ̃tʁ]: 2861

venu [v°ny]: 2618, 2951

vérifier [veʁifje]: 2383

vérité [veʁite]: 2098

verrouillé [veʁuje]: 2018, 2149

verrouillée [veʁuje]: 2018

verrouiller [veʁuje]: 2018, 2027

vers [vɛʁ]: 2951, 3000

vert [vɛʁ]: 2035

vêtements [vɛt°mɑ̃]: 2145, 2579, 2901, 2913

vêtue [vety]: 2501

veuillez [vœje]: 2114

veulent [vœl]: 2511

veut [vø]: 2037, 2215, 2323, 2444, 2756, 2790, 2797, 2883

veuve [vœv]: 2514

veux [vø]: 2274, 2344, 2346, 2372, 2431, 2502, 2504, 2512, 2619, 2714, 2732, 2941

veux-tu [vø ty]: 2374

viande [vjɑ̃d]: 2214, 2285

victimes [viktim]: 2879

vide [vid]: 2406

vie [vi]: 2297, 2380, 2457, 2485, 2879, 2923, 2994

vieil [vjɛj]: 2856

vieilles [vjɛj]: 2945

viendra [vjɛ̃dʁa]: 2685

vienne [vjɛn]: 2917

viennent [vjɛn]: 2381

viens [vjɛ̃]: 2567, 2644, 2724

vient-elle [vjɛ̃ t‿ɛl]: 2626

vies [vi]: 2473

vieux [vjø]: 2595

village [vilaʒ]: 2034

ville [vil]: 2062, 2170, 2216, 2257, 2472, 2521, 2532, 2585, 2780, 2966

villes [vil]: 2546

vingt [vɛ̃]: 2251, 2782, 2966

vingt-cinq [vɛ̃tsɛ̃k]: 2707

vingt-six [vɛ̃tsis]: 2249

vingt-trois [vɛ̃tʁwa]: 2703

violents [vjolɑ̃]: 2885

vis [vis]: 2390
visa [viza]: 2123
visage [vizaʒ]: 2995
visite [vizit]: 2273, 2762, 2933
visiter [vizite]: 2328, 2503
vit [vi]: 2086, 2371, 2406, 2893
vite [vit]: 2076, 2259, 2618, 2624, 2670
vitesse [vitɛs]: 2749, 2750, 2767
vivent [viv]: 2286, 2386, 2476
vivons [vivɔ̃]: 2095, 2487, 2978
vivre [vivʁ]: 2026, 2050, 2062, 2087, 2122, 2125, 2390, 2423, 2522, 2776, 2777, 2892, 2978
vocabulaire [vokabylɛʁ]: 2250, 2251
voir [vwa]: 2491, 2502
voir [vwaʁ]: 2110, 2144, 2159, 2421, 2491, 2492, 2502, 2519, 2527, 2625, 2626, 2634, 2698, 2926
vois [vwa]: 2466, 2653, 2669, 2707, 2708
voisin [vwazɛ̃]: 2241, 2242
voisines [vwazin]: 2369
voisins [vwazɛ̃]: 2369
voiture [vwatyʁ]: 2017, 2065, 2094, 2115, 2150, 2176, 2186, 2211, 2219, 2322, 2374, 2515, 2601, 2652, 2670, 2706, 2741, 2767... +3
voitures [vwatyʁ]: 2473, 2757, 2911
vol [vɔl]: 2119, 2162, 2272, 2383, 2388, 2647, 2736, 2968
volé [vole]: 2121, 2549
volée [vole]: 2219
voler [vole]: 2666
voleur [volœʁ]: 2677
volons [volɔ̃]: 2749
vont [vɔ̃]: 2574, 2712, 2738
votre [vɔtʁ]: 2474, 2995
voudrais [vudʁɛ]: 2256
voudrais-tu [vudʁɛ ty]: 2645, 2849
voulaient [vulɛ]: 2988

voulais [vulɛ]: 2212, 2491, 2492, 2503, 2519, 2759, 2917
voulait [vulɛ]: 2934
voulions [vuljɔ̃]: 2588
vouloir [vulwaʁ]: 2684
vous [vu]: 2023, 2114, 2181, 2353, 2355, 2449, 2495, 2967, 2995
voyage [vwajaʒ]: 2160, 2168, 2236, 2368, 2519, 2678, 2852, 2962, 2971
voyagé [vwajaʒe]: 2376
voyageais [vwajaʒɛ]: 2228
voyager [vwajaʒe]: 2061
voyages [vwajaʒ]: 2235, 2613, 2997
voyons [vwajɔ̃]: 2461
vrai [vʁɛ]: 2498
vraiment [vʁɛmɑ̃]: 2157, 2559, 2658, 2671, 2793, 2796, 2927, 2988, 2997
vrais [vʁɛ]: 2979
vu [vy]: 2057, 2120, 2186, 2187, 2188, 2189, 2190, 2212, 2215, 2510, 2531, 2591, 2625, 2753, 2757, 2782
vus [vy]: 2195, 2241, 2524
week-end [wikɛnd]: 2082, 2653
y [i]: 2261, 2383, 2391, 2406, 2503, 2582, 2621, 2791, 2982
y [l̩i]: 2028, 2030, 2087, 2169, 2223, 2224, 2260, 2271, 2379, 2380, 2388, 2389, 2423, 2460, 2472, 2490, 2522, 2605, 2640, 2641... +7
y [n̩i]: 2073
y [ʁ̩i]: 2422
y [t̩i]: 2385, 2386
y [z̩i]: 2004, 2212, 2503, 2668
ya [l̩ja]: 2973
yens [jɛn]: 2951
yeux [z̩jø]: 2032
yoga [joga]: 2926
york [jɔʁk]: 2318, 2328
zoo [zoo]: 2523, 2739